# BEFORE THE STORY

## Interviewing and Communication Skills
## for Journalists

# BEFORE THE STORY

## Interviewing and Communication Skills for Journalists

George M. Killenberg
*University of South Florida*

Rob Anderson
*Southern Illinois University at Edwardsville*

St. Martin's Press
*New York*

Editor: Mark Gallaher
Project Editor: Beverly Hinton
Production Supervisor: Chris Pearson
Text Design: Nancy Sugihara
Cover Design: Tom McKeveny
Cover Photo: Stephen Morton/Silver Image

Manufactured in the United States of America.

32109

fedcb

*Library of Congress Cataloging-in-Publication Data*

Killenberg, George M.
    Before the story.

        1. Interviewing in journalism. 2. Communication.
I. Anderson, Rob, 1945–     . II. Title.
PN4784.I6K55 1989        070.4'3        88–29907
ISBN 0-312-02545-9
    0-312-01238-1 (pbk.)

For information, write:
St. Martin's Press, Inc.
175 Fifth Avenue
New York, NY 10010

ISBN: 0-312-02545-9
    0-312-01238-1 (pbk.)

# Preface

*N*ewsweek called it "The Great TV Shout-Out." *USA Today* asked, "Who got mugged?" *Editor & Publisher* wondered, "Has the interview . . . , which once was supposed to elicit information for the public, been reduced to the status of 'who won?' " The news-making event was a live, nine-minute confrontation between Vice President George Bush and his interviewer, CBS anchor Dan Rather, shortly before the first primary of the 1988 presidential campaign.

Bush objected to the content of some early questions and to Rather's insistent interruptions to press for specifics. Rather seemed to object to Bush's reluctance to address the issues specifically and decided not to let the vice president elaborate without—in his view—responding directly to his questions.

Millions of viewers who were accustomed to network news inter-views neatly edited and packaged from videotape were treated to a rare drama enacted spontaneously and emotionally. Interviewer and interviewee jousted with raised voices, refusals to yield the floor, and personal put-downs. Each side insisted it was somehow set up by the other. Bush claimed the network misled him about the sub-stance of the interview and slanted the issues unfairly; Rather and CBS claimed that Bush was fully informed the questions would be tough and that the candidate orchestrated the interview's combative tone—live, at his request—to enhance his image as a tough leader.

What's most surprising about the Rather-Bush episode is not that media and politicians were mistrustful of each other or that this mistrust would surface in a face-to-face interview. That happens often, though the public seldom sees it displayed so nakedly or venomously. The unusual fact about this clash was that the *process* of an interview became the news. The interview's *content,* the ostensible purpose for the program, took a back seat to how the interviewer related to the interviewee.

Rather's performance eventually led to a broader discussion of how journalists generally go about their work. Difficult, important questions were raised and debated: What is the purpose of an interview? Is it at all reasonable to think in terms of "winning" or "losing" an interview? How crucial is listening? Is good journalism always polite journalism? How is communication in an interview affected by biases and unstated motives? What ethical principles should guide a journalist in choosing questions and pressing for answers? Where are the distinctions between fairness, toughness and callous disrespect?

Similar questions have confronted us over the years as we've taught reporting, interviewing and interpersonal communication. They guided our writing of *Before the Story,* but we never expected them to become front-page news just as we were wrapping up the manuscript.

*Before the Story* was born of our fifteen-year friendship, our previous collaborations as authors, our shared concern for students, and some long lunches. One of us had long taught reporting, but with an emphasis on news-gathering and writing techniques. The other had taught interviewing and various interpersonal communication courses without making many applications to the tasks of reporters.

Two articles we wrote for *Journalism Educator* taught us that we had something to say to each other and, together, to others. We learned that journalistic interviewing can be more than rote questioning and answering, more than manipulation, more than tricks and counterpunches. An adversarial or mistrustful style of interviewing, though at times necessary, is an inadequate model for journalists faced with assignments that range from the happy arrival of New Year's babies to the tragedies of divorce and custody fights. For most stories a reporter will tackle, a concern for *dialogue,* a sensitivity to people's needs, a willingness to listen and the ability to communicate clearly and nonjudgmentally will be the soundest preparation. Journalistic interviewing is not too different from everyday conversation in this regard.

Does a dialogical approach mean conflict in an interview is necessarily bad? Of course not. Interviewers must be assertive, as Dan Rather reminds us. Some stories are too big or too protected for a polite-at-all-costs interviewer. Journalists must sometimes struggle even to *obtain* a person's view or a more truthful account of an event. If anything, interpersonal competence will allow journalists to be more effective on those occasions when firmness and persistence are demanded. Careful listening sets up more incisive questions. Understanding the nonverbal clues to an interviewee's discomfort allows you to supply more detail in your final story. Sensitivity to some possible signals of deception could alert you to check out a story with other sources of information. And sensitivity to the other's reaction to you might tell you when to back off or when a line of questioning is counterproductive.

The Bush-Rather confrontation is unsettling. On the one hand, it reminds us of the fundamental importance of the subject of this book. On the other hand, the event reminds us of the ambiguity of the profession. We know what Rather did, and how Bush reacted— and vice versa. But do we know for certain what Rather *should* have done, once caught in the heat of the interview? Should he have kept his temper, stayed cordial, not interrupted, not raised his voice at the vice president? Was this an example of an embarrassingly bad interview? Or could it be argued that this type of interview showed us a forceful (mean? strong? defensive? candid? evasive?) side of Bush we wouldn't have seen otherwise, and thus was somewhat effective?

A book can make suggestions, but we can't tell you what is correct to do in all cases. Each situation makes different demands, and you begin to allow for differing personalities and goals. So don't look here for answers. Look for questions and dilemmas to which you provide personalized responses; look for challenges to what you've assumed to be true; look for approaches that have worked well for other successful journalists; and look for ways to develop your own view of what person-to-person journalism is about.

## ACKNOWLEDGMENTS

Few books spring primarily from the creative insight of their authors. While we all hope for creativity, authors should acknowledge how often they are merely gatherers and collectors of influences. Most communication is a simultaneous process of shaping and being shaped. The beginning of a book is a good place to recognize how we were "shaped." Many people—family, friends and colleagues (not mutually exclusive groups)—contributed to this project, some in ways they couldn't predict and some in ways perhaps not fully appreciated.

Our families helped us immeasurably. "The book" was a constant presence in two households; plans always seemed to be made and changed around it, and this often rude guest disrupted the lives of our wives and children probably more than we had a right to ask. Their patience, support and love are reflected in these pages. Thanks to Penny, Andrew, Kristen, Anne and Mark Killenberg, and to Dona, Eric and Neil Anderson.

Our students and former students gave us many of the ideas we present here as "original." They might have thought they were "taking" ideas from us at the very times we knew they were giving so freely. Their commitment to their careers, to clear and sensitive communication and to persistent questioning (". . . but *why* is that a better way?") helped us to focus on central issues. More specifically, a number of students assisted us in conducting and compiling the results of the interviews for this book. Our thanks go to: Bobbi Ahrens, Carol Althoff, Mike Archibald, Lesley Bell, Misha Benavides, Andrew Cingolani, Megan Collins, Cheryl L. Eaton, Sharon Henson, Gary S. King, Lydia Martin, Melodie L. Powers, Frank Purcell, Mark Purdey, Therese M. Sedlak, John Twombly, Nicole K. Vaughn and Lisa Diane White.

Two insightful professionals served as informal reviewers of our manuscript as it developed. One was Mike's father, George A. Killenberg, former executive editor of the *St. Louis Globe-Democrat*. While supporting the idea of a more communication-oriented approach to journalism, he always reminded us to keep the working reporter in mind. Practical, keep it practical, he said. We hope we have. The other was Dr. Noreen Carrocci, associate professor and chair of the Department of Communication at St. Louis University. Neither was hesitant to point out where our writing or thinking was just plain stupid. Authors need such friends, especially when they're right and supportive at the same time.

We prepared for *Before the Story* by interviewing (and asking students to interview) a number of working journalists and public news figures. Their observations enliven and personalize many sections of the book. With journalists we were curious about such things as:

What were their different styles and pet peeves? How did they learn their craft? When did people seem to be most willing to talk? Were there special danger signals within an interview? With public officials and celebrities we wondered, for example: What encourages them to trust an interviewer? When do they feel defensive or double-crossed? Do they expect a reporter to be a person, too? What kinds of talk have an "opening" effect? We are grateful for the cooperation of the following journalists: Safir Ahmed, Charles Bosworth Jr., Jim Floyd, Pat Gauen, Ray Hartmann, Jeff Herman, Beverly L. Isom, George A. Killenberg, Mary Delach Leonard, Bill McClellan, Jim Orso, Tommye Walter and Sue Ann Wood. We also thank the public figures and frequent interviewees who generously contributed their time and ideas to give the book a too-often-neglected perspective: Marcus J. Albrecht, Eric W. Althoff, Don Baker, Edward Bushmeyer, Bennett Dickmann, Harry Gallatin, G. Lynn Lashbrook, Suzie Mathieu, John Mehan, Thomas Purcell, Julius Rhodes and Randy Rushing.

*Before the Story* was conceived, in a sense, by two articles we wrote for *Journalism Educator* some years ago. We want to acknowledge the receptivity and encouragement of that journal's editors, Thomas A. Bowers and LaRue W. Gilleland, and to report that we have borrowed and rejuvenated many of those earlier ideas.

Finally, we express thanks to two caring editors at St. Martin's Press, Mark Gallaher and Nancy Perry. Without their encouragement you wouldn't be holding this book right now. Without their expertise, you might be holding a vastly inferior one. Mark not only applied his impressive editorial skill but also coordinated the work of reviewers who examined and responded to the manuscript of various stages of preparation. *Before the Story* is clearer, more direct, more accurate and more interesting because of their work, too. Our final thanks to Terrance L. Albrecht, University of Washington; J. Laurence Day, University of Kansas; Martin L. Gibson, University of Texas; John Griffith, University of Florida; Samuel V. Kennedy, Syracuse University; Daryl Moen, University of Missouri at Columbia; Tom Nugent, University of Maryland—Baltimore County; Eric M. Odendahl, San Diego State University; Robert E. Simmons, Boston University; and Jean Ward, University of Minnesota.

George M. Killenberg
*University of South Florida*

Rob Anderson
*Southern Illinois University at Edwardsville*

# Contents

CHAPTER  FOUR

## An Ear for News: Reporters as Listeners   89

CHAPTER  FIVE

## Assessing People and Information: On Not Getting Fooled, Most of the Time   121

CHAPTER  SIX

## Handle with Care: Interviews with Special Challenges   137

CHAPTER SEVEN

CHAPTER EIGHT

# BEFORE THE STORY
## Interviewing and Communication Skills for Journalists

# CHAPTER ONE

# Reporters as Communicators

## The Possibilities for Inter-view

In an antiseptic nursing home cafeteria, a feature writer from the Daily Dispatch fidgets uncomfortably on a chair across from the town's oldest citizen, who is celebrating his 100th birthday. Separating them are vast differences of experience and environment. Will those differences cripple the interview?

A thousand miles away, a city editor beckons to a young reporter who's putting the finishing touches on a city council story. "I have a tough assignment for you," the city editor says. "A 2-year-old in Middletown drowned in a neighbor's swimming pool. I need someone to talk to the parents." The reporter cringes. She knew she'd probably have to interview grief-stricken people someday; the day has arrived. "Will I be able to handle this?" she asks herself.

In a steamy office at the county courthouse, a political writer is about to face a gruff county treasurer known for chewing up journalists. He must question the official about the misappropriation of traffic-ticket fines collected by the county. The reporter braces for the treasurer's customary tactics of evasiveness and intimidation, wondering whether he will be able to stay cool.

Every day, reporters face tests of their ability to communicate. They may interview a television evangelist in the morning and a needle-scarred junkie in the afternoon. They are expected to know the difference between Dwight Gooden's ERA and Gloria Steinem's ERA. A reporter who drives a spotless Honda Accord might be called upon to communicate with a bag lady who pushes a dented shopping cart; a reporter from Dubuque must find a common language in order to interview a street kid who runs with a Chicago gang; or a straight reporter may interview a gay activist. Deadlines and competition to get stories first complicate their work.

In the Roaring '20s era of "Front Page" journalism, a reporter could get by with chutzpah and a gift for gab. It was an era of the pencil-and-pad reporter—the reporter as stenographer. Journalism did not take itself as seriously as it does today, nor did people need the press as much to help them understand a simpler world. Today's Information Age overwhelms the public with complex issues and events. What are the moral and social implications of surrogate motherhood? Should there be a right to die? Is racism growing, decades after Martin Luther King Jr.'s assassination? Will AIDS imperil humankind? Increasingly, the public turns to news media for answers. People depend on the ability of reporters to observe, to question, to listen and, most of all, to understand.

Successful, respected reporters tend to be proficient at interpersonal communication. But their success is often based on intuition and experience, not education or knowledge. While experience and intuition do count, reporters need knowledge to complement experience. Knowledge, if nothing else, teaches us how to interpret experience. William Zinsser says interviewing is at least half "purely mechanical." The rest, he says, can be learned with experience: "Interviewing is one of those skills that you can only get better at."[1] That's a hard assumption to accept. Probably every working reporter can think of a colleague with impressive experience who is an incompetent, inattentive interviewer. In fact, too many reporters suffer from the "old pro" syndrome. They've been interviewing people so long that they've started relying on formulas, cutting corners and assuming the truth of stereotypes.

Reporters generally are better prepared to collect facts resourcefully and write stories with zip and style. Their teachers and editors drill them to track down tips, draft leads, organize information and write for deadlines. Not surprisingly, when journalists gather to discuss their craft, the focus is on writing. They won't praise each other for the ability to converse or listen to people. The compliment usually is, "Great story, Bill," not "Great interview." Of course, this is understandable, given that the story is seen as the "product." But the steps taken—or not taken—*before the story is written* contribute substantially to the product, although sometimes in subtle ways.

What happens *before the story* is not only consequential; it is far more complex than many reporters recognize or appreciate. For example, reporters should watch for nonverbal messages and understand what they might mean. They should know how to listen actively and nonjudgmentally. They should be aware of the power of first impressions. Learning these and other nuances of communication may make the difference between success and failure as a journalist. A reporter who is as proficient at communication as he or she is at writing can expect payoffs that include increased confidence as an interviewer, fuller cooperation by interviewees, sharper perceptual power and, ultimately, more accurate, more complete stories.

## REPORTERS AND THE PUBLIC

Journalists no longer are proud graduates of the school of hard knocks. Most of them are well-educated, polished, committed professionals. Yet, paradoxically, methods and attitudes from the old days linger, causing problems in reputation and practice for today's reporters.

The image of the ugly reporter can't be denied or escaped. Television and movies portray reporters as insensitive, rude clods. Politicians condemn reporters for being scandal-mongers. Public-opinion polls find widespread disapproval of the behavior of journalists. In 1985, for example, a study commissioned by the American Society of Newspaper Editors reported that 78 percent of the respondents felt reporters were "just concerned about getting a good story." A respondent in Tallahassee, Fla., said, "They pick on people. When somebody has a small problem and the media leaps upon it, I think it ruins a lot of people's happiness. They overdo it." Another person commented, "They will take something that a political leader has said, and twist it around and put words in that person's mouth."[2]

Is the image deserved? To some extent, yes. Journalists continue to operate in ways that frequently alienate the public.

### The Confrontational Stance

A confrontational, "us vs. them" attitude still underlies much reporting. Part of the problem is that reporters are by nature—or by training—suspicious and skeptical. Moreover, they are conditioned to ferret out the news even if the cost is dear. Compassion, sensitivity, caring and patience—attributes important to most successful communication relationships—are not among the most rewarded characteristics of reporters, who are more likely to be praised by colleagues for being aggressive, calculating and even manipulative. On the job and in the classroom, reporters are encouraged to be firm and in control.

Young reporters *ought* to be taught an assertive, determined style—but with an accompanying flexiblity to moderate that tough-minded style at appropriate times. As Arthur Wible, publisher of the Dallas Times Herald, points out, novices sometimes confuse toughness with effectiveness. "I don't think [reporting] demands being a bull in a china shop to get the story," he said. "Instead, you might say, 'Hey, why don't we get a cup of coffee? I don't have all the answers to this, and I'd like your help.' "[3]

That is sound advice, yet much of the language of journalism training reinforces the perception that reporters should arm and gird themselves when pursuing a story. In the words of one author, "It is time now to consider what the reporter can do in newsgathering situations to stack the deck more in his or her favor."[4] Another journalism book advises reporters to "draft a battle plan."[5] Still another says, "Journalists know the tricks used by news sources, and continuously develop countertactics."[6] Stack the deck. Draft a battle plan. Develop countertactics. Should reporting be a contest or war exercise? Rarely. Few interviews are with overtly uncooperative or hostile news subjects.

Herbert Gans refers to the journalistic interview as a "tug-of-war." According to Gans, "While sources attempt to 'manage' the news, putting the best light on themselves, journalists concurrently 'manage' sources in order to extract the information they want."[7] He describes the kind of aggressive, hard-nosed approach necessary to obtain some stories. The popularity of "60 Minutes" comes from the public's reasonable desire to have otherwise protected and perhaps devious officials and celebrities exposed to greater scrutiny. But this approach cannot be the model for most journalistic interviewing. Confrontation is occasionally important, but communication—the search for understanding—is the overriding concern.

## Arrogance, Elitism and Isolation

An unpleasant air of superiority accompanies some journalists. "I've noticed an arrogance," said one metropolitan newspaper reporter we interviewed. "It's based on an attitude that 'I represent the public. You owe me an answer.' It's like somebody handing you a license to poke into other people's business. Reporters I know usually outgrow this stage, though."[8]

Washington Post reporter Lou Cannon, however, wonders how easily it is outgrown. "The reporter's view that he is performing a sacred calling can cloak him with an annoying self-righteousness about his mission which ordinary Americans find disturbing."[9] Arrogance may be cloaked in noble-sounding platitudes, such as "the public's right to know." A former editor of The Quill refers to this form of arrogance as a "missionary's orientation."[10] But a reporter's zeal to become a self-appointed reformer clearly can interfere with the ability to be evenhanded and open-minded. The reformer can become a First Amendment chauvinist, unreasoning and bellicose as he or she seeks the Truth and protects society from evildoers. Chauvinistic reporters are likely to tune out criticisms that might help them become better at their work.

The reporter's sense of self-importance can go beyond the power-trip complex. At times it is a case of false superiority. Stuart Schwarz, a journalism professor who became a newspaper consultant, offers this picture: "I go into newsrooms and I see all these reporters and editors sitting around and making fun of people. They're always talking about some stupid councilman or laughing at the lady who brought in the eggplant that looks like Richard Nixon. But that's life. Life is an eggplant that looks like Nixon. Newspaper people have a tremendous lack of respect for ordinary people. We have a combination of idealism and ignorance, and that's American journalism."[11]

Perhaps it isn't, as Schwartz says, "a tremendous lack of respect for ordinary people." It could be a tremendous lack of involvement with ordinary people. H. Eugene Goodwin, author of Groping for Ethics in Journalism, refers to journalists as an "isolated elite." The isolation, he says, is both physical and social. "Because of bomb threats and other problems with 'crazies,' virtually all urban news organizations have hired security guards to protect them. Unfortunately, they also protect them from people who may have news and information but who never get into the fortress."[12] Too many reporters seek refuge in the newsroom as if they are afraid of being contaminated by contact with outsiders.

Reporters tend to be young, white, suburban (or urban chic), liberal. They also tend to be male, though to a much lesser extent in recent years.[13] Not surprisingly, a fairly stable set of values and attitudes characterizes American newsrooms, further isolating reporters. A 1986 study concluded that journalists belong to a "largely homogeneous group that is cosmopolitan in background and liberal in outlook."[14] Of course, the public benefits from bright, urbane, motivated reporters. Problems arise, though, when reporters lose touch with the mainstream of community life. A study sponsored by the American Society of Newspaper Editors concluded that a "substantial subset" of journalists, particularly editors and young reporters, are insulated from their public.[15] Similarly, Everette Dennis and Arnold Ismach found that reporters in the Minneapolis–St. Paul area "had little direct knowledge of how people unlike themselves worked, lived or played." They encourage reporters to seek "touchstones" of reality, such as riding the bus, attending a small-town fair, touring a factory or watching a soap opera.[16]

A more recent variety of isolationism stems from the celebrity status some highly paid, highly visible journalists attain. This was evident in a 1984 encounter between CBS anchor Dan Rather and Sen. Alan Cranston, then a presidential candidate. The two were conversing when a CBS aide approached Cranston and said, "Senator, Mr. Rather will only have time for one more question."[17] Journalists like Rather may not seek or enjoy celebrity status, but their wealth, clout and prestige reinforce the attitude of arrogance people associate with journalism. Not surprisingly, some researchers found evidence of *narcissism* among today's high-powered journalists.[18] If this research is valid, then it helps explain why some journalists appear distant and egocentric. Elitism and narcissism can cause reporters to devalue "lesser" people and their ideas.

When reporters stand apart from others and fail to build bridges of everyday involvement with ordinary people, the consequences can be serious. Intelligent and cosmopolitan reporters will miss or misinterpret stories if they're not "people-smart."

## The Limits of Objectivity

Another potential obstacle to a healthy communication climate is something that is usually thought of as one of the cornerstones of good journalism—objectivity. When reporters define *objectivity,* it usually is in terms of disinterest, detachment and noninvolvement. Reporters compulsively seeking this type of objectivity may create barriers between themselves and their news subjects. David Hawpe, managing editor of the Louisville Courier-Journal, fears the pursuit of objectivity "is turning reporters into simple vehicles of transmission."[19] Although bias obviously is dangerous, reporters should not be excessively afraid of close rapport in an interview.

More significantly, reporters who believe that objectivity—in the form of an absence of bias—is possible, might only be deluding themselves. Reporters who can admit their prejudices are better equipped to recognize the emotional filters though which information and people are assessed and cataloged.

The devotee to objectivity may come to treat news "sources" as objects. Stories are "dug up," or people are considered reservoirs to be pumped dry. But such impersonal, cold treatment rarely goes unnoticed. Two men we interviewed describe their problems with this assumption. For example, a union official quickly sizes up reporters by their demeanor: "With some reporters there's a distance, a lack of involvement. I ask myself, 'Am I dealing with an idiot or just one who doesn't give a damn about what I have to say?' " A retired executive editor said, "The callousness of reporters increases in proportion to the distance and lack of contact with the people they write about. As a general rule, the reporters most sensitive to treating people decently are those on runs (beats) who have to face their news subjects the day the story appears and who have to deal with those same news subjects day in and day out."

A reporter's work naturally depends on interaction with others. That interaction is aided when there is empathy—a sincere attempt to identify with the other person's experiences and emotions. If empathy is lacking in some aspects of journalism, it could be the result of misguided "objectivity," or what columnist Max Lerner calls the relentless pursuit of factuality. "For decades," he says, "we have been pursuing all the ascertainable facts—scorching the earth, fiercely, for facts."[20] Today's reporter cannot simply rely on conveying facts or recording what he or she sees or hears. Understanding human motivation is just as essential. "It is interesting," writes media observer Michael Kirkhorn, "how often the word 'empathy' appears in tributes and testimonials to journalists of outstanding reputation."[21]

## REPORTING AS A FORM OF DIALOGUE

If some of the traditional ways and means of journalism are flawed or ineffective, what might be alternative approaches to reporting? A starting point is to weigh the implications of the term *newsgathering*. *Gathering* suggests a harvest—an act of one person "taking" or "collecting" from another. If someone is merely a "source," then he or she might be seen as existing only in the role of news "supplier" to the reporter. Fruitful communication, however, occurs between people, not between roles. News is not sitting out there, waiting to be harvested. More often than not, newsworthy information *emerges* from successful talk. News, in this sense, is more like a relationship than an object. News, in fact, is often a *co-creation* of journalists and those they interview.

Instead of thinking in terms of *gathering* news, reporters might benefit from viewing the process as *discovering* news. "Discovery" is usually a fulfilling learning experience. The word suggests finding out something new about a person or place; indeed, it may be a surprisingly pleasant discovery. Studs Terkel, a journalist who evidently sees the difference between newsgathering and discovery, describes how he collected information for a book. "I realized quite early in this adventure that interviews, conventionally conducted, were meaningless. Conditioned clichés were certain to come. The question-and-answer technique may be of value in determining favored detergents, toothpaste, and deodorants, but not in the discovery of men and women. It was simply a case of making conversation. And listening."[22] Combining the concept of *discovering* news with the concept of news as a *co-creation* is likely to result in talk that invites unanticipated ideas and moves the interview in unexpected, productive directions.

The journalistic interview at its best, as Studs Terkel demonstrates, is a form of dialogue. *Dialogue* can be defined in various ways, but authorities on the subject would say real dialogue must be grounded in an attitude of *mutuality*.[23] Thus, an interview could be thought of literally as an "inter-view" in which partners share a view or perception with one another. The idea of partnership in an interview, however, is probably foreign to most reporters. Reporters are likely to treat interviews as *their* domain: They establish a purpose, plan questions and control the interview without taking into account that someone else is equally involved in the outcome. But an interview, if it is to be dialogue, is not something one person does to another. It is something done together.

Granted, not every act of communication between reporters and those they interview can or should develop to the level of dialogue. That takes time and effort. Both parties are often rushed and can't, for good reason, make the commitments needed for true dialogue. When there is time, though, dialogue is rewarding. Charles Kuralt, for example, is able to unlock the essential feelings of people in everyday life by allowing dialogue to occur. As he puts it, "I have tried to go slow, stick to the back roads, take time to meet people, listen to yarns."[24]

Unfortunately, reporters' methods can become too structured and automatic for dialogue to occur. Reporters have to be willing to relax, be natural and let dialogue develop. Columnist Bob Greene once wanted to do a story about an 86-year-old man who sent eloquent letters to world leaders. Greene saw him as an anachronism in an age of apathy. But the man didn't want to be interviewed, saying, "Please . . . no." Greene honored his request, but out of admiration and curiosity, he went to talk to the man anyway. "For a non-interview, talking with him was the most fun I've had during an interview all year. I could palpably feel the difference between our conversation and the dozens of other conversations I have each week."[25] Did Greene, dispensing with his normal businesslike approach to interviews, experience the satisfaction and enjoyment of dialogue? When people, showing mutual respect and interest, converse, their partnership can be expected to result in better stories.

Even in difficult or confrontational circumstances, the essential ingredients of dialogue—sensitivity, respect for people, and the willingness to listen—can develop. An interviewer seeking dialogue can often diminish a news subject's negativity by seeing the interviewee as more than a means to the journalist's narrow goal. Reporters who value and attempt to engage in dialogue will only reluctantly put an interviewee in the position of being grilled, interrogated or judged. Above all, reporters who practice dialogue will attempt to understand the interviewee's feelings and motivations, even if these are not directly relevant to the "story."

Dialogue may sound like idealistic journalism. And it is easier to practice when you're a Charles Kuralt, who is not tracking down wrongdoers or trying to get a straight answer from a politician. As Kuralt realistically observes, "If I come upon a real news story, I call some real reporter to come cover it. I was a real reporter once. . . . Real reporters have to stick their noses in where they're not wanted, ask embarrassing questions, dodge bullets, contend with deadlines, and worry about the competition."[26] Does that mean real reporters are hard-boiled types who shun dialogue? No. Going after "real news stories" doesn't preclude the type of dialogue practiced by a Charles Kuralt.

## A TRANSACTIONAL VIEW OF REPORTING

Dialogue depends upon a "transactional" understanding of communication. Often, though, all of us—journalists included—pattern our communication in simpler, narrower terms. Before exploring what *transactional* implies, it will help to look at two alternative views of communication. These are not just scholarly inventions; they are descriptions of everyday informal philosophies available to us all, whatever our jobs or tasks.

Some people seem to follow a *linear model,* in which communication is conceived as something one person *does to* another. This also could be labeled a "target" or "one-way" model. It assumes that good communication merely involves aiming clear messages at one another. It's a model typically found in the behavior of order-givers and interpersonal manipulators. In fact, critics say many reporters view communication from this perspective.

A less simplistic approach is the *exchange model.* Here, "senders" and "receivers" are thought to be mere message-traders, and communication is the process of back-and-forth exchange in which one message more or less causes another. It works this way: "I speak and you listen, then you speak and I listen." This approach characterizes how many people communicate, including reporters. The advantage of this model over the linear approach is the incorporation of "feedback"—a message used to gauge the success of previous messages. But the shortcoming of the exchange model is that it misleadingly oversimplifies the process of communication.

The *transactional model,* however, recognizes that messages are generated and received simultaneously in a variety of verbal and nonverbal ways.[27] In the context of the interview, participants are not separate at all. They are partners and co-creators of a common meaning to which both, in a sense, belong. Who one person will "be" in a transaction, and what he or she will communicate, is not wholly a personal choice. It is determined by the dynamics of the relationship.

*Relationship,* although it has become a faddish word, is really the key to understanding transactional communication. Instead of merely asking such questions as "What do *I* want?" or "What does *he* mean?" you need to ask, "What is my relationship to this other person and to this event?" and "How is my presence here affecting this person's talk?" Journalists cannot assume that they first talk and then listen, taking turns with whoever is being interviewed. The communicative reporter will be listening at all times—to himself or herself as well as to the interviewee. The communicative reporter will know that a so-called reluctant interviewee may be reluctant only in relationship with *this* particular interviewer; the reluctance (or exuberance, or interest, or boredom) cannot be perceived in isolation from the relationship or event in which it is experienced.

## THE MANY FACES OF EFFECTIVE COMMUNICATION

There are many productive paths to a story and many role models for reporters. There isn't a single right way to communicate in an interview. Some of journalism's superstars regularly break normal expectations for interpersonal communication. Barbara Walters, for instance, has a reputation for asking highly personal questions. In the 1970s, Bob Woodward and Carl Bernstein stuck their feet in doorways and talked their way into homes of reluctant informants in their Watergate probe. Oriana Fallaci sometimes ignores even a basic "rule" of reporting—save your toughest questions for last. She began an interview with Gen. Leopoldo Galtieri, the Argentine president who provoked the Falklands War, with a seemingly inflammatory question: "President Galtieri, when you think of what you have done—I mean the hundreds of kids who have died and will die, and the new detonator you have placed in this part of the planet . . . —tell me: Don't you ask yourself if it was worthwhile? Don't you ever say to yourself, 'Maybe I made a mistake?' Don't you feel a regret?"[28]

Fallaci and the others have had notable success, but their idiosyncratic styles (which evidently work for them) are a form of communication brinkmanship that certainly should not be modeled indiscriminately by beginning reporters. Interviewers can learn from the methods of Fallaci or Mike Wallace, just as ballplayers can learn from the batting stance of George Brett or Pete Rose. But reporters, like ballplayers, should master the basics first and then develop a personal style.

As *Before the Story* explores the issues, problems and strategies in human communication, some conventional wisdom of journalism must be assessed critically. Too much is at stake if journalists are incomplete, or worse, intrusive or thoughtless communicators. This book is dedicated to helping journalists improve as communicators so that we all might understand this complex world more fully.

### Notes

[1]William Zinsser, *On Writing Well,* 2nd ed. (New York: Harper & Row, 1980), p. 79.

[2]*Newspaper Credibility: Building Reader Trust, A National Study Commissioned by The American Society of Newspaper Editors* (Minneapolis, Minn.: MORI Research [1985]), pp. 16 and 27.

³Quoted in Elizabeth Franklin, "Minding Your Manners: A New Politeness Hits the Press," *Washington Journalism Review,* December 1986, p. 34.

⁴Herbert Strentz, *News Reporters and News Sources: What Happens Before the Story Is Written* (Ames, Iowa: Iowa State University Press, 1978), p. 42.

⁵Judith Bolch and Kay Miller, *Investigative and In-depth Reporting* (New York: Hastings House, 1978), p. 59.

⁶Mitchell V. Charnley and Blair Charnley, *Reporting,* 2nd ed. (New York: Holt, Rinehart and Winston, 1979), p. 9.

⁷Herbert J. Gans, *Deciding What's News: A Study of CBS Evening News, NBC Nightly News, Newsweek, and Time* (New York: Pantheon Books, 1979), p. 117.

⁸This quotation and others not accompanied by a note come from interviews conducted by the authors or their students. In most cases, we decided to identify the interviewees by position or title rather than by name.

⁹Lou Cannon, *Reporting: An Inside View.* (Sacramento: California Journal Press, 1977), p. 31.

¹⁰Ron Dorfman, "If the Question Is, Who Won?—Everybody Loses," *The Quill,* November 1986, p. 19.

¹¹Quoted in Dennis Holder, "Give the Readers What They Want," *Washington Journalism Review,* June 1983, p. 38.

¹²H. Eugene Goodwin, *Groping for Ethics in Journalism* (Ames, Iowa; Iowa State University Press, 1983), p. 284.

¹³John W. C. Johnstone et al., *The News People: A Sociological Portrait of American Journalists and Their Work* (Urbana: University of Illinois Press, 1976), p. 185. See, as well, David H. Weaver and G. Cleveland Wilhoit, *The American Journalist* (Bloomington, Ind.: Indiana University Press, 1986).

¹⁴S. Robert Lichter, Stanley Rothman, and Linda S. Lichter, *The Media Elite* (Bethesda, Md.: Adler & Adler, 1986), p. 53.

¹⁵Judee K. Burgoon, Michael Burgoon, David B. Buller and Charles K. Atkin, "Communication Practices of Journalists: Interaction With Public, Other Journalists," *Journalism Quarterly* 64 (Spring 1987): 125–132, 275.

¹⁶Everette E. Dennis and Arnold H. Ismach, *Reporting Processes and Practices* (Belmont, Calif.: Wadsworth, 1981), pp. 329–331.

¹⁷Quoted in Lichter, Rothman, and Lichter, *The Media Elite,* p. 27.

¹⁸Lichter, Rothman, and Lichter, *The Media Elite,* pp. 103–108.

[19]David Hawpe, "Point-of-view Journalism," *Editor & Publisher,* Sept. 8, 1984, p. 40.

[20]Quoted in Robert N. Bostrom, ed., *Competence in Communication: A Multidisciplinary Approach* (Beverly Hills: Sage Publications, 1984), p. 98.

[21]Michael Kirkhorn, "The Search for a Competent Press," in Bostrom, *Competence in Communication,* p. 87.

[22]Studs Terkel, *Division Street: America* (New York: Avon Discus Books, 1970), p. 21.

[23]Martin Buber, *The Knowledge of Man: A Philosophy of the Interhuman,* trans. Maurice Friedman and Ronald Gregor Smith (New York: Harper & Row, 1965); Charles T. Brown and Paul W. Keller, *Monologue to Dialogue,* 2nd ed. (Englewood Cliffs, N.J.: Prentice-Hall, 1979).

[24]Charles Kuralt, *On the Road with Charles Kuralt* (New York: G. P. Putnam's Sons, 1985), p. 14.

[25]Bob Greene, "Non-Interview Was Best of All," *Chicago Tribune,* May 20, 1986, sec. D, p. D1.

[26]Kuralt, *On the Road with Charles Kuralt,* p. 14.

[27]See Karen Rasmussen, "A Transactional Perspective," in Donald K. Darnell and Wayne Brockriede, *Persons Communicating* (Englewood Cliffs, N.J.: Prentice-Hall, 1976), pp. 28–35. For other explanations of transaction, see John Stewart and Gary D'Angelo, *Together: Communicating Interpersonally,* 2nd ed. (Reading, Mass.: Addison-Wesley, 1980); Charles M. Rossiter Jr. and W. Barnett Pearce, *Communicating Personally: A Theory of Interpersonal Communication and Human Relationships* (Indianapolis: Bobbs-Merrill, 1975); and for the philosophical basis for much of this work, John Dewey and Arthur F. Bentley, *Knowing and the Known* (Boston: Beacon Press, 1949). The transactional view will be applied to problems of journalistic listening in Chapter 4.

[28]Oriana Fallaci, "The Argentine General Who Never Fought in a War," *Washington Post,* June 13, 1982, sec. C, p. C1.

# Meeting People

## Off on the Right Foot

**I**t is 2 P.M. and city hall is quiet.

Anna Quirk, a young reporter in a neatly tailored suit, glances at her watch, pleased that she is precisely on time for her appointment with the mayor. The reporter is new to the city hall beat, and her first assignment is touchy. She must ask the mayor, Ed Wagner, about a potential conflict of interest. The city's liability coverage is handled by an insurance agency owned by the mayor's son-in-law.

"Good afternoon, Mayor," she says as she stands by Wagner's open door. "Come in, young lady," the mayor says. Resting his cigar in an ashtray, he rises behind his desk to greet Quirk. She notices the odor first, and winces slightly.

It is not quite a gunfighter's showdown, but both the reporter and the mayor are sizing each other up, somewhat warily. Although they have never met until now, they already know something about one another, and neither is favorably impressed.

Around the newsroom, Mayor Wagner is known for playing the horses, pounding backs and cutting deals. He butchers English and reads the National Enquirer. Quirk is not surprised to hear that his favorite pastime is bowling. How did such an unpolished man ever manage to get re-elected three times? she wonders.

The mayor, too, did some checking. The reporter is two years out of journalism school, which alone is enough reason to distrust her. He remembers when reporters would drink beer with him after city

15

council meetings and were not offended by off-color jokes. The mayor figures he is about to face another idealistic do-gooder who knows nothing about the game of politics. What's worse is that this one wears a skirt.

As they approach, the reporter and the mayor continue to measure one another, confirming and reinforcing secondhand impressions and combining them with what they are now observing. For one thing, the reporter finds the "young lady" greeting condescending. The mayor, who didn't miss the reporter's reaction to the cigar, tells himself, "I'm not going to put it out for some damn woman reporter." Of course, it still may be possible for the two to set aside their first impressions, many based on stereotypes, and move to a relationship based on fuller, more objective appraisals. But given the unsteady start, the odds of that happening are not good.

Understandably, reporters tend to de-emphasize the importance of the meeting stage in their eagerness to get down to the business of asking questions. But what happens before the questioning begins is hardly trivial. A reporter's first attempts at communication may determine how the relationship develops—or whether it develops at all. If put off by a reporter's manner or greeting, a person who was otherwise quite willing to talk may answer cryptically, mutter "no comment" or slam the door. Reporters not only must know how to approach people confidently and competently. They must also know how to read initial moods and nonverbal messages, build rapport and overcome obstacles to more substantial communication. Most important of all, reporters need to realize that the relationship which unfolds depends on an *interplay* of first impressions and first steps taken by *both* parties. The reporter's impressions and actions will, in part, influence the mayor's impressions and actions—and vice versa. Too much is at stake, even in a handshake, to take the meeting stage lightly.

## THE MIRROR TEST

Reporters who want to get off on the right foot ought first to take a careful look into a mirror of introspection. Everyone acquires attitudes, values, assumptions and stereotypes that can be traced back to the formative years of childhood and family life. Our views of others are influenced by these socialized habits of behavior and perception. William L. Rivers offers journalists this advice: "An honest man who seeks the truth can balance some of his biases by cold self-examination."[1] A "cold self-examination" might include asking yourself a series of questions. Where did I grow up? (Was it a neighborhood where members of particular racial or ethnic groups weren't welcomed?) What was my family life like? (Did you grow up despising alcoholics because your uncle got drunk most weekends and bullied your aunt?) What were my parents' attitudes and beliefs? (Did your father impress upon you that any able-bodied person ought to be able to rise above poverty?)

More than 50 years ago, one of journalism's most astute commentators, Walter Lippmann, described how many people, including reporters, perceive the world: "For the most part we do not first see, and then define; we define first and then see. In the great blooming, buzzing confusion of the outer world we pick out what our culture has already defined for us, and we tend to perceive that which we have picked out in the form stereotyped for us by our culture."[2] Time has not changed human behavior.

Acknowledging that you are a closet racist or homophobic will not necessarily mean you will be able to exorcise your biases. But you should be less likely to let them poison relationships and distort your reporting by dictating whom you choose to interview, what questions you elect to ask, how well you listen, and how you interpret information. Will a reporter reared by a UAW official view a story about declining union membership differently from a reporter whose family owns a small steel mill? Probably. But both reporters, if honest about self-examination, will resist feelings and attitudes that might subvert their attempts to produce stories that are accurate, complete, fair and balanced.

## OBTAINING INTERVIEWS

Reporters turn to traditional providers of news frequently—perhaps too frequently. Notice how often the same well-used experts appear on interview programs, newscasts or the pages of the metropolitan press. These are professional sources, some of whom, such as Henry Kissinger or Carl Sagan, make a good living from being interviewed. Most localities have their own authorities on various subjects, always available to comment for publication or broadcast. Reporters may be lulled into routines by such availability, relying on the same subjects again and again. It's the path of least trouble or resistance. Introspective reporters, though, explore why they elect to interview Mr. X instead of Ms. Y or Mr. Z.

Reporters should realize that they tend to confer a type of "expert" status on those they ordain as interviewees, thus encouraging other reporters to turn to the same people. Two problems arise from this practice. First, some potential interviewees may attempt to manipulate themselves into an undeserved level of prestige and influence simply by becoming available for you to question. A second and related problem is that journalists apparently rely heavily on males holding executive positions in government.[3] Such a reliance suggests a bias toward a narrow definition of newsmakers; in turn, these elite newsmakers become further legitimized. You can minimize this effect by seeking diverse sources of news.

Journalists also are inclined to turn to news subjects who are, among other things, attractive, reliable, articulate, knowledgeable, honest, friendly, accessible and compatible. Certainly, those are valid grounds for deciding who to interview, but what do such criteria say about people reporters choose *not* to interview? At the courthouse, for example, you may prefer to talk to the attractive, eloquent Harvard law school graduate who speaks "your language," but there may be just as much to learn from the disheveled, cigar-chomping politician who demeaningly calls you "kid." Most people will avoid others they don't like, respect or readily understand, but reporters must resist operating that way. Cultural compatibility or interpersonal attractiveness should never be your criteria to determine whose thoughts and words are newsworthy—and whose are not.

After determining who to interview, the next step is convincing your choice to talk or agree to a meeting. You'll find that various circumstances and approaches may either increase or decrease your chances of gaining cooperation. They range from your status as a journalist to the "rules of the game" set by some interview subjects.

❑ Your status. A novice reporter or obscure freelancer, no matter how gifted, will be at a disadvantage in obtaining an interview, especially from the high and mighty. Barbara Walters can ring up world leaders; you, however, might have trouble getting through to the mayor of Kalamazoo. Reporters should be realistic about their opportunities, but an apt maxim applies: Nothing ventured, nothing gained.

❑ Who you represent. Even well-known, well-regarded journalists find paths to a news subject blocked if they represent the "wrong" media organization. A politician might be quite willing to discuss AIDS with the Washington Post but not with a reporter from a gay activist weekly. At times, the sins of another reporter or editor may haunt you. That was the experience of a Texas Monthly writer who introduced himself to football star Roger Staubach. "Oh, yeah, Texas Monthly," Staubach said. "They gave me some kind of award last year. 'Best Wimp.' "[4]

Sometimes the problem is one of recognition. When Hunter Thompson arrived in Washington, D.C., in 1971 as correspondent for Rolling Stone, few people, he said, would return his calls. Why? Rolling Stone was a new magazine and certainly not one found on the typical upper-crust Washingtonian's coffee table. Some people associated Rolling Stone with the English rock group.[5]

When situations like these arise, build credibility for yourself, your publication and your audience. A reporter not known to the interviewee might mention that she's done several similar stories for different publications. Or a reporter from a mid-sized newspaper might win over a television actress—or her press agent—by saying, "Our newspaper is read by 85 percent of the adults in a six-county region, and most of them watch your program on Saturday nights. You have quite a following here—and so does our newspaper."

❏ What's the payoff? People often weigh interview requests in terms of benefits to them—recognition, material gain or advocacy. If there's little to be gained, a celebrated figure can afford to say no. Your success at meeting someone and obtaining an interview might depend on finding an irresistible reward. Truman Capote paid two death-row inmates $50 each for their interviews that resulted in the best seller *In Cold Blood*.[6] This isn't an endorsement of "checkbook" journalism; psychological rewards can be just as persuasive. One reporter said he almost always induced public speakers to answer his questions by using variations of this approach: "Sir, you flew 2,000 miles to put your ideas across to the 250 people in this audience. I'm trying to put your ideas across to 250,000 people who read our newspaper. Won't you help me?"

❏ What are the risks? Even if there is an evident payoff, a newsmaker might figure the potential risks tip the balance. Who wouldn't think twice about an interview with Mike Wallace, given his reputation of going for the jugular? Henry Kissinger once agreed to a session with Oriana Fallaci, noted for her inquisitorial style of interviewing. Fallaci led him into a discussion of his "Lone Ranger" style of diplomacy. Later, in embarrassment, Kissinger said it was one of the dumbest moves he'd made.[7] Imagine yourself in the position of the person you hope to interview and weigh the risks. You might find a way of easing apprehension. If you've never met the person you plan to interview, you might suggest that he talk to a trusted colleague who knows your work and who can verify that you are a competent, fair journalist.

❑ Time and place. In a world of "one-minute" managers, "frequent flyers" and "power" lunches, convincing a busy person to reserve time for an interview may be a challenge. Worthwhile interviews, however, can take place in a cab or during a brisk walk to a boarding gate. You might have to eliminate an interviewee's excuses: "Senator, I'll talk to you any time or place you say." Being resourceful and opportunistic is important. A student reporter, for example, gained an interview with Supreme Court Justice William O. Douglas by hitching a ride with the university driver assigned to take Douglas to the airport. Another student went to Bob Hope's motel room after a concert and ended up with a brief interview after helping carry Hope's luggage to a waiting car.

❑ Rules of the game. People who are deluged with reporters' requests often establish elaborate guidelines and conditions before submitting to an interview. A condition might be, for example, reviewing a copy of the story before publication, something most reporters would find unacceptable. Another condition might be a ban on sensitive topics. A Chicago Tribune reporter who wanted an interview with talk-show hostess Joan Rivers was instructed that certain topics, one being Johnny Carson, were verboten. Rivers quit as Carson's fill-in to launch a competing talk show. "If you're going to ask her about Johnny Carson and all that, don't bother," Rivers' publicist warned. "It will be the shortest interview on record. She'll walk out."[8] Many reporters would be—and should be—unwilling to agree to rules that restrict their ability to report. If someone says, "I'll talk to you only on the condition that our conversation be kept anonymous," you might have to decline. "My newspaper won't agree to those terms," you reply. Don't give up, though. Frequently, a supposed hardliner on interviews can't resist talking.

Here are some additional suggestions about obtaining interviews:

❑ Don't request a formal "interview." Many reporters just call or approach a person, identify themselves and start talking, easing into the interview. Others may ask for "help," "advice," "input," or "thoughts." Requesting an interview may sound too official, formal and, perhaps most important, too time-consuming. An informal, indirect approach is advised, as long as you reveal both your identity and the purpose of the conversation. Be sure your interviewees know they are speaking for the record, if that's the case.

❑ Knock on the door. Leonard Ray Teel and Ron Taylor say getting some interviews may "require the gall of a snake oil salesman" while others may call for the "honest sympathy of a priest." Among the strategies they suggest are the "end-around" (making the secretary—or any other protector—your friend and ally); the "sit-in" (camping out in someone's office, and even bringing your lunch to show you're determined); and the "face-off" (facing repeated rejection in your attempts to obtain critical facts, you finally might be forced to barge in).[9] Whenever engaging in behavior that could be interpreted as inconsiderate or boorish, reporters should have ready explanations and sincere apologies.

❑ Don't hide your hand unnecessarily. Like poker players, reporters sometimes play their cards close to the vest. Protecting your hand is sound strategy in cards but not always in journalism. In order to gain an interview, you ought to be prepared to state your purpose, outline key questions you intend to ask, set a realistic time limit, provide an incentive and establish your credibility. That may sound like too much territory to cover, but all of those steps can be accomplished in a couple of minutes.

Reporter: "Mayor Jones, this is Tom Brown of the Post. I'm looking into accusations of patronage in your administration. I know this is a sensitive subject, but my reporting won't be balanced until I talk to you. I'd especially like to discuss the job your uncle holds at city hall. I know you're very busy, but if you can give me 20 minutes, I'd be grateful. The charges against you may be political; that's why I want you to know I'm determined to be fair in handling this story."

❑ Be persistent. Television and movie portrayals make a reporter's job harder. Hollywood's journalists are shown hounding the hero or heroine, who ends up pushing through a tangle of cameras and tape recorders, saying, "No comment, no comment." "No comment" ought to be the epitaph for some newsmakers. The best advice when faced with such obstinacy is to *keep talking*. The reporter who persists often ends up with a useful comment.

Don't be too quick to say goodbye or walk away in the face of rejection. Many people are programmed to say "no"; really, it's hard for anyone to hang up or slam the door in the face of a pleasant, calm but persistent reporter. And remember that it's your *right* to ask, just as it is the other person's right to decline.

❑ Try a circling pattern. Several reporters we talked to said that before approaching a potentially unwilling interviewee they first question surrounding figures in the story, learning all they can. Then, thoroughly prepared, they call the central figure, summarizing what they've learned and from whom—taking care, of course, not to violate any confidential communication. Few news subjects can resist responding under those conditions, especially if they dispute some of the details you've presented ("That's all wrong. Let me tell you what happened . . . ."). Such a method might work well, for example, in approaching a chief executive officer about sexual harassment in the corporation. In fact, if you go to the executive without talking to others first, you may be told, "This is the first I've heard of it. I really can't comment unless you have something more specific to discuss."

## FORMING FIRST IMPRESSIONS

One of the most crucial yet underestimated stages in the process of meeting people is the formation of first impressions. Reporters must be especially careful to evaluate and question their initial reactions to others. Of course, everyone relies on instincts and hunches from time to time. But be skeptical about this kind of description of reporters' powers of intuition: "The experienced reporter generally can size up a person with some reliability in a matter of seconds. Is the person a nut? Is the person honest? What's he hustling? What's she going to try to hide? What you read in the person's eyes, in the mannerisms, often is a reliable clue to how the interview must be handled."[10] A matter of seconds? First impressions are more complicated than that and may be biased by a number of conditions.

### Prior Impressions

A reporter's first impressions are often based on fragmentary information acquired *prior to meeting* an interviewee face to face. Ideally, a reporter would imitate The New Yorker's John McPhee, "who tries to be as blank as his notebook pages, totally devoid of preconceptions."[11] Reporters are right, however, to do homework before an interview as long as they understand the danger of being misled by first impressions.

Reporters learn about those they'll interview in at least four ways, each of which is somehow inadequate:

**Superficial Observation.** Often reporters get a chance to "know" a future news subject by means of casual contact. A reporter, for example, sees a candidate for the state legislature kissing babies and teasing silver-haired women, and concludes, "That guy is a phony." When it comes time to interview the candidate, will the reporter disregard signs of the politician's sincerity, seeing only the phoniness he observed from a distance?

**A Trip to the "Morgue."** One of the first things a rookie reporter is likely to hear from the city desk before going out on an assignment is, "Did you check the clips?" In other words, did the reporter stop at the newspaper's library (which some still call the "morgue") to see what others have written or said about the same subject? The newspaper's own clips (articles clipped and filed by names and topics) and printouts of articles from data-base services like NEXIS are useful for background, but remember that they contain someone else's impressions of the person you are about to interview. If you're doing a story about the woman chancellor of the local university, you might find her described in the clips as an "iron butterfly"— "tough," "aloof," and "steel under velvet." Will you then find those characteristics because you anticipate them? Some reporters, recognizing clip material as a potential source of bias, will put off reading it until the interview is over or the story is written. Keep in mind, however, that checking the clips prior to an interview safeguards against oversights, making obvious mistakes and asking questions another reporter asked two weeks earlier.[12]

**Newsroom Pundits.** Opinions abound in a newsroom. Frequently they're unsolicited: "Hey, Sue. I hear you're going to do a piece on the police chief. Watch out for that jerk. He hasn't given me a straight answer in five years." Will Sue approach the chief primed to deal with deception and evasiveness?

**Guilt—or Innocence—by Association.** Assumptions based on someone's friends or business connections could be misleading. For example, if you see the city's director of public works having dinner with a contractor known for an uncanny knack of low bidding on municipal jobs, you might be tempted to conclude that a cozy relationship exists. When you interview the public works director, will his explanations fall on your skeptical ears?

Reporters, like anyone else relying on prior or secondhand impressions, will process details they have learned through what psychologists call "implicit personality theory." This refers to the human tendency to attribute motives and traits to others in a seemingly consistent way. For example, when we are told that someone is "warm" or "cold," we tend automatically to assume that certain associated traits will apply to that person. Are "cold" persons "generous" or "stingy"? We would probably assume "stingy." Are "warm" persons "kind" or "cruel"? We'd likely say, "kind."[13] Withholding judgment may allow you to see the generosity in the IRS agent you'd assumed was "cold"—or see the ill will in actions taken by the "gentle, warm" social worker.

## Visual Inventory

The next level of first-impression formation occurs at the point of introduction. As strangers meet, they assess each other by conducting a visual inventory that might take no more than two seconds.[14] Their immediate perceptions will be based on such observable details as dress, grooming, physical features, facial expressions, manners and behavior. These are merely superficial indicators of what's inside a person, and they may or may not be reliable. Yet people frequently judge others on the basis of such flimsy evidence. Suppose a male interviewee is wearing an earring, which a reporter inaccurately equates with homosexuality. The earring might trigger a series of reactions and behaviors on the reporter's part that can jeopardize the interview. To avoid the trap of mistaken impressions, reporters should understand how even subtle surface signs can affect them.

**Physical Features.** Physical attractiveness influences first impressions, which should come as no great revelation. Although tastes differ, researchers have found considerable agreement when they asked people to rate photographs on a numerical scale of attractiveness.[15] The significant finding, though, was that survey participants used far more positive adjectives, such as "happy," "confident" and "perceptive," in describing attractive people than they did in describing unattractive ones. If reporters react similarly, they can expect to respond less favorably to physically unattractive people. Unchecked, this invites misjudgments, unfairness and a tendency to "write people off." One of our student reporters said she couldn't concentrate on interviewing an older man whose teeth were so bad they sickened her. Had she, though, directed her attention to his eyes, she might have found them unexpectedly expressive, youthful and absorbing.

Other physical features, such as body build, shape impressions. In one study, adults were shown silhouette drawings of three body builds—soft, fat, round; tall, thin, fragile; and muscular, athletic—and asked to assign character traits. The athletic types were characterized by adjectives like "energetic," "bold" and "strong." The thin types were described in largely negative terms—"suspicious," "nervous" and "pessimistic." Overweight types were associated with a mix of positive and negative traits; they were judged "warmhearted" and "good natured" but also "greedy for affection" and "dependent on others."[16] Be careful not to overestimate someone who looks like an Olympic athlete or to underestimate someone who looks like he eats a gallon of ice cream for a mid-morning snack.

Height also plays a role. People tend to measure prestige in terms of height—taller individuals are associated with higher status. In one study, corporate job recruiters were asked to choose between two hypothetical male applicants with identical qualifications. The only difference was that one was listed as 6-foot-1 and the other as 5-foot-5. Only 1 percent of the recruiters chose the shorter man.[17] Studies like this one suggest that taller people, especially males, are viewed more favorably; shortness frequently is seen as a handicap. Being aware of human response to height will help reporters clarify and perhaps control their reactions to interviewees. Remind yourself: The taller supervisor may be more passive and unassertive, and there's no reason a diminutive teacher can't handle a class of football players.

**Dress and Grooming.** Research confirms that grooming, clothing and decorative accessories affect first impressions.[18] Most of us know from experience that occasionally others judge us—and treat us—according to our attire. Salespeople, for example, usually give well-dressed customers more attention and more respect. Logic may tell you that clothes don't—or shouldn't—make the man or woman. The fact remains that how you look does count.

Impressions based on clothing and grooming work on reporters, too. Reporters ought to resist judging others by their clothing or appearance. Instead, try to assess why news subjects are groomed and dressed as they are. Someone with orange-colored spiked hair and tight leather pants is "saying" something. Don't dismiss him as a freak or a flake. Under the leather may be a thoughtful, level-headed individual.

Clothes communicate messages and sometimes reflect the personality or attitudes of the wearer. There are reporters, for instance, who pride themselves on being nonconformists, including in how they dress. Perhaps they are rebelling against the dress-for-success mentality. Then there are those who affect a "look," whether it be college chic, blue collar or L. L. Bean. Finally, some are just plain tacky; mix-and-unmatch polyester is their style.

No matter how reporters dress—and why they dress the way they do—each should ask this question: "Do I want to risk offending or alienating an interviewee by drawing attention to my clothing or appearance?" As a general rule, choose clothing that is appropriate in a professional business setting—a jacket and tie for men and a suit or dress for women. Most people expect such attire. Try to remain inconspicuous or even "neutral" in the color and style of your clothes. Avoid anything in dress or grooming that would be considered unfavorably because you're perceived as pretentious, flashy, sloppy or rebellious. A male reporter who wears jeans and a sport shirt to interview a corporate officer may prompt an internalized reaction: "Why is this reporter so impertinent in his dress? It's almost as if he's making an anti-establishment statement."

Occasionally, it is important for reporters to match dress to the situation. During the urban riots of the 1960s, reporters quickly learned that clothing was an issue. A postmortem report by the Detroit Free Press noted: "Many staffers felt that a coat and tie automatically made them part of the power structure and diminished chances of getting information from the people it was hardest to get it from—the rioters."[19] We spoke with a reporter for a metropolitan newspaper who said he dresses to be comfortable. "I'm a suit-and-tie kind of guy. I don't feel I need to put on bib overalls to interview a farmer. If they see I'm comfortable in the way I dress, they'll be comfortable too." That makes sense, but comfort can't be the only guide; otherwise many people would go to work in pajamas or robes. If you wear a Brooks Brothers suit to interview street people, don't be surprised if rapport is difficult to establish.

**Body Language.** Our first impressions are also derived from such visual cues as posture, gestures and facial expressions. Some people call these nonverbal messages "body language" or "kinesics." Many nonverbal messages are emitted simultaneously when two people meet, and some of those messages are significant, particularly those involving the face.

The eyes, say body-language authorities, are the primary medium of nonverbal communication at the early stages of an encounter.[20] Eye contact can be the beginning step to a relationship. A reporter might interpret avoidance of eye contact as a sign of distance or deceit; conversely, an interviewee might look upon similar behavior by the reporter as rudeness. Neither person may be correct, but the inferences are there nevertheless. Keep in mind that the eye is *simultaneously* a sending and receiving organ for *each* party in a communication encounter.

While eye contact usually enhances communication, intense, prolonged eye contact—a hard stare—can make people uncomfortable, even if that's not the intent. Eye contact can be a means of engagement, but if an interviewer isn't careful, it can become an instrument of disengagement. Moreover, instead of generating trust, unnecessarily purposeful eye contact can create a climate of suspiciousness. Psychiatrist Leonard Zunin has observed: "A meeting of the eyes may start in motion a fast train of assumptions. 'He was undressing me with his eyes,' or 'She seemed to look right through me.' "[21] In addition, there are those who try to play power games with eye contact, somewhat in the way certain people use a vise-grip handshake to be assertive or intimidating. They try to stare someone down in a form of mental arm-wrestling.

Think of the smile, too, as a message promoting first impressions. When people meet, initial contact often involves a smile. Like eye contact, a sincere smile is a step in relationship development. Zunin refers to the smile as "the lubrication for words and the collaborator of the eyes in contact."[22] For reporters, a smile may ease tension and help them approach interviewees in a friendly, relaxed and open way. But because of the often serious nature of their work and because of their orientation to be wary and skeptical, reporters sometimes find it difficult to smile when they should. Just remember—many people are reluctant already to talk with reporters. Do you want to make them more reluctant by a stern or dour expression?

## Unintentional Impressions

People communicate much more than they realize. In fact, through nonverbal behavior you may unintentionally influence the impressions of others in ways that can handicap further communication. Here are some situations that can lead to unintentional impressions:

**Handshakes and initial body contact.** The handshake is usually the only body contact when two people meet. It is an expected, commonplace form of greeting, certainly among men. Although the act of shaking hands is simple, there is a degree of protocol involved. In addition, messages are sent and received in the process, so the handshake becomes a basic form of communication. A limp handshake often turns people off because it could connote indifference. A damp hand could suggest nervousness. A too-powerful grasp may be interpreted as aggression. A prolonged grip, or prolonged pumping, can make your partner uncomfortable, annoyed or even wary. Even an otherwise normal handshake might be viewed as inconsiderate if the recipient is an older person with arthritis.

Since handshakes are not always self-explanatory, our assumptions about people and their motives can influence how we evaluate a handshake. As always, don't rush to judgment. Some people might conclude, for example, that the "glad-hander" is up to no good, but he or she may simply be the demonstrative—yet sincere—type. Since many men are taught by their fathers that a weak grasp is unmanly, the bone-crusher may be overcompensating in a handshake and "mean" nothing in particular by his behavior.

Are there universal rules for handshaking etiquette? No, but observations by anthropologist Desmond Morris may be helpful. Taking an evolutionary point of view, Morris notes that a subordinate chimpanzee will offer its hand to a dominant one as a gesture of appeasement. In humans, he says, it might therefore be appropriate for an inferior, determined by age or status, to offer the hand first. Morris also makes an interesting point about handshaking between a man and a woman. A man, he says, usually will wait for the woman to offer her hand for shaking, as if she were still offering it to be kissed. "However," Morris adds, "not to offer the hand to her first, now that kissing has vanished from the act, is tantamount to saying that he is the officer and she the private, and that she must make the first sign of salute."[23] A man still might prefer to wait for a clue, such as an intentional movement of the arm, before offering his hand. But no matter who's involved, male or female, the object is to shake hands comfortably and simultaneously, so neither party feels awkward.

Other forms of body contact are probably inappropriate when strangers meet. Greetings among acquaintances often include an embrace or pat or an embellishment to the handshake, like touching the elbow with the left hand. But there is an accepted intimacy among friends that is not present when strangers greet each other.

Touch becomes increasingly important as a relationship unfolds. But early in developing relationships, a conservative, non-invasive policy is safest.

**Smoking.** The combination of a smoker and nonsmoker may be volatile: Some nonsmokers deeply resent the use of tobacco in their presence, while some smokers fail to recognize the emotional impact of their behavior. Reporters who smoke should abstain unless it is obvious that the interviewee smokes, too. It's inadvisable even to seek permission to smoke. That puts the interviewee in the uncomfortable position of having to say no or being forced to endure the smoke in order to avoid appearing inhospitable. Resentment could develop in either situation. The reporter who is denied permission might be resentful as well.

What if the interviewee is a smoker and the reporter isn't? The reporter shouldn't show any sign of displeasure. In such a case, think positively: Smoking might stimulate the thought processes in the interviewee or help him or her to relax.

**Territoriality.** People can be very sensitive to what they perceive as invasion of personal territory. Part of our personal territory is the body buffer zone we create to maintain proper distance in relationships. If strangers come too close to us, we feel uncomfortable or even defensive. We also often lay special claim to objects or places within "our" territories. Reporters may unknowingly violate personal zones if they aren't careful. These guidelines may be helpful:

❑ Stay at least 24 to 40 inches away from a new acquaintance. This "personal distance" is considered acceptable for conversations in Western culture.[24] To come any closer might unintentionally communicate an inappropriate degree of intimacy. That's why touch beyond the handshake is not recommended among strangers.

❑ Don't touch any personal objects belonging to the person you're meeting. You might be tempted, for example, to look more closely at a photograph on the person's desk or pick up a book. Your action may be harmless and unmeaningful from your perspective, but the other person might see it as presumptuous familiarity. Even moving an object to make room for your briefcase or tape recorder might be perceived as an invasion of personal space. Ask permission first.

❑ Don't take liberties in someone else's office or home. First, wait until it is clear you are welcome before entering the personal territory of another. Once within someone's domain, show respect for his or her possessions. For example, don't prop your feet on a coffee table or lounge languidly on the settee.

**Tardiness.** One of the worst sins for a reporter is being late to a prearranged meeting. Tardiness communicates multiple messages—most of them negative. The latecomer is likely to be regarded as inconsiderate, unreliable, forgetful or unprofessional. Excuses like "I couldn't find a parking place" sound (and are) feeble. (The ultimate sin is to be late and then have to ask for a pen or a piece of paper for notes.) If, by chance, you are late due to an emergency, an explanation is generally expected. Work it into your small talk introduction in whatever way seems appropriate.

Clearly, research into nonverbal communication has yielded important insights, but be aware that you are still dealing with an inexact science. Two qualifiers, therefore, are in order. First, never assume that an individual nonverbal message "means" anything taken by itself. Context is always crucial. Second, don't overestimate the importance of body language or overinterpret its messages.

## SMALL TALK, LARGE CONSEQUENCES

Reporters are accustomed to meeting people, so they generally go about introductions and the other rituals of greeting automatically, without giving much thought to the process. Initial talk, however, will help structure and in some ways pre-set further communication. Introductions and preliminary conversation transcend social niceties. They signify several things. For one, they may tell us whether the other person is making a commitment to a communicative relationship. A cold and formal introduction—signaled perhaps by physical distance, clipped speech or averted eyes—may be a danger sign. Although messages are being transmitted in both directions, it is particularly important for reporters to do everything in their power to ensure that initial communication is effective and beneficial to the relationship to follow.

### Saying Hello

There are many ways to make introductions, but creativity is probably not advisable at this point. Ideally, the reporter should be socially correct and self-assured. A friendly, semi-formal greeting

("Mr. Cavanaugh, I'm Robert Jones from the Tribune. I'm pleased to meet you.") is usually in order. You seldom will go wrong with such an approach, but an unconventional salutation may flop. The overly anxious reporter is most prone to commit an introductory *faux pas*. A dramatic example can be seen in what happened to Arthur Zich, a writer for National Geographic, who interviewed four armed guerrillas in the Philippines. As Zich told the story:

> The leader extended a bony hand. "I'm Ka Liber, a code name," he said. Ka, I knew, meant comrade. "Small caliber or large?" I joked nervously. Ka Liber did not smile. "You may find out someday," he replied. The young(est) guerrilla kept his rifle pointed at my mid-section throughout the interview.[25]

You probably won't interview many gun-toting people, but an inappropriate introduction on your part may still result in unnecessary hostility or suspicion.

Inappropriate greetings come in other varieties as well. Ours is a casual age in which 6-year-old Nathan greets an octogenarian with "Hi, Martha!" Martha may think little Nathan is cute, but informality isn't well received by everyone. A safer practice is to refer to people by professional title (Captain Davis) or courtesy title and last name (Mr. Jackson). One reporter tells the story of a colleague who made the mistake of calling writer Maya Angelou by her first name: "Ms. Angelou immediately stopped the interview and told the reporter that she (Angelou) was a lot older than the young woman and it was a sign of respect for young people to address their elders formally until given permission to do otherwise." Angelou's scolding left the young reporter unnerved for the rest of the interview.

Another type of inappropriate behavior occurs when reporters try to be chummy by adopting the idiom or presumed style of others. A student reporter unsuccessfully tried to relate to an inmate at the county jail by greeting him as "Yo, Marvin . . . " Marvin, serving time for armed robbery, reacted with derisive laughter. Phil Donahue committed a similar gaffe when he referred to a biker's wife as "your old lady." The biker sternly corrected Donahue. "She's not my 'old lady'; she's my wife." Presumptuousness in your greeting or manners may offend.

Obviously, the first few moments of contact are important, even when greeting someone with whom you are well acquainted. You still should evaluate responses to your verbal approaches and make adjustments if necessary. All of us have experienced saying hello to an acquaintance, and then, based on an instant calculation of a handful of verbal and nonverbal messages, concluded: "Boy, Joe sure is preoccupied this morning." That may be true, or it could be entirely incorrect. Reporters should be alert for messages found in even pro forma greetings. Is the county clerk's curt hello a sign he or she is upset with your story about voter registration irregularities? Or is the curtness caused by a nagging headache? And do you need to deal with what you perceive? You might want to ask the county clerk about the story, and, if necessary, offer the chance to vent any bad feelings.

## Benefits of Small Talk

In a fast-paced world, there's often pressure to dispense with small talk and get down to business. For journalists, deadlines and schedules may prevail; newsmakers are also pressed for time. In established relationships, such as a reporter encountering people on a news beat, small talk isn't as important. But when and where small talk is appropriate, it has benefits reporters should not overlook.

For one, small talk can help establish rapport—a communication environment of trust, comfort and good will. Warranted or not, reporters don't enjoy a reputation for fair play and good manners. In some cases, a wary interviewee will hide behind a defensive shield until the reporter proves to be decent and trustworthy. Small talk, if accomplished smoothly, can help soften or eliminate skeptical feelings. It can also help to humanize reporters. A reporter who rushes headlong into the business of asking questions may seem too much like a news-collecting machine. Robotic or single-minded interviewers are not likely to achieve the personal rapport that leads to comfortable disclosures. Barbara Walters underscores the point when she observes, "Until the celebrity, or anyone for that matter, feels comfortable with you, it's not likely that he will feel like disclosing anything more intimate than his hat size."[26]

Anthropologist Bronislaw Malinowski coined the term *phatic communion* to describe social conversation that is basically noninstrumental.[27] In other words, it doesn't attempt to accomplish any particular goal other than that implied by the term *communion*. This small talk is communication for the sake of its own enjoyment, and therefore it is a form of social lubrication that enables greater possibilities for the relationship.

Small talk also can provide useful clues to the emotional moods and priorities of the conversants. While chatting with the school superintendent, you remark, "Bill, your office seems especially busy these days." The school superintendent responds with fatigue in his voice, "You're right. Trying to balance the damned budget is driving everyone crazy, especially me." Or during a post-game interview in a football coach's office, you notice a Special Olympics ribbon hanging from the conference championship trophy. "Coach, I see you have a Special Olympics ribbon." The coach immediately warms up and tells how his son, who has Down's syndrome, won first place in the 100-yard dash. Until then, you knew nothing about his son, and you see another dimension of the coach's life. And he sees that there's more dimension to your life and interests, too, than just getting quotes about TD's and tailbacks.

Finally, small talk can provide openings and transitions to more penetrating conversation. For example, chitchat about the sweltering weather with the public works director might lead to a serious discussion of the city's water-supply problems—a situation news media had not yet thought to probe.

## Conversational Openers

Some reporters instinctively seem to know what to say. But small talk, though it is enjoyable if natural, isn't always easy. Because first impressions are important, and because small talk paves the way for more significant talk, reporters ought to consider a conversational entree in advance. Saul Pett of the Associated Press uses this technique: "I kind of plan the opening, either with a little humor or something to relax them, or something that will interest them. I think the success of an interview depends on whether you interest the guy."[28] Pett recognizes that initial contact is critical, and he sees it as *his responsibility* to say something that will stimulate the interviewee.

Of course, there is a kind of paradox involved here. If small talk is most effective when natural and spontaneous, can a reporter really use it to "open up" the interviewee? The answer is yes, as long as small talk is not used in a contrived fashion. That would be a contradiction: orchestrated spontaneity. It should develop only as part of a reporter's sincere attempt to get to know the other person in the ways natural conversation will allow. Phatic communion is the way "real people" talk, and therefore it is a guideline for reporters' conversation, too.

These suggestions for pre-interview openings come from reporters and communication experts:

❏ Refer to something in the news, especially if it may be of interest to the person you plan to interview or germane to the interview's purpose. Suppose you're meeting the general manager of a local television station. After introductions, you might say, "Did you happen to see the FCC chairman on 'The Today Show' talk about the Fairness Doctrine?" A question of that sort could either prompt a reaction by the general manager ("Yes, I did . . . ") or a request for you to relate what was said ("No, I missed that. What did he say?"). As a result, the conversation, no matter which party takes the next step, should evolve naturally and smoothly to a fuller discussion.

❑ Offer a genuine compliment. Everyone enjoys being appreciated, and praise fosters a positive communication climate. The key, though, is not to engage in praise for manipulative reasons. As Dale Carnegie observed, an expression of appreciation or admiration and one amounting to flattery differ dramatically. "One is sincere and the other insincere," he said. "One comes from the heart out; the other from the teeth out. One is unselfish; the other is universally condemned."[29] An authority on the psychology of meeting people says the praise must be believable.[30] Otherwise, the compliment will give the interviewee an immediate reason to question the reporter's motives.

One way to enhance believability is to avoid compliments that are too general or too effusive. You might say to a politician, "It's such an honor finally to meet a senator with the courage to speak out about our Middle East policy." You would be better off saying, "Ever since I read your book on Middle East policy, I have looked forward to meeting you." Another approach to believability is to offer a balanced compliment. Applying the same example, the reporter might say, "I've admired you ever since I heard you speak on Arab-Israeli relations, although you've certainly upset a lot of people." Using qualifications in bestowing praise will suggest that the reporter is discerning and not attempting to ingratiate.

❑ Build a mood of commonality by mentioning mutual acquaintances or interests. A colleague once videotaped a very preoccupied Walter Cronkite, who entered the hotel room and gruffly said, "Let's get this over with." But someone softened the mood by asking Cronkite if he remembered an old colleague from his newspaper days in Kansas City. Cronkite beamed. "Do you know him?" he said. "How's he doing?" A connection between you and your interviewee can be constructed with comments such as: "Your friend, Mr. Rayburn, says hello," or "Did you enjoy your vacation last month at Sister Bay? We've been going there for years." Thereafter, you'll be less of a stranger, and you'll be engaged in supportive light conversation from which more serious inquiries can grow.

❑ Bring up a sure-to-please topic. Perhaps the person you're meeting has a son or daughter who's a star athlete. You might say, "I see your daughter Jane is doing well this season. Has she decided which college she'll attend?" What parent could resist such a conversational appetizer?

❑ Look for openers in the surroundings or actions of the person you're meeting. When interviewer John Brady arrived at film critic Rex Reed's apartment, Reed was opening mail and muttering about the ridiculous invitations he frequently received. "What sort of wild invitations have you turned down lately?" Brady asked.[31] Openings like Brady's, however, can't be planned. They depend on a reporter's talent at improvisation.

Reporters interested in improving their conversational improvisation might try to "spy" on their own non-professional private conversation. Try to be alert to your natural style of starting conversations with friends and intimates. Make a list of your prominent habits and behaviors. Then imagine you were responsible for "interviewing" these people; decide which aspects of your so-called private or personal style might be transferred profitably to your professional style.

## Testing the Water

Small talk can dampen a relationship if done poorly. To minimize the potential problems of small talk, here are some guidelines:

❑ Stick to pleasant, noncontroversial subjects. Comments about religion, sex or politics might be too provocative to risk raising. Bring up safe topics, like asking a newcomer to town what he likes about St. Louis.

❑ Avoid offering advice. Don't look around someone's office and say, "You have such a beautiful view from your window. You ought to move your desk to take advantage of it."

❑ Use self-focused talk carefully. You are there to learn about what the interviewee has to say, not to talk about yourself. Nonetheless it can often help to build rapport if the reporter reveals something about himself or herself to the other person. Remember that small talk is *phatic communion,* and communion is meant to be shared. You should try to reveal part of your personal side to the interviewee as well as the other way around. In interviewing the mother of an autistic child, you might talk about your sister, who is dyslexic.

❏ Employ humor cautiously. Humor can be an effective opener provided it's in good taste and the other person has a sense of humor. Saul Pett's skill at conversational openers failed in an interview with labor leader Jimmy Hoffa when he asked Hoffa, "My wife wants to know why you always wear white socks." The icy response was, "Because my feet sweat less in them."[32]

❏ Watch for telltale signs. Small talk irritates some people. They may, unfortunately, consider it too trivial or a waste of time. If that's the case, they probably will reveal their feelings nonverbally, such as by frequently shifting their body positions, or verbally. They may even be blunt: "Let's get on with it."

❏ Don't go too long with small talk. How long is too long? It's not as if you're cooking a three-minute egg. But as a general rule, small talk should last until each of you is at ease and a degree of rapport is established. Then it's time to move gracefully on to more substantive talk, preferably with an appropriate transition. For example, "Speaking of difficult decisions, Senator Townsend, how hard was it for you to vote for the tax measure yesterday?"

The best advice is to approach small talk as a swimmer tests the water with the toe before jumping in.


## A STATE OF READINESS

People assume that reporters are extroverts and skilled conversationalists; reporters supposedly relish meeting people and confidently go about their work. That's not always the case.

Many able reporters work hard to overcome shyness or subdue anxiety. Richard Reeves of the New York Times told the Washington Post's Lou Cannon: "Most of us are terribly curious introverts, and we need an institutional cloak. I could go to a party and never say a word to anyone—I don't know how to begin a conversation. But if I can say, 'Excuse me, I'm Dick Reeves of the Times,' that breaks the ice for me and I can deal with the situation."[33] Cannon himself told an interviewer about his own shyness. "I'm a lot less shy now," he said, "but I was very shy when I started."[34] Joan Didion, noted for her revealing pieces about people and places, is another journalist who feels uncomfortable meeting strangers. "I am bad at interviewing people—I do not like to make telephone calls, and would not like to count the mornings I have sat on some Best Western bed somewhere and tried to force myself to put through a call to the assistant district attorney."[35]

Anxiety and shyness are special problems for novice journalists. A major reason good students abandon journalism is apprehension over meeting people. "I get so nervous going into someone's office my palms sweat and my stomach churns," one student confessed. Reassurance that reporting becomes less stressful with time usually doesn't change such minds. Some reporters are always fighting a case of butterflies, and it is a perfectly natural feeling.

Reporters, if they are to remain reporters very long, must cope with moments of insecurity or stress. But even the most efficient, poised reporters frequently find themselves rushing from one assignment to the next, with little time to catch a breath. A harried reporter may perform poorly. If time and conditions permit, reporters should try to achieve a state of emotional and mental readiness for meeting people. One way is the *PRRP process—prepare, rehearse, relax, pause.*

## Prepare

A reporter can't—and shouldn't—prepare for every eventuality. Sometimes circumstances don't permit much preparation, such as being called out to cover a disaster story. In addition, there should be a degree of spontaneity in conversation. Nonetheless, preparation is a key to approaching an assignment with confidence.

Earlier, we advised planning a conversational opener. But it is important to go further and do some homework. If the person you plan to interview is well publicized, there should be no excuse for failing to gather background information. An interview will immediately falter if you have to ask for a first name, title or some other bit of readily available information. It's not enough to merely know someone's past accomplishments or claim to fame. A reporter should be up to date, which includes knowing something about the other person's latest ventures or plans. (Chapter 3 includes more about preparing for interviews.)

What if there's nothing in the newsroom clips, reference room or computerized information services on your subject? There's still opportunity for preparation, provided the reporter is resourceful. Suppose the person you plan to interview is the inventor of a better mousetrap. Someone, somewhere, at some time has written something about mousetraps, a topic of certain interest to your interviewee. Find it. Beyond that are articles and books about inventors and inventions. Libraries are self-evident aids, but too many reporters have not set foot in one since they finished their last college term paper.[36]

Preparation does more than bolster confidence. It is also a sign of caring and consideration that other people will quickly detect and appreciate. A. J. Liebling, for example, won immediate respect and cooperation from jockey Eddie Arcaro with his first question: "How many holes longer do you keep your left stirrup than your right?" Liebling asked. That opener, Liebling said, launched an hour-long conversation during which Liebling put in about 12 words. "I can see you've been around riders a lot," Arcaro said.[37]

## Rehearse

Public speakers rehearse. Actors rehearse. Lawyers do, too. They know that success depends on being smooth and sure in their delivery. Why shouldn't reporters rehearse those opening lines that can be so difficult to come by if they are just ad libbing? If unsure of what to say or how to say it, you'll struggle to be clear, succinct and at ease. When the words don't come easily, you become even more clumsy in your communication attempts. Communication can start on firmer ground with rehearsal. Of course, conversations can be crippled by excessive rehearsal or forecasting of discoveries. Your goal should be to establish a more "familiar" ground from which the conversation can develop.

Rehearsal can simply be deciding on an opening comment or introduction and how you might phrase it. Reporters tend to be more eloquent at a keyboard than in oral communication, so it makes sense to plan a provisional opening to conversation. It might help to consider it a lead. After all, reporters will often experiment with dozens of lead variations before being satisfied. They realize the lead is the most important part of the story. It will either invite the reader to go on or turn the reader away. A conversation opener has the same effect. If your introductory communication is dull, the interview may go on—but probably without much commitment or interest on the part of the interviewee.

## Relax

Working against a deadline is a leading cause of tension for reporters. Another source of pressure is having to ask questions that might provoke tears or curses. Sensitive reporters rightfully become tense at times prior to interviews. Physician Maxwell Maltz suggests "do-it-yourself tranquilizers" that might help a reporter learn to relax. One method is to construct what Maltz calls a personal "decompression chamber." "Each of us needs a quiet room inside his own mind. . . . It depressurizes you from tensions, worry, pressure, stresses and strains, refreshes you and enables you to return to work better prepared to cope with it."[38] The quiet-room effect usually is established by visualizing a pleasing scene or place, such as a cabin by a cool stream, and putting yourself there for a brief mental vacation. Maltz also suggests hitting the "clear" button in much the same way as we erase the memory on a calculator so that we can face a new situation with a clean slate. His advice is useful in putting aside personal problems, like a fight with a spouse earlier in the day.[39]

In a similar vein, most martial arts disciplines teach a body-awareness method known as "centering." Mind, body and breathing are all known to be connected and interdependent. Fear and worry become bodily problems, such as the headache that develops after driving in rush-hour traffic or taking an exam. Tension in the body inhibits mental relaxation; the resulting mental tension exhibits itself in a tightening of the musculature and a constriction of breathing, sometimes creating a vicious circle of mind and body effects. But centering—actually a simple breathing technique—can break the circle. In an undisturbed moment alone, whether sitting, standing or lying down, allow yourself to follow these steps:

- Imagine a point about two inches below your navel, your "center."
- Breath in from your nose, and imagine that breath traveling slowly to the center.
- Bring the breath slowly back from the center and out the mouth.
- Count the breaths.

What will happen? Most often people who seriously concentrate on the technique find that it clears the mind. (Can you worry about your work when you're focusing on counting the travels of your inner breath stream?) It relaxes the muscles—something that cannot be done by will alone. The centered person thus becomes truly ready for what is to come *next,* rather than being unduly affected by some reservoir of tension or fear that is connected to the *past.*

## Pause

Consistent with centering, try to arrive early and spend a few moments collecting yourself before the interview. The privacy of a rest room is a good place to get ready. You might learn from professional athletes who have their personal pre-game rituals. Some beat on lockers, but many quietly undergo psychological priming, using visualization and positive-thinking techniques. Reporters can go through some mental and physical conditioning, too. Clear your mind of extraneous thoughts. Check your grooming. Loosen your facial muscles. Go over your questions one more time. Think positively about yourself, your interviewee and your story. Then walk assuredly to your meeting, but don't go into the interview with the resolute visage athletes call a "game face." If appropriate, enter with a smile.

## OPENING CLOSED DOORS

Despite your best intentions and efforts, some people are going to be difficult to approach. They may be recalcitrant, manipulative or suspicious. Ultimately, it is your responsibility to open channels of communication. Here is an assortment of observations and suggestions designed to help you when doors appear closed.

### Finding a Pass Key

Reporters often find establishing a relationship hardest when dealing with public officials. Why do reporters struggle to gain access? Why do public officials frequently seem to resist or frustrate the efforts of journalists? The problem, in part, is competing duties. Journalists believe theirs is to serve as the public's watchdog. Public officials, on the other hand, believe their duty is to safeguard the public interest. Reporters usually feel the First Amendment entitles them to special privileges and full access in covering the news. But are reporters realistic in viewing their role in society? Can they reasonably expect to find a welcome mat in front of every door? Reporters should curb any feelings of righteous indignation as they approach government officials and public figures. Don't burst in with guns blazing or kick down the door if people *at first* decline to admit you.

Opening some doors requires firmness, determination and persuasion. Assertive journalism may be needed, but there's a distinction between assertive journalism and aggressive journalism. Training in communication skills often stresses this distinction. "Assertive" behavior means that you simultaneously respect your own rights and the rights of other persons. "Aggressive" behavior, on the other hand, meets your own needs but at the expense of the needs and rights of others.[40] Assertive journalism calls for a persistent approach—with a careful, flexible, empathic touch.

Assertive journalism might take this form:

A reporter calls the police chief to learn more about the reported suicide of one of his officers.

REPORTER: "Chief, I'm sorry to hear about the death of Officer Wilson."

CHIEF: "I not going to say anything more about the case."

REPORTER: "It must be difficult for you talk about what happened."

CHIEF: "It's more than that. You guys in the press are like vultures. Can't you leave it alone?"

REPORTER: "I know it must seem that way sometimes. I think I know what you're going through. A good friend of mine took his life. At the time, I sure didn't feel like answering reporters' questions."

CHIEF: "It's not going to do any good to tell the world what happened. It's tragic, and I don't want his wife and kids to suffer any more than they already have."

REPORTER: "I don't either, chief. Can we sit down and talk about how we can possibly tell this story in a sensitive way?"

Of course, a gentle but assertive approach is no guarantee you will gain cooperation and disclosure, but butting heads and kicking butts won't produce much more than bruises for all parties.

At times, reporters have to be prepared to accept rejection. Just try not to be too casual about rejection. Instead of automatically saying, "That cop just hates the press; that's why he won't talk," a sensitive reporter will probably assume more personal responsibility for an encounter that fails, trying to assess why it failed: "Is it something I've done—or haven't done?"

### Overcoming Another's Apprehensiveness

People who try to dodge reporters often do so out of fear of "having a job done" on them. That's why the errors or bad manners of other reporters may complicate your work. As one observer put it, "Milling around between you and the subject are the ghosts of every reporter who ever misquoted, misled, or mishandled your [person]."[41] Overcoming fears may not be easy, but if you can establish that your motives are honorable and your methods fair, you should gain cooperation more often than not. Mere reassurances may not be enough to put people at ease. You might have to make an unusual demonstration of good intentions, for example, by offering to review your notes with the interviewee for accuracy and understanding.

Here's how one reporter approaches those reluctant to talk. "I try to separate myself from other reporters," he said. "First I fill them [interviewees] in on what I have learned. This helps convince them that I know what I'm talking about." Another reporter cautioned against using ploys on suspicious types. "If you try to fiddle around, it will just be clear to them that you are fiddling around. The best thing to do is say, 'Look, I'll tell you exactly why I'm here.' " Sometimes a direct approach, forsaking small talk and other niceties, is necessary.

With certain stories and interviewees, being patient pays off. Reporter Ann Frank compassionately told the story of Al Perlmutter, a victim of Lou Gehrig's disease, who waged a legal fight for the right to die. At first, people Frank sought to interview turned her away. Some of them chided her for having the nerve to invade the Perlmutter family's privacy. But she didn't badger, trick or anger people into responding. Showing professionalism and sensitivity, Frank ultimately won the respect and support of Perlmutter's neighbors, nurses and friends. Although she never was able to speak to family members, shortly after Al Perlmutter's death his son said, "A young woman, who I never met and who never met me, who never met my father, wrote my Dad's legacy. It's all there."[42]

For some people, especially those unaccustomed to dealing with reporters, nervousness might discourage communication. You should anticipate this in inexperienced interviewees and do your best to put them at ease. One way is to be sure to explain what is going to happen in the interview. Going over some questions you intend to ask may also ease apprehension. Another way is to meet, if possible, in a place that is comfortable for or familiar to the interviewee. Sometimes getting together for coffee or a soft drink is conducive to relaxed, natural conversation.

## Coping with Power Games

Reporters can expect that some people will try to establish authority over them through power games. Nancy M. Henley, author of *Body Politics,* says making people wait is one kind of a power game.[43] Reporters, of course, are used to waiting for people, so a waiting game only becomes a threat to communication at the point when a reporter feels he or she is being intentionally put off. Sociologist Barry Schwartz says being made to wait makes some people feel subordinate.[44] Although a long wait may be an interviewee's way of asserting dominance, reporters should ask themselves whether there might be legitimate reasons for the delay. Waiting may be the price a reporter has to pay to meet a busy, powerful person. If you sit and seethe, your feelings are likely to get in the way of objectively assessing what the person eventually has to say.

Space and distance can also be expressions of power. One example is making a visitor stand at an office doorway. If the tactic is deliberate, then it becomes an act of control and a message that serious communication is not desired. One professor leaves a pile of books on the chair nearest his office door to prevent visitors from settling in. Another example is control by means of office arrangement. In some corporate offices, visitors have to walk a good distance, like a crown subject entering the royal chamber, to reach the news source, who is positioned behind an imposing desk. An executive, according to a reporter who deals with him regularly, appears to assign importance to appointments by deciding where his visitors sit. Some people are invited to chairs in front of his desk (important business transactions); some are led to a sofa (social or intimate conversation); and some are seated at a small, plain table just inside the door to his spacious office (minor, impersonal business matters). The reporter said he usually ended up at the small table, which, to him, at least, represented the executive's low esteem for the reporter's "business."

If you believe you are a target of power games, try to maintain your professional composure. Showing negative feelings may only aggravate the problem. Evaluate evidence of power messages carefully and objectively. There may be a perfectly innocent intent to the behavior you sense to be manipulative.

In Chapter 2 you have seen how the first several minutes of contact between a reporter and a potential interviewee can determine—for good or ill—what is to follow. Reporters who don't understand or appreciate the important elements of meeting people invite problems: less cooperation from interviewees, mistaken impressions and incomplete stories—if they get a story at all. Care and expertise in meeting people will help lay the foundation on which a successful interview can be built.

## Notes

[1] William L. Rivers, *Finding Facts: Interviewing, Observing, Using Reference Sources* (Englewood Cliffs, N.J.: Prentice-Hall, 1975), p. 24.

[2] Walter Lippmann, *Public Opinion* (New York: Macmillan, 1922), p. 81.

[3] Jane Delano Brown, Carl R. Bybee, Stanley T. Wearden, and Dulcie Murdock Straughan, "Invisible Power: Newspaper News Sources and the Limits of Diversity," *Journalism Quarterly* 64 (Spring 1987): 45–54. See, as well, Leon V. Sigal, *Reporters and Officials: The Organization and Politics of Newsmaking* (Lexington, Mass.: D.C. Heath, 1973).

[4] Jan Reid, "The Aging of the All-American Boy: Roger Staubach at Thirty-Five," *Texas Monthly,* October 1977, p. 195; cited in Michael E. Stano and N. L. Reinsch Jr., *Communication in Interviews* (Englewood Cliffs, N.J.: Prentice-Hall, 1982), p. 94.

[5] John Brady, *The Craft of Interviewing* (New York: Vintage Books, 1977), p. 8.

[6] Denis Brian, *Murderers and Other Friendly People* (New York: McGraw-Hill, 1973), p. 89.

[7] Quoted in Melvin Mencher, *News Reporting and Writing,* 2nd ed. (Dubuque, Iowa: Wm. C. Brown, 1981), p. 451.

[8] Cheryl Lavin, "Rivers' Goodbye Not a Minute Too Soon," *Chicago Tribune,* May 17, 1987, Sec. 5, p. 3.

[9] Leonard Ray Teel and Ron Taylor, *Into the Newsroom* (Englewood Cliffs, N.J.: Prentice-Hall, 1983), pp. 84, 85.

[10] Teel and Taylor, *Into the Newsroom,* p. 88.

[11] William L. Howarth, ed., *The John McPhee Reader* (New York: Vintage Books, 1978), p. xvi.

[12] Kathleen A. Hansen, Jean Ward, and Douglas M. McLeod, "Role of the Newspaper Library in the Production of News," *Journalism Quarterly* 64 (Winter 1987): 714–720.

[13]Mark L. Knapp, *Social Intercourse: From Greeting to Goodbye* (Boston: Allyn and Bacon, 1978), p. 91.

[14]David Sudnow, ed., *Studies in Social Interaction* (New York: The Free Press, 1972), p. 259–279.

[15]Karen Dion, Ellen Berscheid, and Elaine Walster, "What Is Beautiful Is Good," *Journal of Personality and Social Psychology* 24 (1973): 285–290.

[16]William D. Wells and Bertram Siegel, "Stereotypical Somatotypes," *Psychological Reports* 8 (1961): 77–78.

[17]Mark L. Knapp, *Nonverbal Communication in Human Interaction,* 2nd ed. (New York: Holt, Rinehart and Winston, 1978), p. 167.

[18]Leonard Zunin with Natalie Zunin, *Contact: The First Four Minutes* (New York: Ballantine Books, 1973), pp. 114–118.

[19]*Reporting the Detroit Riot* (New York: American Newspaper Publishers Association, [1968]), p. 16.

[20]Chris L. Kleinke, *First Impressions: Psychology of Encountering Others* (Englewood Cliffs, N.J.: Prentice-Hall, 1975), p. 21–29.

[21]Zunin, *Contact,* p. 80.

[22]Zunin, *Contact,* p. 83.

[23]Desmond Morris, *Intimate Behavior* (New York: Random House, 1971), p. 141.

[24]Edward Hall, *The Hidden Dimension* (Garden City, N.Y.: Doubleday, 1966), pp. 110–122.

[25]Arthur Zich, "Hope and Danger in the Philippines," *National Geographic,* July 1986, p. 96.

[26]Barbara Walters, *How to Talk with Practically Anybody About Practically Anything* (Garden City, N.Y.: Doubleday, 1970), p. 21.

[27]Bronislaw Malinowski, *Magic, Science and Religion and Other Essays* (Boston: Beacon Press, 1948), p. 249.

[28]Roy Peter Clark, ed. *Best Newspaper Writing of 1981* (St. Petersburg, Fla.: Modern Media Institute, 1981), pp. 25, 26.

[29]Dale Carnegie, *How to Win Friends and Influence People* (New York: Pocket Books, 1972), p. 39.

[30]Kleinke, *First Impressions,* pp. 113–122.

[31]Brady, *The Craft of Interviewing,* p. 52.

[32]Brady, *The Craft of Interviewing,* p. 55.

[33]Quoted in Lou Cannon, *Reporting: An Inside View* (Sacramento: California Journal Press, 1977), p. 12.

[34]Quoted in Shirley Biagi, *NewsTalk I: State-of-the-Art Conversations with Today's Print Journalists* (Belmont, Calif.: Wadsworth, 1986), p. 44.

[35]Joan Didion, *Slouching Toward Bethlehem* (New York: Washington Square Press, 1981), pp. 13, 14.

[36]Several books are available to aid the journalist in research. Among them are Lauren Kessler and Duncan McDonald, *Uncovering News: A Journalist's Search for Information* (Belmont, Calif.: Wadsworth, 1987); John Ullmann and Steve Honeyman, eds., *The Reporter's Handbook: Investigative Guide to Documents and Techniques* (New York: St. Martin's Press, 1983); William L. Rivers, *Finding Facts: Interviewing, Observing, Using Reference Sources* (Englewood Cliffs, N.J.: Prentice-Hall, 1975); and Jean Ward and Kathleen A. Hansen, *Search Strategies in Mass Communication* (New York: Longman, 1987).

[37]A.J. Liebling, *The Most of A.J. Liebling* (New York: Simon and Schuster, 1963), p. 157.

[38]Maxwell Maltz, *Psycho-Cybernetics* (North Hollywood, Calif.: Wilshire, 1969), p. 177.

[39]Maltz, *Psycho-Cybernetics,* p. 180.

[40]See Manuel J. Smith, *When I Say No I Feel Guilty* (New York: Bantam Books, 1975).

[41]Connie Fletcher and Jon Ziomek, "How to Catch a Star," *The Quill,* December 1986, p. 32.

[42]George Kennedy, Daryl R. Moen, and Don Ranly, *The Writing Book* (Englewood Cliffs, N.J.: Prentice-Hall, 1984), pp. 24 and 25.

[43]Nancy M. Henley, *Body Politics: Power, Sex, and Nonverbal Communication* (Englewood Cliffs, N.J.: Prentice-Hall, 1977), pp. 43–54.

[44]Barry Schwartz, "Waiting, Exchange, and Power: The Distribution of Time in Social Systems," *American Journal of Sociology* 79 (1974): 856.

# CHAPTER THREE

# The Question of Questions

## Ask and Ye Shall Receive (Sometimes)

In the midst of major league baseball's drug scandals, a reporter put this question to Whitey Herzog, manager of the St. Louis Cardinals: "Would you rather have a drug-free team that finishes third or have a couple of guys with a quiet drug problem that can help you finish first?"

Herzog's response? "First of all, that's a very stupid question. Secondly, drugs are against the law. I don't want anybody on drugs."[1]

Good question or bad question? Some reporters would applaud the reporter for being direct and asking a pertinent, not impertinent, question. Others would agree with Herzog—the question was stupid. Without passing judgment, it can safely be said that questions like this one are potent instruments of communication. They can unlock long-suppressed feelings. They can energize a relationship. They can also inflict pain. Antagonize. Insult.

In Herzog's case, was the question designed to provoke the manager—interviewing's equivalent of a bean ball? Perhaps the reporter simply threw an unintentional wild pitch. If the reporter merely wanted an answer, he accomplished his objective. But at what price to the relationship? Although the interview continued, how much empathy, trust or respect was lost by asking such a question? Anyone who values communication should understand the powerful potential of questions. A narrow view of question-asking won't suffice. Reporter Sam Donaldson says two thoughts guide him

47

in coverage of the White House. "First, if you don't ask you don't find out; and second, the questions don't do the damage, only the answers do."[2] With apologies to Mr. Donaldson, questions can do damage. A reporter who discounts the need for thoughtfully worded questions may still gain an answer, but perhaps at the cost of unnecessary hostility or reduced trust.

For reporters, *success* at asking questions will determine to a large degree the quality of the story. Even the most gifted writers cannot turn baby babble to Shakespeare. The foundation of good journalism is the quality of reporting, which, in turn, depends on the ability to ask questions that elicit useful answers.

Journalism teachers certainly know that is true. They've seen their students return from assignments nearly empty handed. What went wrong? After all, the students prepared a list of questions as instructed and dutifully asked them, only to collect vague, lifeless answers. When that happens, students tend to blame the interviewee. "That guy was really dull," is a common accusation. Most often, the problem is theirs. Did they ask questions that invited "yes" or "no" answers? By failing to probe, did they miss the opportunity to flesh out a response? Even experienced reporters too readily take for granted their ability to ask questions. Media observer David Shaw of the Los Angeles Times believes "the majority of the nation's press corps plod along, uninspired and uninspiring, asking the same old questions of the same old sources—when they think to ask any questions at all."[3] That indictment is a bit harsh, but, certainly, most reporters can benefit from knowing more about the art of asking questions.

This chapter focuses on the question-asking component of the interview, but it's important to remember that the act of asking questions can't be separated from the complementary act of listening. Communication is an integrated, interdependent process. Think of it as a baseball game in which actions and counteractions influence the outcome of each stage of play. At this point, we are studying pitching, but we must not forget that other forces—say, a swift runner at first base—can affect the infinite possibilities of the game, including the delivery, speed and placement of the pitch.

## HUMAN NATURE AND THE NATURE OF QUESTIONS

Because questions are personal creations that reflect our previous experiences, some questions inadvertently function merely to confirm our preconceptions. Anthropologist S. Elizabeth Bird sees this condition as prevalent in journalism. "Too often, journalists and their editors have a tendency to 'know' what the story will be before they even start work—they may even have leads running around in their heads," she says. "It becomes an easy task to prove that this story is indeed the right one, by asking the right sources the right questions, and managing to ignore other issues that may come up in the course of the interview or event."[4] Journalist Donald Murray believes the problem is "compounded by editors who tell reporters what to find and give them a hard time when they don't fill in the blanks of the editor's stereotype."[5] To avoid a "hard time," some reporters ask the questions they sense the city editor wants asked.

All the blame can't be laid to editors. Suppose there's a stabbing at a suburban high school where blacks are being bused under court-ordered integration. The accused attacker is black; the victim is white. What "angle" will many reporters take? Not surprisingly, interviews with police, teachers and students may bore in on the racial angle, because that's what is *expected.* Moreover, those being interviewed may become unwitting partners in an act of subtle distortion. It works this way: The reporter implants the idea of racial conflict and nurtures it through a line of questioning. The idea grows in the interviewee's mind until the "right" answers come forth.

Here's a real-life example recounted by a principal at whose school a stabbing occurred. A television reporter interviewed a white youth as he was leaving school and asked if any students carried knives. "Oh yeah, lots of kids," he replied. "Which kids?" the reporter asked. "All the black kids," the youth said. Later, in a private talk with the student, the principal learned that the youth had only seen five knives at school and not all were carried by blacks. The news report created racial tension, the principal said. He blamed the reporter: "They put a kid on to make a gross statement like that and that's what broiled the whole thing up." The reporter apparently contributed to the "broil" by failing to challenge what seemed to be a sweeping generalization—"all" blacks carry knives. Was this simply a case of negligent questioning, or did the reporter's stereotypes lead to an automatic, uncritical acceptance of the youth's answer?

Obviously, there's danger of misrepresentation and error when our preconceptions influence the questions asked. Two experienced interviewers offer advice to overcome this tendency: "Ask what you want and need, but be ready to abandon all prefabricated plans as soon as the interview subject opens a new door for you. Go through it."[6] That advice, however, will work only if the reporter gives the person being interviewed opportunity to open the door. Don't let biases block the way. No matter what the story, there isn't going to be a set of "right" questions to ask—or "right" answers to those questions. Reporters may ask similar questions, such as "What happened?" or "What caused the fire?" But there are simply too many differences in reporters and how each sees the world to expect uniformity. Just as some people will say a glass of water is half empty and others will say it's half full, there are reporters who will go to the scene of a fire and ask, "What was lost?" and others who will ask, "What was saved?"

The more reporters understand themselves and human nature, the less likely they will be to underestimate the power of questions or misuse them. Human nature is too complicated to reduce to axioms, but four general observations about people should guide reporters as they ask questions.

## People Want To Be Treated Fairly

In our interviews with news subjects, we heard a common refrain: They want reporters to be fair and accurate. "People don't usually fear interviews," an experienced reporter said. "They fear being made to look foolish or stupid." To news subjects, fair play often simply means common decency. "I want to be treated with respect," a police chief said, "but mostly I want my family to be given respect. They are not responsible for what I say or do and their home is not my office." A civic leader complained about reporters who have called him at home, as late as one o'clock in the morning, "demanding" answers to their questions. "They have no sensitivity; they want continued access," he said. "And when I have been called late at night, I was very unimpressed with their reasons for calling me."

Fair play usually pays off. A man who won $2.5 million in the Illinois lottery said he granted requests for interviews because most reporters were "very nice and polite. I'm just a common guy who won a lot of money and they kept that in mind." But his attitude changed when one reporter went too far.

> I got a letter from a reporter, and he wanted to interview me about what had happened since I won the lottery. He knew that my sister and my wife had died. I was going to do it; I think it's kind of strange myself that all this sickness and death seemed to come with this money. Well, I let him call me and things were okay for a few minutes. Then he asked me how I felt about losing my wife. My wife of 18 years was dead only a few months. How the hell does he think I felt about losing my wife? He even

had the nerve to ask me if the money made it easier. That was it—end of interview for me. I never had anybody, reporter or otherwise, insult me like that in my life.

Even if insensitivity on the reporter's part does not terminate an interview, damage is likely to be done nonetheless. A former NBA coach described how he reacts: "In most cases I have the tendency not to expand, not to be as cooperative as I could be. It's very important for a reporter to abide by all the kinds of personal respect that he would want to be afforded if he were on the other side of being interviewed." Other interviewees said essentially the same thing. When they encounter an offensive reporter, they usually just "go through the motions," answering questions tersely and unenthusiastically.

## People Tend To Respond in Kind

Few people are able to turn the other cheek when someone offends them. Retaliation seems justified, even if it's an act of passive resistance. That's why overly aggressive, argumentative reporters usually will see their behavior reflected in the responses of interviewees. With observation No. 2 in mind, here is advice worth following:

> The thoughtful interviewer will word his [or her] questions so as to:
> Probe, not cross-examine.
> Inquire, not challenge.
> Suggest, not demand.
> Uncover, not trap.
> Draw out, not pump.
> Guide, not dominate.[7]

## No Two People Are Alike

Interviewing authority William C. Donaghy observes, "We tend to classify people together because they wear similar clothes . . . or talk alike, but each person is unique. Research interviewers, for example, often begin to anticipate responses because they have already done a great many interviews with similar people."[8] The same can be said of many reporters. Failure to see the individuality of people may not only result in anticipated answers. It might also lead to standardized, trite questions.

Reporters should, as well, consider how reactions to questions can vary. Some questions, for example, can affect people like a slap in the face. A sharp question might cause one person to strike back or another to cry or still another to turn silent. Questions shouldn't be asked without taking into account the differences in people.

## People Try To Meet Fundamental Needs

Why do people share their thoughts, dreams and, at times, even their most intimate feelings with audiences of millions? Deep-seated needs may drive them, and reporters should be alert for and sensitive to those needs. Some needs are material—to peddle a book, promote a movie or sell a product. On the other hand, people operate to fulfill altruistic needs, too. The actor promoting the new movie may be more concerned about spreading the film's "message" than making a profit. There are times, too, when needs compel people to avoid communication. A sensitive reporter might decide to honor those needs and back off. Associated Press writer Jules Loh once wanted to do a story about the genteel proprietor of a stately boarding house. "Where would the story appear?" the woman asked. "In many papers around the country," Loh replied. To which the woman said, "I think that would be vulgar." According to a colleague of Loh's, "Reporter and gentleman in Loh struggled briefly, and then both quietly withdrew."[9]

Treat people fairly and decently, acknowledge their uniqueness and recognize their needs, including the need to be left alone. Remember that people are fulfilling their own goals by being interviewed, not just yours. Let these thoughts guide you as you approach the various types of interviews to be faced.

## FORMATS FOR INTERVIEWS

The objectives and formats of interviews vary; so, too, must the questions, methods and strategies involved. Here are the most common categories of journalistic interviews and some question-asking implications of each.

### News Interview

Reporters often must work quickly to determine the facts of a news event. They may "interview" a half-dozen people within an hour's time, finding out the who, what, where, why, when and how of the news. These interviews are primarily fact-generating, and, because of deadlines or circumstances, some of the recommended elements of communication, such as small talk, aren't always possible. Nevertheless, the spirit of dialogue—respect for others, caring and a willingness to listen—can and should be present.

In the typical news interview, questions often are not planned. Reporters may first use "filter questions"—inquiries to determine what a witness or participant knows, if anything, about the news event: "Sir, did you actually see the plane crash?"

In news interviews, reporters rely heavily on experience, observation and enterprise in formulating questions. At a residential fire, for example, a reporter might notice that the hoses are connected to a hydrant a block away, not to the hydrant in the front yard. "Why is that?" the fire captain is asked. The explanation: The hydrant is defective, and 20 percent of the city's other hydrants need repair. That's an important element of the fire story, and the start of a separate story on the state of fire protection.

## Investigative Interview

Investigative stories put the reporter's communicative skills to a rigorous test. The subjects generally are sensitive and controversial; there's likely to be an inherent tension and adversarial tone to interviews. Investigative reporting may also require tactics and questions that run counter to the principles of ideal communication. The reporter often can't avoid being manipulative, even devious, in relationships, presenting difficult ethical issues.

## News-feature Interview

News features often are done in a day or less, but they afford reporters time to plan and develop the story. A reporter may go beyond the interview to use other methods of learning about the subject. A reporter, for example, might walk a beat with a policeman before conducting a formal interview. The questions asked for news features include the standard fact-generating ones; however, exploration of feelings, attitudes and even dreams is undertaken as well.

## Profile Interview

A personality profile usually involves reporting by immersion. It may be an intense experience for reporter and subject alike, as they engage in multiple sessions in a variety of settings—home, office or porch. Interviews may be marked by deep probing into emotions, experiences and motivation.

## Other Forms

Reporters ask questions in a variety of other situations. Here are some of them:

**"Meet the Press"-type Format.** Typically in this situation a newsmaker occupies the hot seat, fielding questions and follow-ups. Dialogue isn't easy. Questions come from a variety of directions and perspectives. The interviewee may end up swiveling—physically, emotionally and intellectually—as she or he reacts to each questioner.

**News Conference.** There's often a high degree of artificiality in the communication that occurs in a news conference. Many news conferences are planned and controlled as part of orchestrated public relations effort, which means trust, candor and spontaneity between interviewer and news subject may be sacrificed. Indeed, some corporate executives and public officials rehearse in mock news conferences. Participants can become tense and adversarial, which is why news conferences frequently turn into free-for-alls. Former presidential press spokesman Larry Speakes says White House news conferences are theater. "They're scripted. Reporters ask written questions to which a president gives a rehearsed answer. An 'I gotcha' syndrome prevails."[10] But despite the shortcomings of news conferences, sometimes they are the only means of communication between reporters and newsmakers.

**Roundtable.** The television program "Nightline" is a good example of this format. A panel of experts, some brought together by satellite, interact, with the host as catalyst and moderator. The often spirited exchanges make for dramatic television. It's not a format used by many newspaper or wire service reporters, though, probably because the approach would not "play" well in print.

**Telephone.** Obviously, the dynamics of communication by telephone are different from those in a face-to-face encounter. Although it has its shortcomings, the telephone interview is necessary and valuable; it can even reach the level of dialogue. Telephone communication is discussed more fully in Chapter 7.

**Broadcast.** Many aspects of electronic reporting, such as the presence of an immediate audience, can unnaturally affect interpersonal communication. Still, some of the most memorable and revealing stories have been shared with us in a 19-inch format. The special needs and problems of broadcast interviews are also examined in Chapter 7.

## PLANNING THE INTERVIEW

One rookie reporter used to jot down a few questions on a sheet of copy paper before racing out to cover a story. So much for preparation, planning and strategy. He didn't have any. He embarked on the assignment with only a vague notion of his purpose. Where did he acquire such a bad habit? From watching veteran reporters work, he explained. What this rookie didn't know was that after many years of experience, veteran reporters often don't *appear* to be working hard at forming their questions. Nor do they always write them down on routine assignments. For rookie or veteran, however, pre-interview planning is essential.

No one can tell you precisely *what* to ask any more than you can be told precisely what to say in a marriage proposal. But some suggestions do seem especially helpful.

❑ Develop a tentative focus or theme for your assignment. If you're fortunate enough to gain an interview with Indiana's volatile basketball coach, Bobby Knight, you're not likely to be given the time and cooperation to produce the definitive profile. Let's say you get a 30-minute session. What's your focus? Knight's temper tantrums? His bench-coaching ability? His Marine Corps-style of discipline? His emphasis on academics? The last topic might be your best bet, given Knight's reputation of contempt for reporters. He probably would be more willing to discuss why he opposes long road trips that interfere with his players' exams than to answer questions about why he throws chairs and beats on tables. Narrowing the topic pragmatically is the first step toward knowing what to ask. (During the interview, you may find that the coach actually wants to address those other touchy areas.)

❑ Take as much time as possible to prepare. The unprepared reporter may never get to ask a question. Author John De Voto had agreed to an interview until the young reporter said, "I'm sorry, but I really didn't have time to look this up. Just exactly who are you, Mr. De Voto?" "Young man," said De Voto, "if you don't have the time to look it up in a Who's Who or in your own library and find out, I haven't any time for you."[11]

Computerized data bases now put volumes of information at reporters' fingertips. Before long, nearly all daily newspapers will subscribe to information services like NEXIS, which offer speedy, full-text access to various newspapers, magazines, newsletters and newswires. The growing accessibility to "electronic libraries" virtually eliminates the excuse, "I didn't have time to look this up."

Pre-interview research tells an interviewee that you are thorough and knowledgeable. Inadequate preparation, however, not only suggests a lack of professionalism; it also increases the possibility of error. A study published in Journalism Quarterly cited reporters' failure to do background research as the main cause of subjective errors—errors of emphasis, meaning or completeness.[12]

Preparation goes beyond doing research. You should anticipate questions that will stimulate or challenge. Questions that come too easily to mind are like words and phrases that come too easily to the writer. They're probably trite, and the person you're interviewing has heard them before. Brainstorm before an assignment. Ask your colleagues for ideas, too. Don't settle for the obvious questions. Conversely, don't overlook the obvious. An editor said his pet peeve is obituaries that say, "So-and-so died of a heart attack at St. John's Hospital." The obvious question, he said, is "Where was he and what was he doing when he had the heart attack? Maybe he was jogging or playing tennis. Maybe he was taking a stress test at a doctor's office." Once, according to this editor, a man died of a heart attack while visiting a friend recovering from a heart attack. That ironic twist was overlooked because the reporter failed to ask the obvious question.

Part of your preparation might involve writing out some questions in advance, especially those most essential to your story. A list will be a backstop if you happen to draw a blank and can't think of the questions you intended to ask. Written questions also may help you develop a focus for the interview. But interviews shouldn't be precisely mapped out. Be prepared to amend or abandon some or all of your questions. One student took a list of questions to interview a college soccer coach. The coach asked to see the list, looked it over and then said, "Let's just talk."

Perhaps the coach, experienced at being interviewed by young reporters, realized that too many of them read prepared questions in the same way amateur actors read a script, never letting the interview become a conversation. Handing over your notes for an interviewee to review isn't advised, and it isn't an accepted practice in journalism. The point, though, remains valid: Don't script an interview.

❑ Keep your eventual readers (or viewers, or listeners) in mind. Ask questions the folks at the coffee shop ask when they're discussing the day's news. If the governor signs a bill raising the gasoline tax, motorists will want to know when they'll have to pay a higher price at the pump. A newspaper once reported how a duck hunter drowned when his johnboat went *through the locks*. Locals familiar with the lock operation rightly asked, "How could someone drown going through the locks?" Of course, that was the question the reporter should have asked. Actually, the boat went *over the dam*. Don't underestimate the curiosity and instincts of news consumers; they may pose better questions than many reporters do. A reader frustrated over holes in a personality sketch about a famous entertainer sent an editor two single-spaced pages of unanswered (or unasked) questions, ranging from "Does she fix her own hair or use a wig?" to "She has 'priceless antiques.' Is this her hobby? Does she do the actual shopping for them? Any particular kind or period? Has she a favorite city, either here or abroad, for antique hunting?" The editor rightly wondered why his reporter didn't think to ask similar questions.

The more complicated the story, the more important it is for reporters to keep the readers' questions in mind. As writing coach Donald Murray suggests, "[G]et away from the notes and list the five or so questions the reader will ask. They should not be the questions you hope the reader will ask, but the ones, like it or not, the reader will ask."[13]

❑ Go beyond the facts. Ask questions that seek out concrete examples, details and anecdotes, all of which fuel a lively, readable story. Don't operate like detective Joe Friday on television's old "Dragnet" series, whose standard line was, "We just want the facts, ma'am, nothing but the facts." If you simply ask, "What kind of car do you drive?" the answer might be, "A Volkswagen." By seeking details, however, you may suggest a fuller

answer. "Anything distinctive about it?" The intriguing answer
then might be, "Yeah. It's probably the only VW in town with an
Edsel grille." You say, "Really? Tell me about it."

Miami Herald police beat reporter Edna Buchanan is a Pulit-
zer Prize-winner because she goes beyond the routine facts.
When covering a homicide, one of her standard questions is,
"What was everyone wearing?" She learned to ask that question
the hard way:

> A man was shot and dumped into the street by a killer in a
> pickup truck. The case seemed somewhat routine—if one can ever
> call murder routine. But later I learned that at the time the victim
> was shot he was wearing a black taffeta cocktail dress and red high
> heels. I tracked down the detectives and asked, "Why didn't you
> tell me?"
> 'You didn't ask,' they chorused. Now I always ask.[14]

Your questions should also seek to draw out anecdotal material, especially if you're writing news features. Anecdotes are
stories within your story. They usually relate a dramatic, enter-
taining or touching experience that illustrates someone's character. You might ask a newly named company president to recall
his first job or the team's new pitcher to talk about other positions he's played. But don't expect to ask one question and receive a beautifully told anecdote in return. You may have to ask
10 or more follow-up questions to fully develop the anecdote.

Beginning reporters are usually admonished to get the facts of
an event or story straight. They are told to ask: Who? What?
When? Where? Why? How? These five W's and an H are sacred.
Time, however, should be left for the "what else" question—the
sixth W. The "what else" time is when some of the most fascinating discoveries are made. If your purpose is purely to generate
facts, you'll probably be limited to specific answers to your specific questions. The finer, fuller points may simply not occur to
the interviewee, partly because you haven't invited them to surface. The sixth W doesn't have to be a direct question. It can
emerge as an *attitude* that you are willing to allow other people to
feel the interview is as complete to *them* as it is to *you*. A "what
else" question, even if asked directly, should not be put offhand-
edly, as if the reporter only really cares about the straight-down-
the-line facts. Nor should it be put judgmentally, as though the
reporter knows or suspects the other person is hiding something.

❏ Try to find a site conducive for communication. When time and circumstances permit, seek a face-to-face interview at a place where communication is most likely to flourish. A quiet, empty room offers privacy and minimizes outside distractions. It does not, however, encourage rapport or hold clues to the interviewee's life. Consider, first of all, going to the interviewee's turf. If you interview a scientist at her laboratory, an artist in his studio, or a boxer at the gym, you may encounter frequent interruptions or the influence of an audience of colleagues. But being interviewed in familiar surroundings should help the interviewee relax and be natural. Moreover, the surroundings are likely to suggest questions to observant reporters.

For a personality piece, you'll probably want to plan on interviews and conversation in more than one setting. A plastic surgeon may present one side of her personality in the doctor's lounge. A side you never anticipated may emerge when the site of your conversation shifts to the surgeon's farm.

❏ Keep abreast of a variety of topics. If you're doing a feature about living in Alaska, your questions will be much more insightful if you've read John McPhee's *Coming into the Country* and Joe McGinniss' *Going to Extremes*. The words of one of Life magazine's most prolific interviewers, Lincoln Barnett, are pertinent: "The reporter who is inquisitive and not proud, unwilling to set any sphere of knowledge outside his interest, unhappily aware of the great clamorous voids of his ignorance, and tormented by the fact that he seldom has time to do more than scratch the surface of any domain he invades—this reporter usually knows what to ask."[15] Barnett's advice also implies that recognizing your ignorance is especially important. Most newsmakers will respect reporters who admit their ignorance; they won't respect those who pretend to be knowledgeable. If an interviewee talks about the Gulf of Tonkin Resolution and you've never heard of it, you'd better ask.

## TYPES OF QUESTIONS

Questions come in as many models as automobiles. Some are high-powered. Others are economical and compact. Most of us can't have an automobile for all occasions, but we can select questions from all over the lot. First, we'll explore the generic categories of questions;

then we'll look more closely at particular types of questions, such as hypothetical ones. Interviewers invariably use a mix of questions. But it helps to know the possible benefits and liabilities of your choices.

## Open-ended Questions

Open-ended questions do not restrict either the content or form of answers. An exaggerated version of the open-ended question is, "Tell me about yourself," but they can be more focused, too. You might ask, "Tell me about your love for antique cars." Among the advantages of open-ended questions:

- They enable the interviewee to do most of the talking, and, just as important, they enable the reporter to listen and observe.
- They are usually non-threatening.
- They allow the interviewee to reveal voluntarily information, attitudes and feelings the interviewer may not have anticipated.
- They encourage the individual to marshal thoughts, knowledge and experiences to formulate an answer to a question he or she may have never considered before.

On the other hand, open-ended questions, because they tend to take longer to answer, may have to be avoided when a reporter has a deadline to meet. There are other disadvantages to open-ended questions.

- They might overwhelm people who are unaccustomed to answering general questions. Even experienced, prepared interviewees stumble over open-ended questions. PBS newscaster Robert MacNeil says the question might be as "simple" as this one: What's wrong with television news? "If you have just spent a year researching and writing a book on that topic," says MacNeil, "you don't know quite where to begin."[16]
- They might encourage rambling, disorganized responses that are hard to interpret.
- They may require you to interrupt or redirect the interview, which could offend the person you're interviewing.

In general, though, cogent open-ended questions deepen and nurture communication. They may go far to build rapport and to uncap feelings.

## Closed Questions

When reporters need unadorned facts, *closed questions* are useful. They focus answers: "Who is your favorite author?" or "Which team will win the Super Bowl?" Closed questions are often easy to ask and easy to answer. The reporter retains tight control over the interview, which may be necessary. Other advantages of closed questions:

- They allow the reporter to seek a specific piece of information without waiting for the interviewee to volunteer it.
- They are good warm-up questions; they don't require strenuous mental gymnastics.
- They are usually less time-consuming because the answers tend to be brief.

Closed questions, however, rarely permit the growth of a communication relationship. A rapid-fire delivery of closed questions may suggest to the interviewee that you're only interested in pumping him or her for information. Some closed questions are bipolar, restricting answers to a "yes" or "no": "Do you like your job?" Here are additional shortcomings of closed questions:

- They don't request explanations or justifications, making it almost too easy for people to answer superficially.
- They aren't likely to be very satisfying or challenging to a sensitive, articulate interviewee.
- They may yield too little detail, ultimately costing more time because so many follow-up questions are necessary.

Closed questions are frequently used when a reporter is covering a breaking news story and a fast compilation of the essential details is more important than gaining depth of information. Closed questions are also appropriate when a reporter is merely seeking to confirm details or plug gaps in a story.

## Direct and Indirect Questions

Reporters are reputed to be very direct. They're trained to bore in on a subject. However, while a frontal, straightforward approach is appropriate and valuable in some encounters, it may be too blunt or too sharp to elicit a full, candid answer. Direct questions are most suitable when the interviewee is willing and able to answer. "Do you enjoy political life?" is a direct question most politicians won't object to addressing. But if the question ("Is politics an ego trip for you?") is threatening, embarrassing or insulting, you probably won't get an answer—at least not one you expect. Moreover, you risk damaging further communication. Consider actress Angie Dickinson's response to a very direct question by a TV Guide writer, who asked if Dickinson ever had an affair with President Kennedy. Dickinson sharply answered, "I think [that question] is disrespectful, sacrilegious. He was a married man and the president of the United States. I don't advertise who my loves are. . . . I'm not going to tell anyone what happens in my bed. That's ridiculous."[17] Admittedly, the writer obtained an answer and a powerful quotation. But she angered Dickinson in the process. Would an indirect approach to the subject have been successful? Perhaps. Let's examine how indirect questions work.

One researcher, for example, eased into a direct question to find out if someone ever shoplifted. First was a series of questions to measure attitudes about shoplifting. Then the focus tightened:

> "Please try to recall the time when you were a teenager. Do you recall personally knowing anyone who took something from a store without paying for it?"

> "How about yourself? Did you ever consider taking anything from a store without paying for it?"

If the response was "yes," the direct question was asked.

> "Did you actually take it?"[18]

The indirect approach will certainly lessen the sting of a touchy or tough question. And you might be surprised by the results. Here's how Barbara Walters got actress Judy Garland to talk about her unhappy childhood:

> I asked her how young people in show business today compared to her friends in the days when she was starting in vaudeville. And I got an answer that still makes me feel sad every time I recall the interview. "We all started too young in those days," she said. And then she added with a tiny smile, "You know my mother was the stage mother of all time. She really was a witch. If I had a stomach ache and didn't want to go on, she'd say, 'get out on that stage or I'll wrap you around a bedpost.' "[19]

Walters reminds us that an indirect question about the problems of others may encourage interviewees to talk directly and personally about themselves.

Indirect questions are sometimes identifiable by the absence of a question mark. You might be interviewing a "straight-A" student who holds down a 30-hour-a-week job in the evenings. You say, "It must be tough to study when your job takes up so much time and energy." Such a question is really a statement or a comment, and it might end with an upward inflection by the speaker. It is an invitation for the interviewee to elaborate. Furthermore, it has the advantage of widening the territory available to your interviewee while reducing the formality of direct questioning.

Use of indirect questions, especially those of the statement variety, might refreshingly vary the reporter's typical question-answer approach. If your questions don't feel like questions, that might be an advantage. The reporter becomes less of a "questioner" and more a normal participant in conversation. Your communication is likely to be more relaxed and intimate, which will encourage more responsiveness.

## Probes

Probes are secondary questions that help fill out or follow up answers to primary questions. Probes can even be nonverbal, such as a nod of the head, indicating, "I understand." Many inexperienced reporters ask adequate "primary" questions; they falter in asking "catalyst" questions that bring an answer to its fullest potential. For example, they might ask a teacher they're interviewing: "Have you ever been physically threatened in the classroom?" The question, of course, invites a "yes" or "no" answer, so you must be prepared to probe. If the answer is yes, the probe might simply be, "I'm curious" or "What happened?" Keep in mind that it may take a number of probes to flesh out a response, especially when anecdotal information is sought.

Probes play many roles. Some are intended to amplify. Some are meant to be provocative. Some are designed to show the reporter's responsiveness. The power of the probe question is seen in Ted Koppel's interview that cost a baseball executive his job. Koppel's guest on "Nightline," Al Campanis, vice president of the Los Angeles Dodgers, was asked why few blacks held leadership jobs in professional baseball. Campanis responded, "I truly believe that they may not have some of the necessities to be, let's say, a field manager, or perhaps a general manager." Koppel could have moved to another question, but, as he should have, he probed, inquiring, "Do you really believe that?" Campanis surprised Koppel by responding, "Well, I don't say all of them, but they certainly are short.

How many quarterbacks do you have? How many pitchers do you have that are black?"[20] Few probes will have the impact of Koppel's, but most probes are quite effective. Here are the main types and some examples.

**Clarification Probes.** When an answer is unclear or ambiguous you must be prepared to obtain clarification. If you don't, you'll be flirting with one of journalism's greatest sins—to assume. Clarification probes take these forms:

❏ *"Let me see if I understand you. You mean that . . . "* With this probe you paraphrase what you've heard from the interviewee, testing to see if you understand each other clearly and accurately. Of all probes, this one is the best insurance against errors. Interviewees often find such a probe reassurance that the reporter is committed to accuracy. A reassured interviewee is likely to be a more responsive interviewee.

❏ *"Could you help me better understand what you mean by that? An example would help me."* Often the best method of gaining clarification is to ask for an example or illustration. Even a hypothetical or frivolous one can put you back "on track" effectively. If the interviewee is unable to come up with one, offer one of your own and note the reaction to your example.

❏ *"Alderman Jones, your assessment of the cost of the new fire station differs dramatically from the mayor's. Do you have figures or documents you can show me?"* Some clarification probes seek additional information or data.

**Amplification Probes.** Many answers to initial questions are underdeveloped; they may need to be cultivated by probes. People don't usually provide an organized, complete response to questions exploring broad, touchy or involved topics. You can anticipate that many interviewees will need help, encouragement or coaxing to answer fully. All you may have to do is say, "Please go on." Here are some other typical amplification probes.

❏ *"Why do you say you're 'angry' about losing the election?"* This is a probe that echoes or restates what the interviewee has just said. With it, you are able to indicate the specific aspect of the answer you want amplified.

❏ *"How did you feel when that happened?"* "How do you feel" probes are often associated with the callous side of journalism, such as asking a mother who lost her child in an accident, "How do you feel?" But used appropriately and sensitively, probes to amplify feelings are important. What if the mother lost her child to a drunk driver? Her feelings may be important and even surprising. "Am I angry? No, I'm numb, and if anything, I feel sorry for the boy who killed my son. He'll carry his guilt with him forever." Could you have predicted this reaction on the basis of the event alone?

❏ *"You favor a tax increase? As you probably read in the* Times, *critics predict it will hurt many people."* Occasionally, you may find it helpful to tie your probes together in a broader, perhaps unfamiliar context for the interviewee. With this approach, you tactfully supply facts ("According to yesterday's Congressional Record . . . ") that may help the interviewee amplify a response.

**Confrontation Probes.** Alert reporters will encounter inconsistencies, contradictions or evasiveness in interviews. When that happens, confrontation probes are needed. "Confrontation" suggests a clash—something potentially unpleasant. But confrontation probes needn't be painful. Instead of a blunt approach ("You're wrong"), you might be indirect ("Are you sure that's correct?").

Reporters may need to be diplomatic and logically agile in posing confrontation probes. Suppose a reporter is interviewing an FBI official about the bureau's alleged surveillance of media people. The reporter asks, "Mr. Horver, did you ever authorize wire taps on journalists?"

HORVER: "Who said we authorized wire taps?"

REPORTER: "Did you, Mr. Horver?"

HORVER: "It's possible that it happened."

REPORTER: "Are you saying that you *did,* Mr. Horver?"

Even when stated politely, a confrontation probe may prematurely end an interview. If you detect answers early in the interview that are contradictory or evasive, you might want to wait until your relationship is more established before probing them.

**Argumentative Probes.** Playing devil's advocate—intentionally defending a point of view for argument's sake even though it may not be your own—can enhance or dash communication. Try to determine if the person you're interviewing appreciates argumentation before using it. In addition, indicate, if you can, that you are arguing in a spirit of good will. One way to do that would be to say, "General, to play devil's advocate, let me ask you . . ."

**Silent Probes.** Novice reporters may assume that silence is a danger signal in an interview. Admittedly, silence can make you feel awkward and compel you to fill the void. Resist the urge; silence may be fruitful. For one thing, it allows people time to think. The result might be a better response. Silence keeps you from disrupting an interviewee's train of thought. By being attentively quiet, you communicate that you are waiting for more to be said.

A study of students ranging from first grade to college found that the quality of class discussion can be markedly improved if teachers wait up to three seconds after asking a question—and after a response. "Wait time," as it is called, increased the length of student responses between 300 and 700 percent, resulted in more speculative thinking, and led to greater use of evidence and logical argument.[21] Reporters who use *wait time* may achieve comparable results.

When do you use silence? There are clues. For example, if the interviewee leans back in the chair and gazes at the ceiling, he or she is probably organizing thoughts. Allow time for this. Another clue is paralanguage—nonverbal sounds. When someone utters a prolonged "aaahhh" or "hmmm," it suggests he or she is groping for the right words or ideas. Silent probes normally should be based on positive goals, not negative ones, such as trying to get someone to sweat or squirm.

**Passive Probes.** When people are engaged in conversation, they send signs of being involved, using brief, neutral expressions like "really," "uh huh" or "I see." Passive probes like these encourage conversation. In the reporter's case, passive probes are helpful when you have to encourage someone whose views you oppose, such as a Ku Klux Klan leader or a jailed terrorist. Expressing passivity and neutrality may show the interviewee that you are nonjudgmental.

Facial expressions, gestures and body movement can function as passive probes. A frown may indicate, "I'm confused. Clarify, please." Rubbing your chin could say, "Hmmm. That's interesting. Go on." Leaning forward, coupled with an intent gaze, communicates, "I'm with you. I'm intrigued. Tell me more." Just remember that nonverbal probes can be misread. An interviewee might interpret your frown negatively: "He's frowning because he is upset with what I said." To avoid misunderstanding, you might have to follow a nonverbal probe with a verbal one for clarification.

## Bridges

Bridges are transitional devices that, when done well, move the interview smoothly in a different direction. Bridges are important in maintaining good will in an interview. You don't want people to get the impression that you are roughly and abruptly steering them through the interview. An example of a smooth bridge would be, "Bishop Ryan, earlier in our talk you mentioned that today's Catholics are facing many agonizing choices. Is abortion one of those agonizing choices?" Bridges are two-way, however. Your interviewee may effectively use a bridge to avoid a troublesome question or to introduce a new subject. A reporter might ask, "Coach Thompson, do you approve of Coach Jones' recruiting methods?" The coach might respond, "I don't know about Coach Jones, but let me tell you what we do." You're now on Coach Thompson's field of play. Listen, but build the new bridge you need: "Thanks for the insight into your methods. They sound quite different from what Jones does. Could you comment on that difference?"

## GOOD QUESTIONS OR BAD QUESTIONS?

Books about interviewing usually suggest questions to avoid. The most obvious are those that are structurally defective—questions that are too long, too complicated or too abstract. A more serious, second level of "bad" questions are those that can damage a communicative relationship. Yet even "bad" questions are useful in certain circumstances.

### Hypothetical Questions

The "what if" question can be brusquely dismissed by some interviewees: "That's a hypothetical question, and I don't answer hypothetical questions." Media consultants Jack Hilton and Mary Knoblauch say most politicians "have been trained to sniff a hypothetical question a mile away."[22] It's not that hypothetical questions automatically offend people; more likely they pose risks that the interviewee might say something foolish or damaging. Hilton and Knoblauch advise media interviewees to "save the 'what if' games for your children and grandchildren."[23]

Does this mean reporters should avoid hypothetical questions entirely? After all, reporters are supposed to be dealing primarily with reality, not fantasy. Used sparingly and strategically, hypothetical questions can especially stimulate people who are creative and explorative in their jobs and lives. Speculation has its value; a well-crafted scenario presented to a scientist might lead to a lively, enlightening and even prophetic discussion: "Professor Green, picture for me what will happen if the ozone layer is destroyed."

## Leading Questions

Leading questions suggest their own expected answers. Under most circumstances, leading questions should be avoided. They raise at least two detrimental possibilities: They tend to invalidate answers because you've primed the pump too much, or they offend people who see them as acts of manipulation ("You're putting words in my mouth.").

Leading questions come in several forms. Some "lead" by using loaded words: "What do you think about the way the mayor 'orchestrated' the passage of the tax bill?" Others limit the range of responses possible: "Are you married or single?" Since "divorced," "widowed," and "separated" are not included in the question, people in these subcategories of being unmarried will be "led" to say "single." Still others attempt to entrap. A student interviewer tried to trick a varsity coach into confirming that two of his players were in a brawl at keg party, as rumor had it. "How are you going to discipline the two?" the student asked, hoping to bluff the coach into an admission. The coach, seeing through the ploy, answered in an annoyed tone, "Joe, I know what you're trying to do and I don't like it." Finally, there are questions with leading or specious prefaces: "Since the number of unwed mothers is rising so dramatically, don't you think it's time to set up birth-control clinics in high schools?" A perceptive interviewee may sharply challenge your question, asking, "Who says the number of unwed mothers is rising dramatically?"

Leading questions are risky with perhaps one exception: They can be used to ease the reluctance to talk about embarrassing or hurtful subjects. Sex researcher Alfred Kinsey began interviews by asking *when* the subject first engaged in sexual activity. As Kinsey explains, "Since it becomes apparent from the form of our question that we would not be surprised if he had had such experience, there seems to be less reason for denying it."[24] (Of course, Kinsey's approach might give a respondent more reason for humoring the interviewer's presumptions or answering untruthfully to avoid looking like an odd-ball.) A variation is the leading question that encourages responses in a suggestive yet sensitive manner, like a doctor saying to an apprehensive patient, "It hurts there, doesn't it?"[25]

## Apologetic Questions

Beginning a question with an apology ("I hate to raise such a personal question") may show sensitivity on your part, but it also invites the person you're interviewing to decide not to answer. Unless you feel it is absolutely important to soften the edge of your question, don't preface it with a *mea culpa*. You may produce suspiciousness or wariness where none previously existed.

## Provocative Questions

A questionable reporting strategy is to provoke or anger someone into giving a fuller, more emotional answer. Calculated attempts to provoke are a gamble that can be costly; they could get you tossed out of an office, and they certainly won't win you many friends. Still, there are reporters who think the payoff occasionally is worth the gamble. Chicago Tribune reporter Neil Mehler, for example, says he sometimes uses an outrageous question in the hope of producing a candid, spontaneous answer. That method is especially effective, he says, when dealing with people who aren't used to being interviewed. As he explains:

> [A] village manager left the employ of a municipality I was covering. It was of some interest to me and others whether he had been fired or had left on his own. I put the question to a village trustee this way: 'You finally got rid of Mr. X." He shot back, with obvious anger, 'We didn't get rid of him!" I had an answer that, I'm satisfied, was truthful and put down all speculation. The same answer said with less emotion would not have satisfied me as to the truth of the matter.[26]

Before using questions as truth detectors, consider whether an honest answer is obtainable by less manipulative methods. In the long run, reporters who are forthright will probably receive forthright answers in return.

## Dumb Questions

No reporter wants to be known for asking a dumb question, but if you ask enough questions, some of them are bound to be dumb. Since reporters often work unobserved by the public and colleagues, many dumb questions are heard only by the interviewee. When dumb questions do surface, it is most often at press conferences. During media day at the 1988 Super Bowl, a Washington Redskins lineman was asked, "If you were a tree, what kind would you be?" Annoyed, the player growled in reply, "Speak my language, man."[27] Don't assume that only sportswriters ask dumb questions. In the 1988 presidential primaries, a reporter asked Sen. Paul Simon, "If you came back to Earth as an animal, what animal would it be?"[28]

Then again, "dumb" may be in the eye of the beholder. Television journalist Linda Ellerbee recalled one of the dumbest questions she'd ever heard. It was put to first lady Betty Ford as a press conference was about to end. As Ellerbee describes it, "What needed to be asked was asked and answered. No news was made. Everyone there was ready for the thing to end. But there was this one reporter who kept asking useless questions, the final useless question being, 'Mrs. Ford, have your children used marijuana?' " What a dumb question, Ellerbee thought. "You could hear the murmurs all over the room. Everybody exchanged looks. They were right. It would have been a dumb question—if the president's wife had not answered, 'Yes.' "[29]

## CONDUCTING THE INTERVIEW

Three important considerations go into conducting an interview: the interviewer's style, the delivery of questions and the organization of the interview. How you conduct an interview is likely to be determined by your personality, the personality of the interviewee and the circumstances of the interview, so there isn't a definitive model to follow. But some advice and alternatives might help you decide how to proceed.

### Style and Roles

Should interviewers take on roles, like actors, when they question people? There are different schools of thought on that point. Some interviewing experts and reporters say, "Be natural." Others believe that role-playing is essential. "Being natural is the worst advice," they say. Indeed, notable interviewers like Ted Koppel use different approaches, depending on the circumstances. Koppel can be relentless and blunt when questioning a hardened political figure, but patient and gentle when interviewing a teenaged mother.

Roles and naturalness, however, can coexist. Consider how frequently people undertake different roles in their relationships. Parents, for example, may be stern with their children when disciplining and tender when consoling. The main point is to be genuine and honest in your roles. Then you won't be guilty of manipulation, such as pretending to be a sympathetic friend or confidant. In addition, you won't run the risk of being detected "playing games."

When reporters do play games it's often because they *assume* the other person won't be forthcoming. Then, too, many news subjects feel reporters are out to "get them." Merge those attitudes and it's no wonder reporters and news subjects look on an interview as a contest of survival skills. Reporters who pride themselves on outfoxing people with a bluff or ploy may get some juicy information, but eventually they'll get a reputation for not being "straightshooters." Few people will speak to them, and those who do will be especially guarded.

What if you have to interview a person whose views you disdain? Should you pretend to be friendly or agreeable? A better role is one of neutrality. Of course, you could be perfectly honest and tell the interviewee how you feel. But why broadcast your biases or preconceptions? If you broadcast them, you may never get the story. Act nonjudgmentally and be receptive.

Some reporters think playing dumb is a justifiable way of getting people to open up. Actor Peter Falk played that kind of role to stardom as television's "Columbo," a homicide detective who snared murder suspects by appearing to be a bumbler. Still, reporters who play act generally fool no one but themselves. What if, in truth, you're more like Columbo than Mike Wallace? Actually, you might be better off than a smooth-talking colleague. As Joan Didion, a regular contributor to Esquire, says, "My only advantage as a reporter is that I am so physically small, so temperamentally unobtrusive, and so neurotically inarticulate that people tend to forget that my presence runs counter to their best interests."[30]

## Delivery of Questions

Naturally, reporters are most concerned about the substance of questions. They should also pay attention to *how* questions are asked. Three elements—phrasing, inflection and timing—affect the delivery of questions.

**Phrasing.** Phrasing of a question can influence the fullness, accuracy and honesty of answers. Choice of words is most important. Studies show that wording can distort responses. Parents who are asked, "Do you control television viewing by your children?" are more likely to answer, "No." But if you ask, "Do you allow your children to watch whatever they please?" they are more likely to admit they do "control" viewing, at least to some extent. Emotionally loaded words normally should be avoided. It is one thing to ask, "Do you believe in mercy killing?" The response might be significantly different if you ask, "Do you believe in euthanasia?"

ABC correspondent Sam Donaldson demonstrates how word choice can make the difference in getting an answer—or getting no answer at all. In questioning President Reagan as to whether Reagan hoped to "remove" the Sandinista government in Nicaragua, Donaldson deliberately avoided the word "overthrow." Reagan answered, "Well, remove in the sense of its present structure, in which it is a communist totalitarian state and it is not a government chosen by the people. . . . " According to Donaldson, "The word remove had not triggered the same warning bells in Reagan's mind that the word overthrow would have, and he had delivered the unvarnished truth about his policy."[31] Be aware, though, that Donaldson was not just playing semantic games in which the two words were equivalent. The words *remove* and *overthrow* are not synonymous. Those overthrown are certainly removed, but many leaders removed aren't subjected to the victimization or violence connoted by being overthrown.

Stanley L. Payne has come up with what he calls a "rogue's gallery" of problem words in questions. Even innocent sounding words like "you," he says, can be misinterpreted. Several repairmen, for example, were separately asked, "How many radio sets did you repair last month?" Payne says that the phrasing of that question seemed perfectly fine until one repairman said, "Who do you mean, me or the whole shop?"[32] For this repairman, "you" had a *collective* meaning. Another problem word is "only." It is one of several words, including "all" and "never," that are too judgmental or absolute (all-inclusive or all-exclusive) for some people. "Only" sounds (and may be) prejudicial: "Senator, how do you respond to people who wonder why you were present to vote on *only* 65 percent of the bills this session?" You might try testing your ability to detect problem words. Devise a list of questions and then have friends check them to see if you've overlooked words or phrases that involve ambiguity, double meanings or bias.

Assume that you and your interviewees don't share the same

vocabulary. Use simple, everyday words whenever possible. You may have to compromise and forego using the "best" word in favor of one that is more likely to ensure an accurate response. When you must use words you suspect are unfamiliar, provide a definition within the context of your question. For instance, the reporter could say, "Some people don't believe in euthanasia—mercifully ending the life of dying, suffering patients. Do you believe in it?" Even when you believe there's no language problem, stay alert for signs that your partner doesn't understand you, like a puzzled look or an inappropriate answer. Finally, minimize, if you can, any embarrassment over misunderstanding a question. Take responsibility, saying, "I probably didn't make myself clear enough. Let me rephrase that question."

**Inflection.** A simple "why" question demonstrates how inflection can alter your meaning—and the meaning as perceived by the person you're interviewing. Payne recommends repeating the question "Why do you say that?", putting inflectional stress on each word.[33] For example, "Why do you SAY that?" may suggest dismay on your part and that, in turn, may upset the interviewee. Inferences may be drawn from each use of inflection:

WHY do you say that? (Inferred meaning: "I'm not sure of your reasons.")

Why DO you say that? (Inferred meaning: "I'm somewhat surprised to hear that from you.")

Why do YOU say that? (Inferred meaning: "Why not let others take that position?" or "I don't understand your personal involvement in this topic.")

Why do you SAY that? (Inferred meaning: "Saying it may get you in trouble," or "It's better left unsaid.")

Why do you say THAT? (Inferred meaning: "Some inconsistency exists here," or "Couldn't you say something else?")

Be aware of how the tone, pitch and inflection of your voice affect communication. With practice and skill, vocal signals can be used strategically to gain fuller responses. Upward inflection at the end of a question, for example, will likely communicate your interest in hearing what the other person has to say. Inflection can also suggest empathy. "WHY did you want to hurt yourself?" delivered in a sympathetic tone, can communicate caring and compassion. On the other hand, intonation—the pitch of your voice—can suggest displeasure as well, which, indeed, might be your intent.

**Timing.** The sequence of asking questions—timing—isn't as important as the other elements. There are occasions, though, when reporters have to be aware of timing. Veteran reporters usually advise asking "tough" questions at the end of the interview lest the interview abruptly conclude the moment the "bomb" is dropped. A more sensible approach is to try to establish rapport so that no question explodes in the face of person being interviewed. When there's no time or reasonable likelihood of achieving rapport, questions may hit hard by necessity. Do you save them for the end of the interview? Probably, but keep in mind that some relationships are so fragile that you might be better off asking your toughest questions immediately. If you wait, even a seemingly innocent question might end the interview before you get to your point.

### Organizing the Interview

Most reporters informally organize interviews, following these loose guidelines: Start with a warm-up of small talk (see Chapter 2); move to easy, fact-generating questions; ease into your main, "must-ask" questions; and gently, if possible, pose your toughest questions last. Talk-show host David Frost prefers to organize his interviews by three categories of notes. "First," he says, "specific questions I knew must be asked. Second, more general areas I knew I would like to experiment with. And third, the verbatim quotes—usually from the interviewee—that I knew I might want to call upon. But they were all only road maps, not blueprints."[34] Frost said the organization and preparation allowed him to pursue any promising new angle that emerged. If you adopt a method like Frost's, don't become so committed to your plan that you can't set it aside and let the natural flow of the dialogue carry you. Although drafting questions in advance is important, many questions grow naturally from the dynamics of the conversation.

Interviewing experts Charles J. Stewart and William B. Cash Jr. say the normal methods of outlining also may be helpful: time sequence; space sequence; cause-to-effect sequence; problem-solution sequence; or topical sequence.[35] Your organization of questions might employ two or more sequences within a single interview. Let's say the interview is with a plant manager about the closing of the factory. At first your questions might follow a topical sequence—when will the factory close, how many will lose jobs, what will happen to the plant? Next, you might explore cause and effect—what will be the ripple effect on the community and other businesses?

Ending an interview isn't something reporters normally plan. Ideally, endings come naturally, with the reporter and interviewee recognizing that the interview is nearly over. In most cases, though, two rules should govern: Exit gracefully, and don't overstay your welcome. Here are some suggestions for applying those rules.

❑ End your interview on time. If you agreed on a 30-minute interview, be prepared to stop at that point. Failing to do so might cause a busy interviewee to lose attentiveness, turning—mentally at least—to the duties that still must be met that day. Worse, it might force the interviewee into the awkward position of breaking off the interview. By saying, "I see our time is about up. I have just a question or two more," you may set up a response, "Oh, I have a bit more time. Don't worry." If you don't—and you still have questions to cover—schedule another interview.

❑ Look for exit signs. When the interview has nearly run its course, signal your intention to conclude. "I just have one more question I'd like to ask." Even if you feel there's much more to discuss, you have to watch for signals sent by the interviewee. Fidgeting, brief answers and shifting of body position all suggest fatigue or loss of interest. Going on will probably yield little more in substantial information. You might just have to call it a day.

❑ Try to conclude on a positive note. Consider closing the interview with an easy or pleasing topic, especially if you sense a need to ease any negative feelings from previous questions. A session with a professor might end with the reporter asking about the pet project of the professor's son: "How's your son doing with his fund raising for the United Way?"

❑ Stay alert and involved until you say goodbye. After you put away your tape recorder or notebook, the conversation may continue at the doorway. Veteran reporters have found that newsmakers often relax and are more expressive after the formal stage of the interview appears over. At the very least, casual conversation at the doorway has its rapport value.

❑ Make a good final impression. One way is to demonstrate that you care about being thorough and accurate. As the interview ends, summarize important points for clarification. ("Let me be sure I understood what you meant when you said. . . . ") Give the interviewee the opportunity to add thoughts. ("Is there anything I've failed to ask that you'd like to cover?") Another sign of thoroughness is to say, "As I go over my notes, I may need to call you to ask a few more questions later, OK?"

Show your appreciation for the interview with a sincere thank you and, if appropriate, a genuine compliment. ("Talking to you really helped me understand how municipal bonds are issued.") You might send a brief note of thanks. Reporters often operate as though people, especially public figures, are obligated to talk with them. A more thoughtful approach is to think of their cooperation as a *favor* rather than an *obligation*.

## RECORDING ANSWERS TO QUESTIONS

There are three principal methods reporters use to record answers to questions: delayed note taking, electronic taping and conventional note taking. In some cases, a reporter may use all three in the course of the same interview. Print reporters, however, are most accustomed to using paper and pencil, and veteran newsmakers are, likewise, accustomed to the reporter's note taking. Nonetheless, each method has it advantages and disadvantages, which will be examined.

### Delayed Note Taking

Truman Capote, author of the nonfiction novel *In Cold Blood,* resorted to memorization and delayed note taking because in his experience interviewees became tense whenever he began taking notes.[36] Capote trained himself by listening intently to others, immediately writing down all that he recalled, and then comparing his notes to a tape-recording of the conversation. He said he eventually achieved an accuracy of 97 percent. Capote's approach underscores the main advantage of delayed note taking—it reduces inhibitions and self-consciousness for the interviewee.

Delayed note taking offers these additional advantages:

- It is useful when taking notes or when tape recording is awkward or impossible. Memorization might be necessary if the interview takes place on the run, with a reporter following a news subject as they walk briskly through an airport, for example, or if the surroundings, like background noise in a factory, prevent tape recording.

- It allows the reporter to absorb background information without the encumbrances of a recorder or notebook. Sometimes it's valuable for a reporter to sit back and, without pressure, listen for the purposes of understanding, comprehension and reflection.

- It lessens the possibility of what is known as "the interviewer effect." Studies show that interview subjects who know they are being recorded or quoted tend to answer questions to satisfy what they *believe* the interviewer *wants,* not necessarily saying what they really think or feel.[37]

- It enables a reporter to "record" important details without a signal to the news subject. Interviewees often are alert for cues from reporters, and they may become more guarded if they sense the reporter is keenly interested in a particular remark. Reporters know this, and some will stop taking notes and rely on memorization when they fear the news subject is reacting unnaturally to note taking.

The many disadvantages of delayed note taking often discourage reporters from its use. Chief among these is that it increases the potential for errors. For most reporters, memory is too unreliable. And while memorization does, indeed, reduce anxiety for *some* interviewees, people who are used to dealing with reporters are uncomfortable and suspicious when there's no notebook or tape recorder. Even reporters with an uncanny power of recall should make limited use of memorization. The notebook and tape recorder are important symbols in establishing and maintaining trust between reporter and interviewee.

There are other disadvantages to delayed note taking:

- It inhibits collection of direct quotations.

- It discourages the reporter from using what are called "probe notes"—reminders of points that should be clarified or expanded upon later in the interview.[38] If a reporter simultaneously attempts to retain probe notes and store verbatim information, the difficulty of memorization is compounded.

- It takes time. After his interviews, Capote would return to his motel room and spend hours, in some cases, transcribing. Reporters rarely enjoy the luxury of time.

## Tape Recording

Some reporters won't work without a tape recorder any more than a high-wire artist would work without a safety net. Other reporters would never think of using a recorder. Reporter-author John McPhee, for one, shuns them. According to a friend, "He never uses tape recorders when interviewing, for they inhibit some people and are too subverbal for his purposes. The writing process must begin with words—a scrap of talk, bits of description, odd facts and inferences—and only a pencil and notebook will answer these needs with literacy and economy."[39] Jack Douglas, author of *Creative Interviewing,* sees tape recorders as friend and foe: "The recorder is both a reassurance of the seriousness of your pursuit and a brutal technological reminder of human separateness that undermines the intimate communion you are trying to create. . . . But it is such a powerful weapon in the fight for truth that it must be used in all situations where it is allowed."[40]

Unquestionably, a tape recorder's presence can be disruptive and depersonalizing. Vladimir Nabokov, author of the novel *Lolita,* colorfully expressed his uneasiness with tape recorders, telling an interviewer, "No, tape recorders are out. No speaking off the Nabocuff. When I see one of those machines, I start hemming and hawing . . . hemming and hawing. Hemmingwaying all over the place."[41] You'd think that celebrated figures would feel at ease with a tape recorder, but Oriana Fallaci found that "getting them to talk in front of a machine that is recording every pause and every breath is, in 50 percent of the cases, fraught with tension." Subjects would "mutter haltingly," "fall silent" or "drown the microphone in a chaos of words. Afterward came the worst moment; when I would listen to the silences and torrents of talk and have to transpose them into normal conversations."[42]

Reservations aside, these days a tape recorder is the reporter's best insurance policy. It provides a permanent, indisputable record of interviews, ensuring accuracy and protecting the reporter in the increasing possibility of litigation. It has other advantages, too.

- It is versatile, particularly when the reporter is physically unable to take notes, such as at a crowded impromptu press conference, in cold weather or where there's too little light.

- It allows for concentrated listening, and it especially frees the reporter to listen for central ideas.

- It allows the reporter to observe the interviewees more carefully and to react to verbal and nonverbal messages.
- It functions as a backup for a reporter's note taking. The tape is used to recheck notes for accuracy, particularly the accuracy of direct quotes.
- It serves as a useful training tool for reporters, enabling them to analyze the effectiveness of their interviewing style.

It is also important to consider the disadvantages of using a tape recorder.

- It tends to discourage candor and naturalness in interviewees. People being recorded are more likely to construct responses cautiously and deliberately, overly conscious that the machine is taking down every word. "I end up talking to the tape recorder instead of the reporter," one news subject said.
- It collects trivial as well as significant detail; it isn't selective.
- It encourages, ironically, laxity and laziness. A tape recorder, although reassuring in many ways, sometimes offers a false sense of security. Moreover, it can cause a reporter to day-dream, lose concentration or relax to the point of disengagement. The tape recorder's presence might lead the reporter to rationalize: "Each word is being taken down; if I miss something now, I can always find it on the tape." That may be true for mere words, but the verbal and nonverbal context won't be found on the tape.
- It can double the reporter's pre-writing preparation, which is probably the main reason print reporters don't use the tape recorder more often. Many get easily frustrated rewinding and fast-forwarding in search of an elusive quotation. (Most tape recorders have counters to help locate points on the tape you wish to review. Counters are helpful—provided you remember to make note of the number on the counter. In the midst of an absorbing interview, you may forget.)
- It tempts Murphy's Law: If anything can go wrong, it will. Besides the possibility of operator error, batteries fail and tapes unravel when you least expect a problem, and when you're least prepared to do something about it.

Despite the tape recorder's shortcomings, its importance as a means of ensuring accuracy cannot be overemphasized.

## Note Taking

Reporters are scribblers. Photographers sometimes call them "pencils." Open a reporter's desk, and you'll see stacks of old notebooks. Although many reporters use a tape recorder for accuracy's sake, their method of choice for recording answers is pen and paper. There are many reasons reporters prefer note taking. Most of all, note taking is the beginning of the process of selecting, analyzing, synthesizing and interpreting information. As they take notes, reporters organize, distill and paraphrase, putting ideas and thoughts into their own words. A story begins to take at least skeletal shape. Writer William Zinsser explains why he stresses note taking: "My tangible reason is that there should be a relationship between a writer and his materials, just as there should be a relationship between an artist and his canvas and his brush. The act of taking notes is, however fragmentary, an act of writing. To bypass the process by having someone talk into a machine is to lose the subtle mystery of seeing words emerge as you put them on paper."[43]

Note taking is not a perfect process, but consider, first, its other advantages.

- It takes less time to review notes than a taped conversation.
- It enables a reporter to keep probe notes, to record visual messages and to underscore other nonverbal details as the interview progresses.
- It keeps the reporter constructively "occupied." Taking notes curbs tendencies by reporters to interrupt or talk too much.
- It induces *some* interviewees to be more expansive and open. Interviewing expert Raymond L. Gorden says interviewees tend to elaborate at points where the interviewer is most intent on taking notes.[44]
- It reassures news subjects that they will be accurately represented.

Note taking poses some significant disadvantages, but most of them can be overcome.

- It distracts reporters who are bent on recording as many comments as possible. They pay excessive attention to the mechanics of note taking, failing to detect central ideas and, more significantly, failing to maintain a relationship with the interviewee.
- It presses reporters to record rapidly—too rapidly at times. When interviewees get excited or passionate, they tend to speak

faster. The words pour out, making it tough for the reporter to keep up; asking the interviewer to slow down might dampen the passion.

• It leads to "essence" quotations, which invite inaccuracies. Using a state official's press conference as an example, a reporter explained, "We all had the essence of what was said and we had direct quotes, but some of the words were different. When I saw what he really said on TV, I had some words wrong and other reporters had some different words wrong, but we all had the essence of what he said." A study of 10 Canadian newspapers introduces a disturbing note about essence quotations.[45] The researcher, Peter Calamai, compared published quotations from a sensational murder trial with the actual trial transcript. The journalists reported the quotes by note taking, since Canadian law prohibits tape recording trials, and none of the reporters knew shorthand. "Trivial" errors in syntax or vocabulary weren't counted. Nevertheless, Calamai found that quotes were misreported in minor or major ways at least half the time. Percentages ranged from one paper that misquoted 45 percent of the time (39 percent of these misquotes were major errors of interpretation or connotation) to another that misquoted 71 percent of the time (67 percent of this paper's misquotes contained major errors). The study is a strong argument for tape recording or formal shorthand. In Australia, journalists often take a "cadetship," a rigorous apprentice program that includes weekly classes in shorthand.[46] Although not required in the American journalist's education, shorthand instruction seems a fairly simple way of increasing accuracy in the news. If you don't know shorthand, at least devise your own abbreviations for commonly used terms and words: & (and); *cd* (could); *w/o* (without); *gov* (government).

• It results in hodgepodge of words, fragments of quotes, symbols and informal shorthand that may look like a cross between graffiti and abstract art. Unless the notes are used immediately after the interview, they might be as interpretable as hieroglyphics at a later date. (The typical reporter's note-taking method is another strong argument for learning formal shorthand.)

## Tips for Recording Answers

Effective reporters can avert some of the problems of keeping an interview record by considering this advice:

❑ Whether you use a tape recorder or notebook, try to prevent your tools from being obtrusive. Place them out of the interviewee's direct line of sight. You might rest a notebook on a crossed leg, keeping the notebook below the interviewee's eye level. Put your tape recorder on a chair; use one with a built-in microphone so you don't have to put a microphone in front of the interviewee.

❑ If you take notes, try to anticipate reactions to your behavior. If you stop taking notes, for example, the interviewee might conclude that you don't care about what's being said. On the other hand, if you too intently take notes, there are interviewees who will stop talking, feeling you're not listening. Keep in mind signals are being transmitted to you as well. For example, if you stop taking notes and the interviewee's eyes focus on your notebook, the silent question might be, "Why aren't you taking this down? I think what I'm saying is important."

❑ If you sense any reservations about the use of a notebook or tape recorder, explain why you're recording the interview. Some reporters will say, "I'm going to take a few notes as we talk so I won't forget what we discussed." That will reassure most interviewees. Another approach is offered by Studs Terkel, who relied heavily on a tape recorder for his oral histories. He minimizes the "threat" of the machine this way: "On occasion, [the tape recorder] might have become an inhibiting factor . . . were it not for my clowning. I'd kick it, not too hard, in the manner of W.C. Fields with a baby or a recalcitrant picket fence. Since the tape recorder did not retaliate, its nonviolent nature was made clear to my companion. With most, its presence had no effect one way or the other."[47]

❑ Don't get so wrapped up in taking notes that you forget the importance of eye contact and nonverbal reinforcements, like a smile, a nod or a raised eyebrow.

A combination of note taking and tape recording works well for some reporters. Reporter Peter Rinearson described his use of both notes and tape: "In many instances, it's not until I transcribe an interview that I understand what was said. When you're taking notes, you get a sentence or two and maybe you miss a sentence. Your mind is turning back and forth between what you're writing and what you're hearing."[48]

Reporters, of course, are divided on methods of recording information. But knowing the advantages and disadvantages will enable you to anticipate problems and select the type of recording that best suits you, the interviewee and the situation.

## LIMITATIONS OF QUESTIONS

Even though questions are basic tools for reporters, don't overestimate their significance or rely on them excessively. Alfred Benjamin, author of *The Helping Interview,* raises an intriguing point that applies to journalists. In general, Benjamin believes interviewers ask too many questions, many of them either meaningless, confusing or impossible to answer. His main reservation, however, is the relentless question-answer cycle interviewers adopt, which he fears depersonalizes communication, inhibiting dialogue. As Benjamin puts it: "[The interviewee] will perceive himself as an object, an object who answers when asked and otherwise keeps his mouth closed—and undoubtedly his mind and heart as well. By initiating the question-answer pattern we are telling the interviewee as plainly as if we put it into words that we are the authority, the expert, and that only we know what is important and relevant for him."[49]

Reporters must ask questions, but Benjamin is correct in his advice to guard against being trapped in a rigid question-answer formula. As a psychologist we know explained, "You can always ask questions." He suggests starting off with informal conversation and careful listening. That advice is echoed by a street-smart character named "Doc" in sociologist William Foote Whyte's classic study of an Italian neighborhood. Doc had introduced Whyte as "a friend" to a group of neighborhood men, including some gamblers. Whyte was accepted as part of the group until he asked a sensitive question about whether the gamblers were paying off the police. He got an icy reaction. Later, Doc told Whyte: "Go easy on that 'who,' 'what,' 'why,' 'when,' 'where' stuff, Bill. You ask those questions, and people will clam up on you. If people accept you, you can just hang around, and you'll learn the answers in the long run without even having to ask the questions."[50]

Whyte learned a valuable lesson:

> I found that this was true. As I sat and listened, I learned the answers to questions that I would not have had the sense to ask if I had been getting my information solely on an interviewing basis. I did not abandon ques-

tioning altogether, of course. I simply learned to judge the sensitiveness of the question and my relationship to the people so that I only asked a question in a sensitive area when I was sure that my relationship to the people involved was very solid."[51]

Reporters who start asking questions immediately, particularly with people who are uncomfortable being questioned, may get the same reaction Whyte experienced.

Questions also may bring out the defensiveness in people. Psychologist Jack R. Gibb says even the simplest of questions can be judgmental or accusatory because, indeed, people are frequently evaluative in their questions.[52] For example, a reporter might ask, "Professor Smith, why did you decide to study the communication habits of whales and not humans?" Intentionally or not, the reporter's question may reflect his opinion that the good professor is wasting time studying whales. Asking questions, of course, is what reporters mainly do; just be aware that questions can raise a specter of defensiveness. Information can emerge through a conversational approach that minimizes the need strictly to ask questions.

Question-asking, then, is not always the most productive or most reliable means of learning about people. Reporters should use a variety of methods to gain understanding, among them conversation, observation and research. When reporters *only* ask questions, the result is usually a story devoid of vigor—the sights, sounds, moods, emotions and action that make for lively reading.

Chapters 4 and 5, particularly, focus on helping you become a well-rounded, perceptive interview *participant,* not a mere *questioner.*

## Notes

[1]"An Interview with Whitey Herzog," *Riverfront Times,* Feb. 11–17, 1987, p. 18a.

[2]Sam Donaldson, *Hold On, Mr. President* (New York: Random House, 1987), p. 20.

[3]David Shaw, *Journalism Today: A Changing Press for a Changing America* (New York: Harper's, 1977), p. 4.

[4]S. Elizabeth Bird, "Anthropological Methods Relevant for Journalists," *Journalism Educator* 41 (Winter 1987), p. 7.

[5]Donald Murray, *Writing For Your Readers* (Chester, Conn.: The Globe Pequot Press, 1983), pp. 30, 31.

[6]Connie Fletcher and Jon Ziomek, "How to Catch a Star," *The Quill,* December 1986, p. 36.

[7]Benjamin Balinsky and Ruth Burger, *The Executive Interview: A Bridge to People* (New York: Harper & Row, 1959), p. 59.

[8]William C. Donaghy, *The Interview: Skills and Applications* (Glenview, Ill.: Scott, Foresman, 1984), p. 19.

[9]Jack Cappon, "Here's the Loh-down on 'Elsewhere in America,' " *The Bulletin of the American Society of Newspaper Editors,* December–January 1981, p. 27.

[10]Larry Speakes, "The Press Gets Its Report Card," *Editor & Publisher,* Feb. 7, 1987, p. 10.

[11]John Brady, *The Craft of Interviewing* (New York: Vintage Books, 1977), p. 36.

[12]Gary C. Lawrence and David L. Grey, "Subjective Inaccuracies in Local News Reporting," *Journalism Quarterly* 46 (Winter 1969): 755.

[13]Murray, *Writing For Your Readers,* p. 85.

[14]Edna Buchanan, *The Corpse Had a Familiar Face* (New York: Random House, 1987), p. 265.

[15]Lincoln Barnett, *Writing on Life: Sixteen Close-ups* (New York: William Sloane Associates, 1951), pp. 13, 14.

[16]Quoted in Jack Hilton and Mary Knoblauch, *On Television! A Survival Guide for Media Interviews* (New York: AMACOM, 1982), foreword.

[17]Quoted in Mary Murphy, "Unlike Marilyn Monroe, 'I'm Strong . . . I'm Sturdy,' " *TV Guide,* May 2, 1987, p. 29.

[18]Don A. Dillman, *Mail and Telephone Surveys: The Total Design Method* (New York: John Wiley & Sons, 1978), p. 107.

[19]Barbara Walters, *How to Talk With Practically Anybody About Practically Anything* (Garden City, N.Y.: Doubleday, 1970), p. 21.

[20]"Dodgers' Campanis: Blacks May Lack 'Necessities' to Be Managers," *Chicago Tribune,* April 8, 1987, Sec. 4, p. 2.

[21]Mary Budd Rowe, "Wait Time: Slowing Down May Be a Way of Speeding Up," *American Educator,* Spring 1987, pp. 38–40.

[22]Hilton and Knoblauch, *On Television!,* p. 128.

[23]Hilton and Knoblauch, p. 129.

[24]Alfred C. Kinsey et al., *Sexual Behavior in the Human Male* (Philadelphia: W.B. Saunders, 1948), pp. 53–55.

[25]Robert L. Kahn and Charles F. Cannell, *The Dynamics of Interviewing* (New York: John Wiley & Sons, 1964), p. 128.

[26]Quoted in Douglas A. Anderson and Bruce D. Itule, *Contemporary News Reporting* (New York: Random House, 1984), p. 56.

[27]Skip Myslenski, "NFL under the Big Top," *Chicago Tribune,* Jan. 27, 1988, Sec. 4, pp. 1 and 3.

[28] Roger Simon, "To Paul Simon, Every Hand Is a Special Hand To Shake," *Chicago Tribune,* Dec. 14, 1987, Sec. 1, p. 5.

[29] Linda Ellerbee, *"And So It Goes": Adventures in Television* (New York: Berkley Books, 1987), p. 37.

[30] Joan Didion, *Slouching Towards Bethlehem* (New York: Washington Square Press, 1981), p. 14.

[31] Donaldson, *Hold On, Mr. President,* pp. 9–10.

[32] Stanley L. Payne, *The Art of Asking Questions* (Princeton: Princeton University Press, 1951), pp. 158–176.

[33] Payne, *The Art of Asking Questions,* pp. 203–204.

[34] David Frost, *"I Gave Them a Sword": Behind the Scenes of the Nixon Interview* (New York: William Morrow, 1978), p. 90.

[35] Charles J. Stewart and William B. Cash Jr., *Interviewing: Principles and Practices,* 3rd ed. (Dubuque, Iowa: Wm. C. Brown, 1982), p. 63.

[36] Roy Paul Nelson, *Articles and Features* (Boston: Houghton Mifflin, 1978), p. 149.

[37] See Herbert H. Hyman et al., *Interviewing in Social Research* (Chicago: University of Chicago Press, 1954).

[38] Raymond L. Gorden, *Interviewing: Strategy, Techniques and Tactics* (Homewood, Ill.: The Dorsey Press, 1980), p. 222.

[39] William L. Howarth, ed., *The John McPhee Reader* (New York: Vintage Books, 1978), p. xvii.

[40] Jack D. Douglas, *Creative Interviewing* (Beverly Hills: Sage Publications, 1985), p. 83.

[41] Alfred Appel, Jr., "Nabokov: A Portrait," *The Atlantic,* November 1971, p. 91; quoted in William L. Rivers, *Finding Facts* (Englewood Cliffs, N.J.: Prentice-Hall, 1975), p. 51.

[42] Oriana Fallaci, *The Egotists: Sixteen Surprising Interviews* (Chicago: Henry Regnery, 1963), p. ix.

[43] William Zinsser, *On Writing Well,* 2nd ed. (New York: Harper & Row, 1980), p. 81.

[44] Gorden, *Interviewing: Strategy, Techniques and Tactics,* pp. 222, 223.

[45] Mark Fitzgerald, "Don't (Mis)quote Me On That!", *Editor & Publisher,* June 6, 1987, p. 114.

[46] Janet Mazur, "An American Journalist Goes 'Down Under,' " *Editor & Publisher,* May 9, 1987, p. 52.

[47] Studs Terkel, *Division Street: America* (New York: Pantheon Books, 1967), p. xxii.

[48] Quoted in Shirley Biagi, *NewsTalk I: State-of-the-Art Conversations with Today's Print Journalists* (Belmont, Calif.: Wadsworth, 1987), p. 30.

[49]Alfred Benjamin, *The Helping Interview,* 2nd ed. (Boston: Houghton Mifflin Company, 1974), p. 66.

[50]William Foote Whyte, *Street Corner Society: The Social Structure of an Italian Slum* (Chicago: University of Chicago Press, 1955), p. 303.

[51]Whyte, *Street Corner Society,* p. 303.

[52]Jack R. Gibb, "Defensive Communication," *Journal of Communication* 11 (1961), 141–148.

# An Ear for News

## Reporters as Listeners

Eudora Welty wrote, "Long before I wrote stories, I listened for stories. Listening *for* them is something more acute than listening *to* them."[1]

In an increasingly complicated and specialized world, the public drama often seems too vast and confusing for us to follow. Busy individuals don't have the time, the energy, the commitment or the information necessary to see the whole picture, so the public is often intimidated by the sheer volume of news. People need to relate global events to local ones, understanding the links between Manila and Main Street. But they need help.

The public depends on journalists to listen carefully and fairly for what is important. Journalism analyzes seemingly isolated facts and opinions, and looks for a larger framework into which to fit these pieces. Journalists also are expected to remain constantly alert to the exceptions and dissonances within the pattern. Nuances are as important to the reporter as bandwagons.

Listening is one of a reporter's *central roles* in a well-functioning society. Journalists in general, and reporters in particular, actually form the conduit through which citizens are allowed to move psychologically through the public drama. It is a powerful responsibility to be society's surrogate listeners.

Surprisingly, the process of listening has received little emphasis in the education of most journalists. An informal survey of 12 contemporary books on reporting revealed that only three listed "listening" or an equivalent term in the index. Only four offered anything more than a passing comment about the importance of listening well. Even books and chapters devoted to the more specialized topic of "interviewing" tend not to stress the lessons to be learned from listening research. Most of these sources tend toward the anecdotal and prescriptive approaches, and emphasize the "ask questions, then write the answers" model of interviewing.

## CONTEXTS OF JOURNALISTIC LISTENING

To one author, the ideal interviewer is one "who can ask 160 or 170 questions over a space of a few hours, then write a coherent, organized, interesting report on what he has learned."[2] This, of course, is true enough as far as it goes. To it must be added the reminder that reporters' questions and comments elicit responses that should be listened to within a series of contexts. These contexts include:

❑ *The personalities of the interview partners.* A remark such as "That question seems inappropriate" might be as agitated and hostile as some personalities will ever get. With them, the reporter would do well to back off, perhaps, thinking,"He's very offended." With other, more direct interviewees, the context of personality might suggest an interpretation like "She's being polite and gentle, inviting a follow-up question." In either case, the meaning is *not* in the words; it is determinable only by interpreting the psychological context of the words.

❑ *The immediate situation.* The pressure of crises, or the presence of certain people, often elicits responses that are regretted or even incomprehensible in more ordinary times. Reporters who aren't sensitive to how an immediate situation might encourage an unrepresentative quote are likely to be technically and textually "correct" more often than they are contextually accurate. An accurate *text* of a quote is not, in a sense, helpful or true if the reporter misses its *context*. A soldier will express different feelings about the war just after he's been shot. And John Brady reports that a sociologist writing "on whether or not elderly persons should live with their children found that replies were affected significantly, depending on whether the children were interviewed alone, the parents were interviewed alone, or the parents and children were interviewed together."[3]

❏ *Expectations and biases*. Actress Geraldine Page told the story of a fan, a dentist, who once came backstage to discuss her performance in "Sweet Bird of Youth." His comment: "I was sitting in the front row and looking up. Most of the time I was studying the fillings in your mouth. I'm curious to know who's been doing your dental work."[4] Instead of being moved by her powerful acting, the man could only respond in the context of his own professional role. Reporters similarly might miss important insights if they can't remove the blinders imposed by working only on one angle of a story.

The ability to listen well, therefore, involves interpreting the other person's meaning, sensing what another's messages may imply even when that person is not fully aware of the implications, and anticipating new meanings generated by dialogue. Although much listening research stresses message reception and information processing,[5] this definition of listening stresses its *activity* and its *creativity* rather than passive reception.

Research has established that 45 percent of a typical person's communication time is spent listening, 30 percent speaking, 16 percent reading and only 9 percent writing.[6] Certainly, professional journalists inflate the writing figure—but not, probably, at the expense of the listening statistic. If anything, journalists should develop more thoroughly this most neglected and least taught[7] of the basic communication processes; instead, they too often overestimate their skill at it. Experts on listening underline the difficulty: "Adult listening behaviors become habitual. Our listening behaviors have been acquired and reinforced over a long period of time. As adults we rarely think about how we listen or consider that it takes time to change old habits. We listen the way we do because we have learned to listen that way."[8]

## LISTENING DISABILITIES OF REPORTERS

There is no foolproof formula for effective listening. Moreover, it is difficult for editors or journalism instructors to measure how well their reporters listen. Punctuation errors or muddled leads are obvious enough in manuscripts, but how can habitually poor listening be identified in an interview perhaps weeks past and miles away?

Of course, some good listeners have never received formal training in listening. But journalism programs that omit listening training risk turning out reporters who fit the following descriptions.

## The Reporter as Stenographer

Some reporters, eager not to miss a word, diminish comprehension and insight because they are too busy listening for words, rather than meaning. They attempt to form, either by note taking or by memory, a near-exact record of the meeting, on the assumption that this record may be recalled later and processed or analyzed for "content." Eye contact with the source is often minimal, and the reporter encourages very little spontaneity. The reporter tries to create a "businesslike" and highly organized interview structure, since this makes the resulting information seem more manageable. The reportorial stenographer, like a court stenographer, tries to avoid an active presence in favor of a *non-person* role. In this role, reporters resemble automatons, programmed to go through the motions necessary to produce a passable story. They ask questions and record answers without becoming intrigued or excited about what they are hearing.

Communication research differentiates between the processes of "hearing" and those of "listening," and the distinction is relevant here. "Hearing" is a physiological process in which aural stimuli are registered. This simple step is as undemanding as it is unrewarding. Given the proper motivations, we are all capable of attending to stimuli, and focusing on them for periods of time. Yet for the purposes of communication, "hearing" becomes important only for what it enables—"listening." People truly listen only when engaged in an inner process of active translation, consideration and interpretation. The stenographer role elevates hearing at the expense of listening, disabling the reporter as a full communicator. This observation is not meant to diminish the importance of accurate and helpful notes, or the need at times to focus on content. But reporters should not expect to remove themselves from active participation in conversational interviews and still be perceived as effective listeners.

## The Lazy Reporter

Many reporters, both veterans and novices, don't fully realize that listening is a complex process. If they have done an adequate job of preparation and research, and if they believe the dubious advice,

"Never ask a question to which you don't know the answer," reporters run the risk of conversational laziness. Becoming lulled by prior information is especially dangerous when the reporter assumes that there is a single, simple predetermined purpose an interviewee can fulfill.

That's the problem—assumption can be the enemy of listening. Effective listeners let themselves be surprised. In fact, they invite surprise, for surprise is a sign of learning. And what, if not learning, is the reporter's primary motivation? One experienced reporter takes an extreme position on being open to surprise. She said that for most interviews she enters the room with only *one* question—the one that will most readily lead her and her interviewee into conversation. From then on, she lets questions and comments emerge from the "flow" of talk, never knowing what she is about to discover through sensitive listening. Beginning interviewers, however, desiring reasonable security and not wanting to forget important issues, will want to do more advance planning of questions and issues than this. The traditional advice about planning an "interview schedule" can often keep reporters on the track during a long interview or focused during one with an ambiguous public official.[9] But this security should not be purchased at the cost of spontaneous learning.

## The Reporter as Inquisitor

Some inexperienced reporters may think the Mike Wallace method is the best way to conduct an interview. Inquisitors are likely to arrive at the interview with ears cocked for confrontation and listening for the worst. In this view, everyone has something to hide, anyone is likely to lie to you, and reporters have to be battlers and controllers. A striking example is provided by Washington Post reporter Walter Pincus, whose story about the U.S.-Iran arms deal was one of the biggest news breakthroughs of the late 1980s. Pincus was interviewed by Lynn Hirschberg in Rolling Stone:

> "Before your first reporting job, did you have any particular journalistic training?"
>
> "I was in counterintelligence in the Army, and our job was to clear people for classified information. I was chasing homosexuals mostly."
>
> "How did you do that?"

"You'd ask people. I became so good at that I became an interroga-
tor, which was a lot of fun. You'd bring somebody in, and the
object was to make them confess. Like some poor top sergeant
who wanted to be cleared so he could dismantle bombs, and he
had apparently committed bigamy. We brought him in for an
hour and a half. There's a whole technique to interrogation—
you keep circling the issue and get closer and closer to it, like in a
bullfight, and finally you ask the question, and as it happened
with this poor guy, he just keeled over and cried and confessed."

"How close is that kind of interrogation to the reporting you do
now?"

"Same thing."[10]

Although the need for interrogation is relatively rare, a poor listener
may be tempted to adopt this role even when inappropriate because
it has the feel of "control" and direction.

Often, such control becomes a self-fulfilling prophecy. That is, we
often get what we expect in social situations because we've "set up"
the outcomes. In educational research, this is sometimes called "the
Pygmalion effect"; teachers who are told that a certain group of
children are especially advanced or bright will subtly alter their
behaviors and expectations in such a way that the children do in fact
perform better on standardized tests. The converse is also true.
Teachers were also found to be capable of *expecting* their students
into inferior performance.[11]

Self-fulfilling prophecies can also occur in a journalistic situation.
Consider, for example, what can happen when a particularly inquisitorial reporter walks into the office of the city's superintendent of
schools for a scheduled interview concerning union negotiations.
He's been told by another reporter that the superintendent is currently suspected of padding his expense account and subsequently
lying about it. "Watch out for this guy," he was told, "because he's
temperamental, hostile even." The reporter, on his guard to stay in
control and not be fooled, asks prepared questions briskly without a
warm-up period. Several times, he interrupts the superintendent
when he believes he's straying too far afield. The interviewer leaves
when the discussion degenerates into silence, and the superintendent announces he has another appointment. Later, the reporter
tells his colleague, "You're right. The guy was definitely hostile and
had something to hide. He got me out of there as fast as he could.
Got some good stuff, though."

Despite all his "control," what our naive reporter got, of course, might have been only what he had preordained by his attitude. Expecting the superintendent to be hostile, he acted defensively from the start. The behavioral cues of defensiveness appeared to the interviewee to be symptoms of hostility. The superintendent naturally responded with annoyance to what he perceived as hostility. The reporter interpreted the annoyance as verification of the "hostility thesis," and acted accordingly. This vicious circle wasted many opportunities for genuine listening and discovery.

Thus, one danger in having a judgmental attitude is that it is usually communicated at some level to the interviewee, even when the reporter believes it's being masked or hidden. Another danger is that an inquisitorial stance can be used as a rationalization for selfish listening, in which a source is pumped for information or an admission, then left vulnerable. Even if the source is thought of as a scoundrel, interviewers who listen as non-judgmentally as possible can expect to hear more and gain more—and get invited back more often—than defensive and contentious ones.

## THE LISTENING ATTITUDE

Although listening is often taught as a behavioral skill of focusing on a message and remembering it, most reporters will be disappointed if they attempt to learn the "do's" of listening, practice them carefully and store them in a strategic repertoire for later use. A faith in technique is seductive, yet dangerous. It's analogous to trusting a hammer to pound a nail. If you miss the nail and pound your thumb instead, how much could you blame the hammer? The hammer "works" only if you *work well with it,* coordinating it with your goal, the nail, the board, your eyes and your disposition. Using techniques or behavioral skills of listening can only work if they are backed by an attitude of genuine interest in the interviewee's perceptions.

So, effective listening, though it can be fostered through certain practices, is less a technique than an attitude. This attitude involves the openness of the listener to the different experience of the speaker. Without this willingness to be surprised, without this receptivity, an interview might as well be scripted and contain no new information for either party, the sterile experience of "going through the motions." The more helpful journalistic attitude is "I don't know . . . yet. Let me hear more." This attitude implies a commitment to stay with the topic and person even though the interpersonal climate might get chilly or the ideas conflict with the reporter's own. The reporter assigns importance to *now,* to *here* and to understanding *this* interchange. There is time later to integrate the new knowledge into a bigger picture. A reporter doesn't know in advance what needs to be known; that, presumably, is the rationale for the interview.

## Information as Transaction

Information comes from successful interviewing. Normally we think of information as bits of facts, figures and quotations. In that sense, information is more like an object. But in another more complex sense, information emerges from and exists because of a relationship between interviewee and interviewer. Information that becomes "news" is an enterprise involving both news "source" and journalistic interpretation. We put "source" in quotation marks to suggest that the real source of news frequently is in the bond between what is said and done in public events *and* its interpretation through reporters' effective listening.

Chapter 1 described a "transactional" basis for viewing communication. Many things customarily identified as objects or events are in reality "transactions" in which the presence of one factor profoundly affects the definition and meaning of another. John Dewey and Arthur Bentley analyze the futility of attempting to understand the processes of speaking and listening in isolation from each other: "In ordinary behavior, in what sense can we examine a talking unless we bring a hearing along with it into account? Or a writing without a reading? Or a buying without a selling? Or a supply without a demand? How can we have a principal without an agent or an agent without a principal? We can, of course, detach any portion of a transaction that we wish, and secure provisional descriptions and partial reports. But all this must be subject to the wider observation of the full process."[12]

In a listening-speaking episode, one person's success as a listener is interwoven with the other person's speaking style, and the converse is equally true. To cite a common example in reporters' lives, public officials don't simply "have something to say," then call an audience together in a press conference to hear it. Instead, the presence of a particular audience will call into play new things to say, new ideas, new attitudes and new directions. Another implication: A public official in an interview may not consciously be concealing a position on a certain issue or lying. He or she may simply have been "invited" to speak about different things in a differing way by the interviewer's listening habits.

Who and what someone "is" in the presence of another person are not only influenced by his or her own personality, habits and strategies. Who one person seems to be is also influenced—subtly but inevitably—by who and what the other person seems to be. If you interview a celebrity, you don't hear *how the celebrity talks.* You hear *how the person talks to you,* and the results may be very different from what would have happened if another reporter conducted the interview.

Here is a variation on the same theme. A number of years ago, a California school district had some difficulties with students labeled by some as "incorrigible."[13] They were removed from their regular classes and placed in a special training program emphasizing behavior modification. District officials told them that their goal was to practice behaviors that would encourage their regular teachers to respond more positively to them. Through role-playing and video analysis, they practiced rewarding their teachers (who would be unaware of the experiment) for giving them positive feedback. Perhaps you can predict the results. Once integrated back into the normal classroom, these students were treated more positively and began doing better in school, both socially and academically. But who were the changers and who were the changed in this experiment? The situation makes no overall sense when you attempt to see the participants in isolation from each other, or as causing the behaviors of others. The students thought they'd changed the teachers, while the teachers were sure the students were changed for the better by participating in the project. But, really, the answer is neither. The changes came from the participants' simultaneously affecting and being affected. Interviews are like that, too.

Reality is always understood differently by different people. Therefore, reporters must be flexible in the way they interpret what they have heard. Accounts may differ because one or more parties want to dissemble, hide the truth or twist an interpretation. Or they may differ simply because all of us are engaged in constant private interpretation of the truth. Reporters participate in a way that goes beyond mere neutral observation. "The news" is not simply "what happened." News is composed of people's fallible mutual attempts to (1) interpret ambiguous circumstances, (2) create an orderly sense out of this ambiguity and (3) communicate this ordered interpretation to an audience.[14] If a reporter interviews Henry Kissinger about a foreign policy decision, it should be obvious that news isn't just what came *before,* but in large part what comes *from* the interview. The reporter's function in this process—though often considered in simplistic conveyer belt or gatekeeper analogies—is as complex and intricate as the listening process itself. This is why listening isn't just an aspect of the job, but the reporter's central role in society.

When two people communicate effectively, then, it is probably the result of a mutual commitment to *understand.* The absence of this commitment on either side subverts the process from both sides. For instance, if a reporter interviews a school board president about her pressing for a certain agreement behind the scenes, the story will obviously be incomplete if (assuming the reporter's basic fairness) the president decides to tell only the part of the story that favors her own interpretation. It would also be incomplete if the reporter listens only to the part of the story that coincides with his or her pre-existing interpretation. These conclusions are part of the conventional wisdom about listening. Be fair; try harder; detect bias; hear it all. The interviewee can subvert or distort the story, and so can the reporter.

A transactional perspective on listening is somewhat more complicated, however. It explains how listening skills involve not just the reception of information; different ways of listening actually stimulate and regulate speaking differently, and thus the conception of information is different, too. When a listener doesn't seem to be interested in a direction the speaker is taking, or if the listener approaches the speaker's point only with cynicism, then each communicator is less likely to think of important things to say—even if he or she wants to be helpful.

## Listening Is Not Agreement

Of course, this kind of listening has little to do with agreement. Interviewers profitably can imagine the other person's points of view, options, feelings, values or goals without agreeing with them or even attempting to develop a personal "position" in relation to them. A subtle temptation occasionally presents itself, however, to the working reporter. Sometimes inventive reporters imply—perhaps by a manipulative, strategic display of "empathy"—that they're on the interviewee's side. They imply that if the other person discloses more, it will be to someone who is an advocate or true believer.

Social science research has long corroborated that people are more willing to communicate with people who like and agree with them. This is not a surprising finding, since it squares with common sense and everyday experience. Reporters, being quick students of human nature, may seize on this insight to get stories by ingratiating themselves artificially with news personalities. One reporter emphasized how much he liked people and wanted to be natural in interviews, but admitted nevertheless that "sweet talk is my specialty." Students of ethics may want to debate the propriety of such behavior. Here, a more direct point is in order. This kind of tactic may be successful in the short run in eliciting information. But a follow-up assignment may present insurmountable problems if the interviewee feels used, objectified or manipulated by a charade of affection staged by the interviewer.

Journalists should realize the reason behind our human willingness to disclose more to those who like us. It is simple; those who like us tend more to "confirm" us as persons and are less likely to treat us as if we were objects or means to their own ends. To be confirmed, simply stated, means that the other person notices our unique feelings and characteristics—and somehow communicates that awareness.[15] It is this confirmation people crave, much more than mere agreement or transitory affection. The reporter who needs information does not need to feign liking the other person if he or she simply confirms in some consistent way the interviewee's status as a unique and important person.

The rest of this chapter will explore ways to encourage disclosure in three common types of journalistic listening.

First, we'll examine what listeners can do at the level of learning new information: We call this "what happened?" listening. Second, we show how interviewers can better discern differences between statements and positions; this is discriminative or "what's different?" listening. Finally, an important but often overlooked aspect of journalistic interviewing is "who are you?" or personality-based listening.

The categories are not mutually exclusive. The interviewer doesn't switch off one in order to attempt another. All three may be involved at a given time, or any one may receive greater emphasis as circumstances dictate. An accident investigation may emphasize informational listening; a presidential press conference demands discriminative listening; and in a celebrity profile interview, personality-based listening is most appropriate.

Remember, too, that these methods aren't prescriptions or recipes that will guarantee success. They aren't techniques tied to automatic outcomes; they are solutions developed by competent listeners to problems they've encountered. You should experiment with the suggestions to discover which work best for you, and in which situations. Modify them to fit your personal style and the context in which you're communicating.

## INFORMATIONAL LISTENING: "WHAT HAPPENED?"

Reporters are charged with a clear fact-determining function. This means they are constantly challenged to listen accurately and to interject minimum distortion to accounts of news events. Several specific suggestions should help guide informational listening:

❑ Prior to questioning an expert, anticipate his or her linguistic habits or special jargon. While you might be ill-advised to try to use this language in conversation as though you were an expert in the field yourself, this preparation will allow you to follow explanations more clearly and accomplish your inner "translation" more smoothly.

Don't foolishly try to deceive the expert into a false image of you; all you're attempting is to form common ground upon which to build an understanding. Since you're usually the one requesting the interview, the prime responsibility for linguistic preparation is yours.

❑ Use perception checks. These are short statements designed to describe and validate your present understanding of what the other person is saying. They allow your interviewee to monitor how well you're following the account, and they invite your partner to correct your listening mistakes, misperceptions or biased interpretations before they have a chance to become embedded in your memory. Perception checks are similar to the "probe" questions described in Chapter 3. They operate as a very cheap verbal smoke alarm—you can often put out the misinterpretation before it spreads its destruction. These are examples of perception checks:

"Now, let me make sure I got it right; *27* percent of your people are now equipped with this new weapon?"

"I believe you said a while ago that the blue car came from the north. Right?"

Perception checks usually operate at the level of restatement. You simply want to be as sure as possible that what you're planning to report corresponds to what the source reported to you. If this sounds elementary, be assured that many experienced reporters—

perhaps out of ignorance, cockiness or laziness—omit this simple step. The public suffers as a result. A city police chief noticed this problem after a series of inaccuracies reached the newspapers following interviews with him. He now tries to compensate for the reporters' failures to check basic facts. "Generally," he said, "I think I can overcome their inattentiveness by redundancy. I will make a point three or four times when I recognize that weakness in them. Usually everything works out fine." It works out fine, of course, except for the wasted time and the loss of confidence in reporters' communicative abilities.

❏ Determine the speaker's core ideas and the speaking patterns into which they fit. As you listen, place individual or isolated facts in the context of the major points the speaker is making. In your zeal to get the *full* story, it is possible to drown in a sea of trivia. Remember that details are most important in the pattern they form. No listener will remember everything, but the truly effective one won't miss the main themes.

If listening to an extended speech or series of answers in a press conference, for example, be especially alert for how the speaker organizes ideas or structures explanations. Some illustrative questions to ask yourself:

- Does the speaker continually return to a point?
- Does the speaker emphasize or highlight certain points with words like "actually," "really" and "essentially?"
- Does the speaker consistently seem absolutely certain about his or her conclusions? Or exhibit a pattern of waffling?
- Does the speaker seem preoccupied with statistical proofs to the exclusion of other forms of evidence?
- Does the speaker phrase most of his or her reasoning in cause-affect terms?
- Does the speaker tend toward abstractions more than concrete examples?
- Does the speaker exhibit emotional involvements that could affect his or her memory or accounts of events?

❏ Listen with your mind, not your notes. Methods of recording answers to questions were discussed in Chapter 3. But a reminder here is useful in the context of listening. Notes are often helpful if they are taken unobtrusively. They can serve as a reassuring reminder to the interviewee that the meeting is important to you, and you want to get the facts right. But can they be a crutch, too? Worse, can note taking sometimes poison genuine communication? Jack Mendelsohn's experience interviewing theologian Martin Buber illustrates a somewhat extreme but nevertheless instructive position:

> As he began to talk, I scribbled furiously. Suddenly there was silence, and when I looked up, Buber was smiling. "Mr. Mendelsohn," he said, "either you can take notes without really listening, or you can really listen without taking notes." It was said with no trace of harshness. Firmly, I closed my notebook and "really listened." He said; "Throughout the world, there is a spiritual front on which a secret, silent struggle is being waged between the desire to be on life's side and the desire to destroy. This is the most important front of all—more than any military, political, or economic front. It is the front on which *souls are moulded.*"
>
> My question was the obvious one: "What can individuals do to tip the balance?"
>
> Buber gazed out the window for a moment; then he turned to me and said: "No one can chart a day-to-day course for anyone else. Life can only be determined by each situation as it arises. We all have our chances. From the time we rise in the morning until the time we retire at night we have meetings with others. Sometimes we even meet ourselves! We see our families at breakfast. We go to work with others. We meet people in the streets. We attend gatherings with others. Always there are others. What we do with each of these meetings is what counts. The future is more determined by this than by ideologies and proclamations.[16]

Not only was Mendelsohn admonished gently to put away his notes, but the expansive response Buber gave became itself a commentary on why notes can interfere with our "chances" for meetings. Notes, if taken obtrusively, can reduce the spontaneity of meeting, increase the relational distance between communicators. Buber's advice is sound, but how can a reporter close his or her notebook and still capture lengthy verbatim quotes? A tape recorder might be the answer.

❏ Use your "listening spare time." Human speech proceeds at a snail's pace when compared with the speed of thought. Speech is linear, sequential, redundant and punctuated by many pauses; it is usually produced at about 125 to 180 words per minute (180 wpm would seem *quite* fast). In contrast, the self-talk of thought can be processed at four or more times that rate.[17] Researcher Ralph Nichols says that it might seem reasonable to instruct listeners to slow their thought processes to match the rate of incoming words. But he dismisses that advice as impossible. The speed of thought can't be managed as if controlled by a faucet. Actually, this rapidity turns into an advantage for listeners, if managed properly. Nichols reminds us that "the differential between thinking and speaking rates means that our brains work with hundreds of words in addition to those we hear, assembling thoughts other than those spoken to us. To put it another way, we can listen and still have spare time for thinking."[18]

This spare time can be used for concentration, or squandered on irrelevancies. We all know the potential irrelevancies: Our own bills to pay, worry about another story we're investigating, whether or not the car will start. But what are the possibilities for concentration?

First, the listener can use the spare time to *infer motivations for behavior exhibited by the speaker.* For example, an interviewee may consistently tell jokes when insecure about his or her answers. You can listen to the joke *as a joke,* giving it your attention—and you can think about what the joke might mean in the larger pattern of the speaker's motivations.

Second, listening spare time might be used to enhance *memory.* One specific technique described by many experts on listening, *chunking,* can serve as a good example.[19] Chunking makes it possible for a listener to find ways to reduce the number of units that need to be integrated into memory, by establishing a pattern and/or finding meaningful "sense" to join some units. For example, if you're expecting to remember that a telephone number is 277-1965, must you remember seven numbers in the proper order? No—most of us probably wouldn't even try. The phone company has already recognized our memory difficulties by "pre-chunking" the data into two sub-numbers of three and four digits each. Instead of seven so-called "inputs" to our memory, we have two or three, depending on whether we can process 1965 as a single unit. The number 1965, of course, is more easily recalled as a unit if that happens to be the year you were born, or if it has other significance to you. Keeping track of the assorted details a reporter encounters daily might be easier for those who are skilled at chunking.

A third way of using listening spare time is to *compare what you are currently listening to and learning with what you already know.* You needn't remove your focus from this speaker at this time to note divergences from previous stories, contradictions between the interviewee's account today and her statement last Thursday, and the like. This possibility is often missed by those who consider listening to be simply the *reception* of messages. If you're participating actively in the give-and-take of an interview conversation, this comparative function of listening can suggest to you new questions and new topical avenues to explore.

❑ Understand the effects of interruptions. Conversational interruptions are common, and, if handled properly, won't damage relationships. Reporters, though, are notorious interrupters, probably because they're conditioned to take charge of interviews. ABC's Ted Koppel, for example, often breaks into a guest's monologue on "Nightline," saying, "Senator, you're not answering my question," or "Ambassador, you're straying; let's get back to the topic." Of course, reporters, especially broadcast reporters, are under great pressure to keep an interview on track and on schedule. Knowing the nature of journalistic interviews, experienced newsmakers usually aren't bothered by interruptions. Still, some interviewers are so insensitive and abrasive in breaking in that they may even provoke the interviewee to say, "Please, let me finish!"

Usually it's safest to avoid interrupting in conversation if possible. But an inflexible rule ignores the fact that during the natural ebb and flow of most conversations, interruptions are inevitable and even useful at times. If an interruption appears to come from a communicator's genuine enthusiasm for the topic or the other person, it is rarely seen as a cause for irritation or anger. When people are really engaged in conversation, they are constantly contributing, reacting, confirming, having new ideas, wanting to participate. Interruptions in such instances can either contribute to the exchange or go unnoticed.

Do interrupters lack listening discipline? Sometimes. Most commonly, interviewers interrupt strategically when they've decided what's being said is insignificant or irrelevant. They break in because they conclude the conversation is not going where they think it should go. As reporters listen, they are right to assess information, and naturally they'll make value judgments about answers. But reporters who approach a story "knowing" what to ask and anticipating answers are more likely to interrupt for the wrong reasons. What the reporter finds irrelevant may be of utmost importance to the speaker. There are times to interrupt and times to listen intently. While no one can always be sure when it's necessary or acceptable to interrupt, some of the following guidelines might be helpful.

*Signals.* Watch for signals that your partner is finished speaking or is willing to turn the "floor" over to you momentarily. Speech researchers call these "turn-yielding" cues. Some are obvious; some very subtle. Speakers about to (or willing to) yield the floor to another speaker tend to:

- Raise or lower intonation at the end of clauses.
- Draw out or "drawl" final syllables of clauses.
- Stop or relax hand gestures.
- Utter such expressions as "you know," "so," "but, uh," and "anyway."
- Interject a note of finality suggested by increased volume and/or falling pitch.
- Use complete grammatical clauses.

Additionally, in information-sharing conversations between strangers or people of different status (much journalistic interviewing fits this description, of course), renewed eye gaze appears to be a reliable indicator of the willingness to yield a turn.

Journalists sometimes interview uncooperative subjects who try to monopolize the conversation. According to Margaret McLaughlin's summary of conversational routines, such speakers will "keep the floor" and suppress new questions by such tactics as overly grand gestures and the avoidance of eye contact.[20] An interruption may be the only realistic option in such instances.

Silence is not always a clear or reliable sign of turn-yielding, especially if it isn't accompanied by a sense of finality or eye contact. Sometimes, when we're searching for the right words to make a point, we stop speaking, but communicate in other ways (gazing upward to a prolonged "ahhh," for example) that we're still formulating the idea. If the other person starts to speak, it will be experienced as an interruption; it *is* possible to interrupt silence, since speakers intuitively know that silence is as much a part of the flow of their speech as are the words.

*Reactions.* React to answers that indicate there is misunderstanding between the two of you. Reporters who don't get an "acceptable" answer to a question may conclude that the interviewee is stonewalling—but this is not necessarily a time for interruption. Give your partner the benefit of the doubt. Interrupt to determine if there's a problem of interpretation, but be tactful. Instead of accusing, "You're not answering the question," try shifting responsibility to yourself: "Excuse me, but maybe I didn't make my question clear enough. Let me rephrase it. . . ."

*Self-Control.* Keep your mind and tongue from racing ahead. Like a preoccupied driver, you may find yourself mentally speeding, unaware that you've just missed an important highway sign. Exercise self-control and keep your thoughts in check until you're sure the respondent has had a chance to speak fully.

Let passionate speakers spend themselves. Moments of eloquent intensity are meant to be left alone. Even when eloquence is absent, don't interrupt someone with the need to get something off the chest; let him or her release the strong or consuming emotion without being disarmed by interruption. Your decision will be appreciated.

*Acceptable interruptions.* Avoid using touch or other nonverbal methods to interrupt. Verbal interruptions are usually less invasive and less objectionable. Stopping someone by tapping an arm or knee is usually considered too aggressive, especially if a male interrupts a female this way. Even less direct nonverbal messages, such as gesturing to indicate "halt" or "time out" or vigorously shaking your head as if to say, "no, no" may be perceived as crude and obvious. Christen Brown, a communication consultant who trains executives and public personalities in how and when to interrupt sensitively, advocates "alignment tactics." She suggests you find something in your partner's speech with which you can agree, then establish verbal entree with polite agreement interjections such as "exactly!" or "yes." You then append what you need to state. If that fails, a tactful "excuse me" will establish for most people your need to talk.[21]

Finally, of course, it is important to listen and watch for signals that your partner wishes to interrupt you. Reporters should be doing more listening than asking, but when speaking, stay alert for "turn-requesting" cues. Verbal signals should be obvious enough—suspended words like "well . . . " "yes, but . . . " or "you see . . . " Slight, rapid nods of the head can also serve this function. Another such request is a forward shift of the body from the waist. It may say, "I'm with you, but I'm eager to make my point." Remember that your role is to listen. Yield the platform.

## DISCRIMINATIVE LISTENING: "WHAT'S DIFFERENT?"

Some interviews are conducted for reasons other than to collect information. Journalists need to compare a politician's current position with the one he or she stressed on the campaign trail. They want to ask about discrepancies between the figures reported in June and those reported in July by different workers in the same office. They want to discover why one eyewitness described an assailant as middle-aged and short while another saw a young, tall man instead. Before the story is written, reporters must not only get the facts straight but account for the differences in interpretations, too. The journalist-as-listener must be a critic, an evaluator and a comparison shopper.

Douglas Cater claims that "for the reporter, the basic quest is to discover and highlight traces of disunity," and thus a reporter must think "in terms of thesis and antithesis."[22] Doing so requires a special kind of listening and a special perspective on what is "really" happening in the world.

Various eyewitnesses see different versions of an event because for each one, it existed as a separate event. A famous example of this is Albert Hastorf and Hadley Cantril's case study of perceptions of a football game between Dartmouth and Princeton, originally reported in the Journal of Abnormal and Social Psychology. After this particularly rough game, undergraduates from both schools were interviewed to determine what they "saw." The perceptions were so divergent, yet so consistent with the affiliations of the students, that Hastorf and Cantril reported: "It seems clear that the "game" actually was many different games and that each version of the events that transpired was just as 'real' to a particular person as other versions were to other people. . . . In brief, the data here indicate that there is no such 'thing' as a 'game' existing 'out there' in its own right which people merely 'observe.' "[23]

A journalist's responsibility, given such complexities, is to develop a listening style that expects differing interpretations, to be alert to their distinctiveness and to be able to notice the nuances of meaning that define them. A recent article in Journalism Educator explored the similarities between ethnographers (researchers who participate within cultures and record relevant habits, mores, attitudes and rituals) and reporters by claiming that "both realize that one's 'neutral' observations cannot be accepted at face value and that it is always necessary to cross-check and verify information. As one journalist commented, 'Immaculate perception is unachievable for either ethnographers or journalists.' "[24] Journalistic listening must be discriminative and evaluative listening that persistently asks, "What's different?" How can this be done? Several recommendations are especially relevant:

❏ Be a critic. This is the most important suggestion, because a critical attitude helps you develop the other discriminative listening skills. Being a critic does not mean being cynical or nay-saying. Basically it means being an informed and sensitive listener who is willing to explore the implications and values behind the statements of others. "Sensitive skepticism" describes the appropriate critical bent in journalism. Reporter Adrian Peracchio differentiates between skepticism and cynicism in reporting when he states that "the very last thing that I would want in a reporter is cynicism. Skepticism, yes." He defines skepticism as "listening to everything and accepting very little of it until you can ascertain whether it's true or not, keeping a lot in mind. Cynicism is the foregone conclusion in your mind that everything you listen to is pure crap."[25]

Sensitive skepticism does not contradict an empathic style of communication, as the following question demonstrates: "Pardon me, Doctor. I know you're very emotional about this lawsuit right now and that this is a bad time to talk. But while I have the chance, I have to ask—why hadn't you mentioned the second opinion before today? That seems to be quite important in this matter." Simultaneously, this inquiry identifies with the emotional state of the interviewee, yet verifies that you are not about to overlook important details or possible contradictions. You're not on the person's side, nor against it, but your question demonstrates that your interviewee *has* a side.

❏ Curb your impulse to argue. Journalists, as intelligent citizens, have opinions on a wide variety of topics. They also have the unique opportunity to meet the newsmakers who are at the center of these issues, and perhaps come to symbolize them. No wonder some interviews turn into struggles between two entrenched ideologies instead of the elaboration and understanding of a particular perspective.

You cannot listen effectively to another's position if you are intent only on refutation. A book about how to listen well identifies this tendency toward refutation and argument as one of the clear characteristics of bad listeners. The authors' simple but too rarely heeded advice: "Hold your fire."[26] One reporter described to us a colleague who was very argumentative with interviewees. "I found it appalling," the reporter said, "because he ended up arguing with the guy rather than listening to him. I think he was trying to impress him. Unless you're really in a tough situation, that is totally useless. You're cutting yourself off from your source of information." He then told of another reporter covering city hall who, on the job for only a day and a half, walked into an office and said, "OK, I know somebody in this office is stealing. Tell me about it." Officials privately asked, "Is this guy crazy?" He was—in that he refused to take a sane approach to sensitivity in interviewing.

❑ Be alert to fallacies of reasoning. Among the most common of fallacies are the following examples of twisted logic.

*Post hoc ergo propter hoc.* This phrase (literally, "after this, therefore because of this") refers to the assumption that the fact one event follows another means the first event caused the second. Using this kind of reasoning, a governor, for example, can assert that a positive event that followed his or her election took place *because of* it. "I was elected in November, and under my economic guidance the state's unemployment rate dropped two percentage points in June." Does the governor have something to be proud of? Do you accept this explanation and report it without a follow-up question? You'd better not; the explanation may be flawed by *post hoc* reasoning. The unemployment rate might have been declining even before the governor took office, or perhaps a new federal program not influenced at all by the governor's action caused the improvement.

*Ad hominem attacks.* This fallacy (literally "to the man") involves an attack on the character of one's opponent rather than a response to the issues raised in a public forum. A journalist will often notice such reasoning when asking a newsmaker to reply to attacks on his or her positions. A possible reply: "That's the kind of attack you'd expect from someone who's been under indictment twice for tax fraud, isn't it? I won't dignify that with a comment." Indeed, the character of the attacker might need to be taken into account; but has your current interviewee answered the charges? Has the issue itself been clarified in any way? No, and it takes a careful critic in the interviewer's seat to point this out tactfully.

*Ad populum statements.* These are appeals based on the (valid) assumption that humans make decisions not just on logical grounds but for social reasons as well. That is, if "everyone's doing it" or if "everyone believes it" or if "a recent poll showed that 80 percent of the country approves of it," then many people will begin to shift their beliefs to conform with the majority. As a reporter, however, you're a critic. You should be alert to such assumptions, listening carefully for their implications. Appropriate responses to interviewees who make such assertions might be: "How do you suppose such a majority was built?" "Some experts admit the prevalence of your view on safe sex, yet claim it is dangerous for today's youth. How do you respond?"

❑ Survey your own personal biases. Chapters 3 and 5 especially warn about the influence of personal bias on the process of perception. We won't repeat such warnings here but instead will take the opportunity to suggest ways for you to uncover what those individualized biases might be. You understand that perception is selective—we don't perceive everything available to be perceived, but systematically filter out some bits of information in order to maintain personal consistency, balance or "homeostasis." To discover some of your filters, try the following strategies.

- List the terms that are "triggers" for you. That is, these words seem to create create an almost automatic reaction, positive or negative. (Of course, no word can literally make you feel a certain way. It is our own socialization and personalities that give certain words power. In the final analysis, the words don't have the power; we do.) Try an experiment. For a day, jot down in your notebook each phrase or term you hear that gets a strong reaction from you. What might you start with? Liberal? Jock? Blonde bimbo? Management? AIDS? Bitch? Coke? Strike? The terms you note are your clues to personal emotional hot spots. Be especially alert when you encounter a speaker who uses such terms; he or she may be pulling your emotional triggers and unintentionally exploding your listening power. If ready, you'll avert this loss.

- List the social, ethnic, political or cultural groups for which you believe the stereotypes are basically true. This exercise is effective even if you concede that the stereotype has unfair effects or is not applicable to all representatives of that group. Do you believe that women are really poorer drivers than men? That men are colder and less sensitive than women? That blacks are naturally better athletes? Greeks emotional? Republicans conservative? Southerners more friendly? Jews money-wise? Again, you're providing clues to yourself; you're reminding yourself of when you need to focus on the individual you're interviewing *as a person,* not as a member of a larger group.

- List the social issues you feel strongly about. Listening authority Carl Weaver claims that when you list the issues that move you, you're "probably listing your biases."[27] Is it possible to believe fervently in something and not let it affect your listening acuity? Probably not. Stay on guard.

- Survey the feedback you've received informally about your listening habits. Have friends, family members or colleagues told you lately that you were narrow-minded? Forgetful? That you switch off people when the ball game is on? That you don't take women (or men) seriously? Assume for the sake of argument that there is at least some truth to all these concerns. (There probably is.) You're affected in some of the same ways when an interviewee talks.

❏ Suspect the familiar. That is, if something sounds as if it's the "same old stuff," mentally slap yourself back into focus. You may be lulling yourself into a listening snooze.

One newspaper "lifestyle" editor says this is her main difficulty as a listener. "I've done three or four stories on alcoholism, for example. It's hard to get up for another story on that subject. You 'know' the answers to your questions before they're given. It's very difficult not to race ahead, because you anticipate the answer." She thus could easily miss the unique twist her current respondent could offer, if only heard and invited. Her problem is common among journalists, and this tendency could actually be a more serious problem for experienced reporters than rookie reporters, for whom each interview is a fresh experience.

The ability of the familiar to seduce reporters into assuming they already know a response can also cause an interviewer to interrupt inappropriately. Margaret McLaughlin writes that "When a listener can project not only when an utterance will be completed, but especially how it will be completed, the loss of the motive for listening provides a reason to begin talking immediately."[28] Not only can the journalist miss important information—the assumption of familiarity can lead directly to rudeness. The interruption becomes a tool to cut off the speaker, not to enable further comment.

## PERSONALITY LISTENING: "WHO ARE YOU?"

Some say the first personality interview in the modern journalistic sense was Horace Greeley's profile of Brigham Young, published in the New York Tribune in 1859. Within a few years, other journalists would complain that such an interview "is generally the joint product of some humbug of a hack politician and another humbug of a reporter," and "the most perfect contrivance yet devised to make journalism an offense, a thing of ill savor in all decent nostrils."[29]

Contemporary journalism is more tolerant of the link between personality and news. Consumers of mass media have become obsessed, says historian Daniel Boorstin, with "celebrities," people "well-known for their well-knownness."[30] Whatever the motivations, we want to know more about the people who make news—as people, not as cardboard cutout roles. The human element matters. In a real sense, the modern public wants to participate in the news at a personal level with the newsmakers.

Thus, interviewers often need more than information and a capacity to analyze it. They need a sensitivity to personality. Many interviews in the sports and entertainment worlds are conducted simply to profile the person, and increasingly the human qualities of our politicians are probed in interviews as well. Even while interviewing primarily for information, a journalist should discover who his or her respondents *are* before deciding what is newsworthy in their comments.

Any interviewer will turn up some information about who the interviewee is. Humans constantly broadcast clues to their identities in interpersonal communication, and it would be indeed hard to miss all such signals. Unfortunately, though, some journalists believe their only job is a zealous collection of facts; they'll miss most of the crucial messages people are constantly sending about how they want their experience to be understood. Research tells us that people who are listened to empathically will disclose more, stay longer, trust more deeply and continue to seek out opportunities to converse.

What interviewer worth his or her salt would willingly forego such benefits? As Karl Menninger said many years ago, "Listening is a magnetic and strange thing, a creative force. The friends who listen to us are the ones we move toward, and we want to sit in their radius. When we are listened to, it creates us, makes us unfold and expand."[31] The benefits extend far beyond friendship relationships.

Several approaches can help you become a more effective listener in this realm of personality and its subtle messages.

❑ Avoid premature judgment. The negative effects of judging probably cut short many more interviews than deadlines or insults. But the reporter isn't aware most of the time when it's happening, since it is an impression "leaked" through his or her nonverbal demeanor. An attitude of judgment comes from an unwillingness to approach the person you're interviewing as a unique person with feelings, experiences and problems distinct from all those who superficially seem to be similar in appearance, ideology or ethnic group. If you're judging, it's as if you've already decided what the respondent will say, because you've heard it before. Your expectations and prejudices are "speaking" to you—but the interviewee can't get through. Your lines are busy, with judgment.

What are some clues to judgment? One is when you find yourself saying to yourself, "I can't believe he's so sexist," or "She's so stupid!" or "That's a lie and he knows it." Although it's unrealistic to think you can be totally nonjudgmental in your reactions to others, and although it's unrealistic, too, to believe journalists don't have strong feelings, it's *very* realistic to expect journalists to check their judgments in order to let their respondents' stories emerge.

Probably the key to avoiding the negative effects of premature judgment is the *inner reminder*. You can train yourself to follow a self-talk judgment with an inner reminder in the following ways:

> *"I can't believe he's so sexist."* (Inner reminders: "I wonder about the environment in which he was raised." "I wonder if I'm oversensitive to that word." "I wonder if he consistently talks this way or if these are unique circumstances.")
>
> *"She's so stupid."* (Inner reminders: "I wonder how she justifies that stand from her vantage point." "I wonder why I have such a heavy investment in my own attitude.")

At times your inner reminders may appear to give more of the benefit of the doubt to people than they deserve. If they in fact don't deserve it, that will soon enough become apparent. You don't need to jump to the conclusion. In the meantime, you'll get further in interviewing if you renounce your premature judgments in favor of imagining the way your interviewee might experience the world.

❏ Focus on confirming the other person's feelings, when appropriate. Journalists Connie Fletcher and Jon Ziomek, discussing celebrity interviews, caution interviewers to "tell the subject that you appreciate the time difficulties he or she is having and that you're glad he or she can talk at all."[32] Later, they reinforce the value of "reflective listening" in emotional situations: "You reflect back the substance of what the person has said, thereby demonstrating that you are tuned in, and that you care. "You were angry. . . . You felt cheated. . . . Your life has been a struggle." The subject rarely says only "yes" to these supportive remarks but will launch into additional explanation of what he or she means, giving you added insights and depth."[33]

Remember that this form of confirmation is not agreement. You are not agreeing with the interviewee that he or she actually is justified in feeling angry or actually *was* cheated, or that you believe the interviewee's life to have been the struggle he or she describes. You're simply demonstrating emotional sincerity as a listener by attempting to confirm *the other person's experience* as he or she experiences it. You're saying, in effect, "As we talk, I'm making my best effort to see it your way." Later, of course, you will have to call it as you see it, adopting your own view, when you write the story.

❏ Focus on nonverbal cues to discover the interviewee's feelings. The world of journalism is usually a world of words. Linguistic competence is paramount, and journalists are rightly verbal creatures. But only about one-third—at most—of the meaning of social interaction is based on words. Most of the meaning we "get" from conversations comes from our awareness of the subtle signals of the *nonverbal* code. One expert even estimates that more than 90 percent of what we communicate takes place outside the verbal channel.[34] Interviewer Oriana Fallaci knows the implications for journalism:

> Listening to someone talk isn't at all like listening to their words played over on a machine. What you hear when you have a face before you is never what you hear when you have before you a winding tape. At times a flashing glance or a movement of the hand

will make the most stupid remark meaningful, but without the hands, the flashing glance, the remark is left in all its disconcerting stupidity. On the other hand, a disagreeable nose, a humble attitude, can at times detract from the value of the richest remark, and without the attitude, the nose, the remark acquires once more its full reassuring richness.[35]

Ignoring a person's nonverbal messages, then, is tantamount to ignoring most of who he or she *is*. Ignoring your own nonverbal messages will keep you perpetually perplexed about why your interviews lead nowhere, or why your good questions don't generate good responses. Although it would take a book on nonverbal communication itself to sensitize you fully to the problems of the nonverbal mode, we can suggest some basic issues. If you want to follow up on specific topics, many excellent books are available.[36] Two areas are most important: first, *your* nonverbal behavior; and second, what you should know about the nonverbal messages of *others*.

First, you should be aware that some visible behaviors tend to be associated with effective listening in North American culture. If you don't exhibit these behaviors for whatever reason (habit, weariness, boredom, illness or whatever), the speaker could easily assume you are not listening well—and will consequently reduce his or her involvement in the interview:

- Listeners tend to lean expectantly toward the speaker; posture is an indicator of attention. A labor organizer said he consciously surveys the posture habits of interviewing reporters. "If they lean back in a chair and are too casual," he observed, "they're not with you. There's a lack of involvement. If you're leaning toward me, we're engaged. Some will just sit there, watching you. Some are riveted on you. I know they're with me."

- Listeners tend to maintain persistent, but not constant, eye contact with speakers; speakers feel they're reaching us if they have access to our eyes.

- Listeners tend to provide periodic confirmative signals, such as a nod or a vocalized uh-huh; in normal conversation, these signals are usually not taken as thorough agreement but as proof that "I'm still with you."

- Listeners tend to focus attention on the speaker by not attempting to complete other tasks simultaneously.

- Listeners tend to place themselves a comfortable and appropriately close distance from speakers; increased personal distance is seen as an unwillingness to communicate.

- Finally, listeners tend to avoid unnecessary barriers between themselves and speakers; sunglasses and crossed arms, however innocently intended, are often perceived by speakers as discouraging further interaction.

❑ Survey your personal habits to determine whether you fit the normal expectations of listeners in our culture. If, for example, it is difficult for you to maintain eye contact or listen without fidgeting, then you may want to practice these elementary behaviors. It will seem trivial at first, but the results will prove such practice invaluable. You'll get the respect of such interviewees as the police chief who described what he looks for in the communication practices of reporters: "I notice eye contact. A lot of people don't do it, but I look for that in people because I like to have direct eye contact. . . . We look for that when interviewing suspects, so I notice that with other people." Or consider the experience of a lottery winner who had a similar desire for normal eye contact from reporters: "Well, one guy came to my house and stared out the window. He had said he wanted to spend an afternoon talking with me. Well, he was at my house, but he stared out the window a little too much to suit me." Do you suppose the resulting story contained many involving or interesting quotations?

Second, what should a reporter look for in the nonverbal behavior of interviewees? Several types of messages seem particularly important for perceptive interviewers. *Paralanguage* is the study of the way we attribute meaning to how words are vocalized— pitch, rate, volume, rhythm. Although words are involved, paralanguage is classified as nonverbal communication because it can create another level of meaning in addition to the meaning of the words themselves. For example, it may be obvious to you what is meant by "I really love my wife." All these words are simple, straightforward and seemingly unambiguous. But this is in print, without paralanguage cues. Any native English speaker could probably say this same sentence in such a way—with sarcasm, perhaps—as to encourage an opposite impression. This, of course, is how we occasionally use insult as a way of indicating friendship: the "insult" is not inflected with vehement intensity or volume, but with rapid, usually high-pitched, offhanded frivolity.

Often such messages also are signaled with appropriate facial expression and body movements. Winks, smiles, waves and nods combine with inflection to convince us that we're liked—to stay with the previous example—even though the verbal "context" is negative. This study of body movement and what it communicates is the province of *kinesics*. Without an understanding of kinesics, interviewers are trapped in the literal, constantly missing the point. A candidate will say he's confident, and you'll miss the shaking papers in his hand when he gestures or his tentative posture.

Knowledge of nonverbal communication is necessary to assess the kind of persons journalists talk with and the kind of information they are likely to receive. In particular, interviewers are often called upon to determine whether interviewees are telling the truth. In the next chapter, we will examine this vexing problem in more detail.

## STAYING A LISTENER

Listening is a matter of choice, and a matter of sensitivity. Given certain basic skills, anyone can decide to become a better listener—and communication research provides clear guidelines for such improvement. When a journalist listens better, the result is not just a more precise hearing of basic information an interviewee wants to share; a more important message is being "broadcast" by an effective listener: "You're important, and I care enough about you and our communication to try to get things straight." Many professional interviewers, unfortunately, haven't considered that listening is more than the reception of messages. Further, they haven't considered how an interviewer's listening style can regulate, in a sense, the speaking style of an interviewee.

We've tried to suggest some practical overt and covert "actions" journalists can take to become better at the three major types of journalistic listening: "What happened?" or informational listening; "what's different?" or discriminative listening; and "who are you?" or personality listening. Ultimately, your goal should be to make sure that those you interview are not tempted to say something like the anonymous words of a popular poster: "I know that you believe you understand what you think I said, but I am not sure you realize that what you heard is not what I meant."

## Notes

[1] Eudora Welty, *One Writer's Beginnings* (New York: Warner Books, 1985), p. 16.

[2] Hugh C. Sherwood, *The Journalistic Interview* (New York: Harper & Row, 1972), p. 3.

[3] John Brady, *The Craft of Interviewing* (New York: Vintage Books, 1976), p. 160.

[4] See Studs Terkel, *Working* (New York: Avon, 1975), pp. xviii–xix.

[5] For examples, see the excellent summaries in Andrew D. Wolvin and Carolyn Gwynn Coakley, *Listening,* 2nd ed. (Dubuque, Iowa: Wm. C. Brown, 1985).

[6] Ralph G. Nichols and Leonard A. Stevens, *Are You Listening?* (New York: McGraw-Hill, 1957), p. 6.

[7] Wolvin and Coakley, *Listening,* pp. 17–19.

[8] Lyman K. Steil, Larry L. Barker, and Kittie W. Watson, *Effective Listening: Key to Your Success* (Reading, Mass.: Addison-Wesley, 1983), p. 6.

[9] See Chapter 3 for more information on asking questions and dealing with answers.

[10] Lynn Hirschberg, "The Power and the Story," *Rolling Stone,* May 21, 1987, p. 46.

[11] Robert Rosenthal and Lenore Jacobson, *Pygmalion in the Classroom* (New York: Holt, Rinehart and Winston, 1968).

[12] John Dewey and Arthur F. Bentley, *Knowing and the Known* (Boston: Beacon Press, 1949), pp. 133–134.

[13] Farnum Gray, Paul S. Graubard, and Harry Rosenberg, "Little Brother Is Changing You," *Psychology Today,* March 1984.

[14] For a similar interpretation, see Tamotsu Shibutani, *Improvised News: A Sociological Study of Rumor* (Indianapolis: Bobbs-Merrill, 1966).

[15] More sophisticated explanations are found in Kenneth N. Leone Cissna and Sr. Suzanne Keating, "Speech Communication Antecedents of Perceived Confirmation," *Western Journal of Speech Communication* 43 (Winter 1979), pp. 48–60; and Maurice Friedman, *The Confirmation of Otherness: In Family, Community and Society* (New York: The Pilgrim Press, 1983).

[16] Jack Mendelsohn, *Being Liberal in an Illiberal Age: Why I am a Unitarian Universalist* (Boston: The Beacon Press, 1985), p. 48.

[17] Wolvin and Coakley, *Listening,* p. 177; Florence I. Wolff, Nadine C. Marsnik, William S. Tacey, and Ralph G. Nichols, *Perceptive Listening* (New York: Holt, Rinehart and Winston, 1983), p. 154.

[18]Nichols and Stevens, *Are You Listening?* p. 79.

[19]George A. Miller, *The Psychology of Communication: Seven Essays* (Baltimore: Penguin Books, 1967), pp. 36–37.

[20]Margaret L. McLaughlin, *Conversation: How Talk is Organized* (Beverly Hills: Sage Publications, 1984), pp. 100, 101.

[21]Beth Ann Krier, "Conversation Interruptus: Critical Social Skill or Just Plain Rudeness?" *Los Angeles Times,* Dec. 14, 1986, Section VI, p. 1.

[22]Douglas Cater, *The Fourth Branch of Government* (New York: Vintage Books, 1959), p. 18.

[23]Albert H. Hastorf and Hadley Cantril, "They Saw a Game: A Case Study," in Hans Toch and Henry Clay Smith, eds., *Social Perception* (New York: D. Van Nostrand, 1968), pp. 70–71.

[24]Bruce T. Grindal and Robin Rhodes, "Journalism and Anthropology Share Several Similarities," *Journalism Educator* 41 (Winter 1987), p. 11.

[25]Quoted in Shirley Biagi, *NewsTalk I: State-of-the-Art Conversations with Today's Print Journalists* (Belmont, Calif.: Wadsworth, 1987), p. 151.

[26]Steil, Barker, and Watson, *Effective Listening,* p. 72.

[27]Carl H. Weaver, *Human Listening: Processes and Behaviors* (Indianapolis: Bobbs-Merrill, 1972), pp. 95–96.

[28]McLaughlin, *Conversation,* pp. 122–123.

[29]Daniel Boorstin, *The Image: A Guide to Pseudo-Events in America* (New York: Harper Colophon Books, 1961), p. 15.

[30]Boorstin, *The Image.*

[31]Karl Menninger, *Love Against Hate* (New York: Harcourt, Brace, 1942), p. 275.

[32]Connie Fletcher and Jon Ziomek, "How to Catch a Star," *The Quill,* December 1986, p. 35.

[33]Fletcher and Ziomek, "How to Catch a Star," p. 36.

[34]Albert Mehrabian, *Silent Messages* (Belmont, Calif.: Wadsworth, 1971), p. 44.

[35]Oriana Fallaci, *The Egotists: Sixteen Surprising Interviews* (Chicago: Henry Regnery, 1968), p. ix.

[36]Mehrabian, *Silent Messages*; Mark L. Knapp, *Nonverbal Communication in Human Interaction* (New York: Holt, Rinehart and Winston, 1978); Edward T. Hall, *The Silent Language* (Greenwich, Conn.: Fawcett, 1959); Edward T. Hall, *The Hidden Dimension* (Garden City, N.Y.: Doubleday, 1966).

# CHAPTER FIVE

# Assessing People and Information

## On Not Getting Fooled, Most of the Time

**A** witness to a beating claims he doesn't know the answer to your question. How do you determine whether: (1) he knows the answer but has something to hide? (2) he knows the answer, but it's easier and more convenient for him to tell you he doesn't? (3) he honestly thinks he doesn't know the answer but could recall pertinent facts with just a little prodding? or, commonly, (4) he has simply misunderstood your question and would have answered it fully except for the confusion?

An activist gives you a long and involved account of a pro-life rally. You are aware of the possibility that part of the response, though probably true in its basic facts, is ultimately self-serving and slanted. No tapes or other records of the rally evidently exist, and other participants are not directly available. Your deadline is nearing. How do you know whether your interviewee is sincere or feeding you a line? Should you delay the story to seek out other participants to interview, or rely on the interviewee's account?

A mayoral candidate parries your every request for specifics on her platform. She doesn't know specifically what position she'll take on the emerging collective bargaining controversy in the schools; she only knows how much she's "aware of the needs of both the children and the district." She adds, "I know how important it is to be fair to both sides in such an emotional time for this city." Should you consider her comments to be diplomatic or evasive? How do you decide whether to press for less ambiguous positions?

Answers to questions like these may often make the difference between filing a comprehensive and stimulating story and filing a flat, emotionless one, or, worse, one that is distorted or inaccurate. This chapter focuses on methods and insights developed by particularly perceptive interviewers—those experienced in analyzing the worth and veracity of information.

## A SENSE FOR DETAIL

Reporters attempting to reconstruct "accurate" accounts of events should realize that various witnesses to those events will inevitably present divergent stories. At the same time, what one reporter hears from an interview will be different from what another would have heard, and different from what that same reporter would have heard at another time or in another place. Is this realization frightening? Sobering? Far from allowing it to immobilize you, simply let it be a reminder to redouble your efforts to seek convergence of these disparate stories. An eye for detail will give you better clues to how the final story might take shape. You'll be less likely to pursue fruitless paths and less likely to be fooled into believing a story has only a single "correct" path to follow.

Remember what editors and readers want in the stories they read. They want vividness, and the key to vividness is specificity. Don't just report that the producer was nervous while talking; count how many cigarettes were lit and almost immediately extinguished in a 20-minute interview. Don't just report that the city manager is busy or that the job is hectic; note how many phone calls and necessary intrusions interrupted a one-hour interview. If an office is cluttered, noticing what kind of papers and books are scattered about—and even the layers of dust on top—can give the story a dimension it would otherwise lack. You can think of other examples. An interesting self-teaching strategy is to videotape televised interviews and try to pick out details of context and behavior that the interviewer misses. Ask yourself, "Which questions or comments might be suggested by these details?"

Sometimes the ability to notice details is crucial to the development of an interview. You develop credibility with most interviewees as you demonstrate that you are fully present and involved in the situation. Noticing, for example, the prominently displayed family pictures on a desk becomes an entree to a more personalized and intimate portion of the conversation. A citation on the wall, appropriately noticed and complimented, can signal to your interviewee that you're willing to be fair and balanced in your story. The interchange will be smoother than you'd anticipated. Noticing that the secretary of state is uncharacteristically wearing a suit to fly to a weekend retreat should lead you to ask about the possibility of interim destinations. Journalists who aren't keen observers won't discover some stories they need and won't write vividly about the ones they do discover.

Once Bob Greene interviewed young movie actress Kristy McNichol by accompanying her, her grandfather, her chauffeur and her boyfriend on shopping trips and dining excursions over two days. His column never commented on anything she said or did, never judged or evaluated her behavior. Yet Green's attention to details of action, statement and situation—reported without ornamentation—was its own kind of commentary. An excerpt:

> In a clothing store called Judy's she led her grandfather to a display showing a skimpy garment made of leather, festooned with metal zippers.
> "Can you see me in this, Grandpa?" she said.
> "Good," her grandfather said.
> "It's not good, it's disgusting," Kristy said.
> "I was just thinking of your great-looking legs," her grandfather said.
> She reached toward her grandfather's mouth. She took out the cigarette he had been smoking. She put it in her mouth and inhaled. She handed it back to her grandfather. She also handed him her purse. "Carry this for me," she said.[1]

Of course, Greene could have streamlined the account by generalizing. But that would have undercut its impact. Everything Greene noticed, from the name of the store through the description of the garment to the exact quote to the grandfather, becomes the core of the story he eventually wrote. The details themselves, and not Green's conclusions about them, carry the story's weight. A less observant journalist obviously would have fewer choices.

Detail is a reporter's constant ally. Reliance on gross estimates or generalizations is dangerous. Look. Notice nuance. See. Ask. Count. William Rivers tells a story about the triumph of detailed noticing over political "crowdsmanship." Richard Nixon flew into Milwaukee to be greeted by a crowd estimated by a Republican aide at 12,000 people. Police estimates were lower—8,000—but not as low as the 5,000 estimate of a reporter at the scene. But someone on the editorial staff of the Milwaukee Journal had developed a finely tuned observational skill; the Journal found an overall crowd photo, and simply *counted the 2,300 heads*.[2]

## RECOGNIZING TRUTHFULNESS AND DECEPTION

Can you tell when someone is lying?

Many people are confident that they can spot liars. They're convinced that liars engage in so-called "shifty" behavior, that people who don't tell the truth are easily found out through their own demonstrated discomfort if not through slips of the tongue. Yet each of us can think of times we thoroughly believed someone, only later to learn of the deception in their statements.

An experienced and respected reporter for a major newspaper said he thought there was no effective way someone can detect if another person is lying. Reporters face special challenges in this regard:

> It's like life, and reporters have no greater ability to detect lies than anyone else. I remember a case a couple of years ago. It was 1985, the tenth anniversary of the fall of South Vietnam. We had a reporter go to the VA Hospital to talk to disabled vets, and he found a guy who gave him a big story about being paralyzed and injured during the war. And the reporter naturally believed him. It turns out that this guy had been to Vietnam, but hadn't been injured over there—but injured stealing welfare checks. There's just no way you can catch a person like that . . . . There's always the tendency to believe people if their story is halfway credible. Of course, some of the stuff can be checked, but it would be too time-consuming. And I run into that fairly frequently, and if it's too time-consuming to check for me, I usually just drop the whole thing.

Detecting deception—or recognizing truthfulness—is a communication skill like all others; we do have moments when the clues all add up and we understand that the other person is probably attempting to deceive us. And there are moments when it feels as if "we don't have a clue."

But there are always clues; most people just aren't well attuned to them. That is where skill comes in. With practice, and with sensitivity to the behavior that researchers have linked to deceptive communication, reporters can become better evaluators of others' intentions. Don't expect to be infallible, and don't develop this skill simply to feed your own cynicism. Don't harass others with accusations of deception where they deserve the benefit of the doubt. This section on lying is included only to serve fair warning to journalists that some deception can be inferred reasonably from behavioral cues, and that on these occasions, you should work especially hard to corroborate that person's story through other sources.

## Which Truth?

Deborah Tannen, an expert on styles of conversation, discusses the inherent complexity of what is often too simplistically branded "the truth."[3] In a revealing hypothetical example, "Ellen" returns to her home town for a wedding and is questioned by several people— relatives and old friends—on how she likes being away at graduate school. Interestingly, she found that in some conversations, she emphasized the positive aspects of her new situation: she liked the city, her courses at the university, her new friends, her basic satisfaction with her new lifestyle. In other conversations, though, she heard herself talking about the negatives. She was alarmed by the dangers of the big city, often felt oppressed in a dingy apartment, was bored and upset over the endless hours of study and didn't have enough money to exist comfortably. She intended to tell no untruths, and indeed, from her perspective, told none. Yet the impressions of Ellen's life that were developed by her listeners were very different.

Everyone is an "Ellen." All humans tell their stories piecemeal; the accounts emerge in ways appropriate to the circumstances. There's no such thing as "the truth, the whole truth, and nothing but the truth." Ellen's existence in the big city *was* positive . . . and it *was* negative. She didn't intend to lie or mislead her family when she stressed the uplifting aspects of city life; she simply wanted them to feel some of the confidence she felt in her new venture. Neither did she lie to her friends when they heard more about the drawbacks; Ellen simply suspected that they were on the verge of envying her too much for her newly developed and rose-tinted independence, and she wanted them to have a more balanced picture of what graduate school was like.

Tannen summarizes the point: "Both pictures were true. That is, they were both composites assembled from pieces of truth. Yet both were untrue, insofar as they omitted the pieces included in the other account, as well as innumerable pieces included in neither. There is no way that Ellen, or anyone, could tell every aspect of the truth.

When constructing a story for a specific occasion, we instinctively identify a main point or goal and include the details that contribute to it."[4]

Most interview situations you'll analyze as a journalist involve this sense of "truth." Even though you've heard a different version of the story elsewhere, or even a different version from this person you're interviewing, consider the possibility that the "versions"—even if they sound contradictory—may be part of a larger "truth." What is true is what is verifiable. But what a person can verify within the complexity of personal experience may be very different from what you can verify using external sources. So, right from the beginning, journalists should be extremely wary about accusations of lying and deception.

## Anticipating Deception

Some people, however, will intend to deceive you. They want to look good, or at least to avoid looking bad. They want to cover mistakes, or at least to avoid the appearance of mistakes. They want to accomplish certain goals, noble and otherwise, that would be unattainable (they believe) without the lies. They want to buy time, or avoid embarrassment. "What ails the truth," H. L. Mencken is reputed to have observed, "is that it is mainly uncomfortable and often dull. The human mind seeks something more amusing and more caressing." This, of course, is an interesting and relatively innocent explanation for lying; we simply try to entertain ourselves in our conversations, to tell a good story, to impress the listeners, to gild the lily, to pat ourselves on the back. The 19th-century American humorist Josh Billings wryly suggested that "there are people so addicted to exaggeration that they can't tell the truth without lying." Their testimony is a grab-bag of maybes for you to sort through.

Author Sissela Bok believes there are certain "bargaining situations" in which participants feel secure that deception is an acceptable practice.[5] Such ground rules of mutual deception govern the relationships between, for example, buyers and sellers at a bazaar, labor and management approaching the bargaining table, and defense and prosecution preparing for a trial. In none of these contexts do the participants feel a compulsion for complete openness and disclosure. In fact, to the extent that the other side becomes fooled or misjudges one's intentions, that is considered *their* problem, not yours. Our normal expectations of truthfulness seem to bypass these special bargaining situations, and even if a participant forswears overt lying for moral or other reasons, omissions or hints designed to mislead are definitely permissible.

Politicians being interviewed by reporters may believe they are involved in such a bargaining relationship and therefore genuinely assume they have a license to mislead. To the extent that their motives seem noble to themselves, or the stakes sufficiently high ("in the interest of national security"), they will justify even overt lies as simply part of the job. President Carter's press secretary, Jody Powell, put it more directly when he claimed that at times a government has not only the right but the obligation to deceive the media.

Powell resorted to lying when Jack Nelson of the Los Angeles Times questioned him about the administration's plans to free the American hostages being held in Iran. "You people really aren't thinking about doing anything drastic like launching a rescue mission, are you?" Nelson asked. Here's Powell's account:

> This was the moment of truth, or, more accurately, of deception. Up to this point, I had only repeated false statements made by others, an admittedly fine distinction, but a distinction nevertheless. Now I was faced with a direct question. With a swallow I hoped was not noticeable, I began to recite all the reasons why a rescue operation would not make sense. They were familiar because they were exactly the ones that it had taken four months to figure out how to overcome.
>
> "If and when we are forced to move militarily, I suspect it will be something like a blockade," I said, "but that decision is a step or two down the road."
>
> I made a mental note to be sure to call Jack and apologize once the operation was completed, hoping he would understand.[6]

Another form of lying occurs when others "put you on." All reporters are duped from time to time, but newcomers to journalism can expect to be a target of some "harmless" deception. People who are frequently interviewed may, out of boredom or spite, play games with reporters. The naive or ill-prepared reporter is most susceptible to put-on lies; he or she may bring up subjects that veteran or knowledgeable reporters know to be myths. An interviewer, for instance, confronts a rock star with, "I understand, Ms. Barnett, that you prefer operatic music to rock 'n' roll." Barnett says to herself, "Here's another dumb reporter who heard I'm into opera. I'm going to have some fun with him." She proceeds to offer a string of outrageous untruths about her "love" of opera.

## Indicators of Deception

Fortunately, some observable behavioral clues tend to signal when a person in Western culture may be lying. Notice the many qualifications purposefully inserted in the preceding sentence: "some," "clues," "tend," "Western culture," "may be lying." Your efforts to detect deception will necessarily be partial and will often be wrong, especially if you become obsessed with the task or lose sight of the context of the supposed "lie." Psychologist Paul Ekman, the foremost contemporary researcher of lies, writes that "any behavior that is a useful clue to deceit will for some few people be a usual part of their behavior."[7] It will *not,* therefore, signal deceit in these people. Another psychologist familiar with what social scientists call the "self-fulfilling prophecy" warns that we're more likely to "discover" lies "when we think we should find them," whether they are there or not.[8] Effective interviewers become aware of the most common motivations and situations for lying. In such situations, they are alert for behaviors that researchers say might indicate deception. Then they compare tentative conclusions with the rest of what they've learned about the emerging story from other sources.

Such warnings aside, what should journalists do to stay alert to the possibility of deception? Which behaviors tend to signal deception? The answer can be divided into verbal and nonverbal factors.

**Verbal Indicators.** According to Ekman, the liar's words often betray him or her to an alert listener.[9] Some important indicators:

❑ A person who is lying may be less consistent; the speaker might fabricate carelessly. Today's statement will contradict last week's assertation, and the statements will be contradictory in implausible ways.

❑ A person who is lying may commit meaningful "slips of the tongue." This Freudian concept describes situations when a speaker unwittingly betrays a suppressed truth or claims something that has unanticipated implications for truthful interpretations. A student asked one professor to postpone an exam because ". . . last night my grandmother lied—I mean died!"[10] But these slips do not always means that the speaker is lying. Communication researcher Michael Motley warns that they can often be explained more by the mind's attempt to choose among various "competing" linguistic options to communicate meaning than by the urge to withhold the truth.[11] Further, Ekman urges us to understand the context for slips before assuming they signal lies, and he also suggests that we shouldn't assume people are telling the truth just because they avoid such slips.

❏ A person who is lying is often under some emotional pressure and might succumb to what Ekman calls "tirades." Under these circumstances, the liar loses his or her "cool" and the speech gushes forth, often revealing information the speaker intended to conceal, or clues to that withheld reservoir. The interview situation, for most people a time of some tension, is an excellent arena in which to observe this tendency.

❏ A person who is lying will often provide excessively "convoluted answers or sophisticated evasions," believes television newsman Tom Brokaw.[12] Excessive indirectness or explanations that ramble may indeed suggest that the speaker is unconvinced, insecure or untruthful. Ekman points out that several studies of deception support Brokaw's hunch, but several others do not. Individuals may simply have a more expansive speech style that should not be confused with deceptive intent. Some specific additional cues some studies have associated with the speech of deception: (1) liars use more "generalizing terms" such as "you know," "that kind of thing," "etcetera, etcetera"; (2) they pause longer before answering questions, and pause more during their answers; and (3) they are less specific in their references to people, behaviors and actual events—speaking instead of such nebulous activities as "had fun" or "just hung out for a while."[13]

**Nonverbal Indicators.** An alert journalist will notice discrepancies between the verbal and nonverbal behaviors of an interviewee. One may say he is not nervous, but his hands are shaking and his voice quivers. Another may say she trusts you and wants you to have the full story, yet ushers you out of the office after only seven minutes of superficial conversation. A self-proclaimed "happy" person may never smile. Such occurrences, known as *mixed messages,* are potent clues for the inferences journalists must make.

Speakers communicate simultaneously in both verbal and nonverbal modes, yet it is the nonverbal channel that never can be switched off. As communication theorists tend to say, despite the double negative, it's impossible to *not-communicate* in another's presence. People constantly interpret the behavior of others as having "message value." (Even if your interviewee remains mute and ignores you, that too is an answer of a sort to your question.) So this ever-present nonverbal channel must be considered as carefully as the words of a conversation. When confronted with contradictions between a speaker's verbal and nonverbal messages, you can usually safely assume the nonverbal message is less easily manipulated by the speaker and therefore a better clue to the truth as the speaker experiences it.

Let's be specific. What might you look for? Here are some examples of nonverbal clues:

- A person who is lying tends to move less than when he or she is telling the truth and will often turn or lean away from the listener.

- A person who is lying tends to talk more slowly than usual, maybe to provide inner practice or rehearsal time for the lies.

- A person who is lying will use the "mouth guard" gesture more than usual (hand obscuring the mouth during speech) and will engage in more facial self-touching.

- A person who is lying may shrug the shoulders more than usual while speaking, gesticulate more broadly and use more varied facial expressions.[14]

Paul Ekman's book, *Telling Lies,* includes a detailed treatment of "Facial Clues to Deceit." Reading subtle facial expressions for emotional meaning is especially difficult and subject to many warnings. If you find this chapter useful, you may want to investigate Ekman's work carefully.[15]

## RECOGNIZING BS AND EVASION

The term *BS,* for many years a crude profanity, is now used almost routinely to refer to a particular kind of *talk.* Not long ago we asked a group of students if they thought *BS* would be an appropriate term to include in a book that might be used as a text. Is it perhaps too offensive? Their unanimous response: What other term defines the same process? Although a few students admitted some discomfort with the term, they said it "fit" our public communication habits very well, perhaps too well. It still offends some people, but for the culture at large, we can scarcely miss its impact.

BS provides a connotation useful for distinguishing manipulative lying and deception from a wide, muddy field of self-serving and unresponsive talk through which an interviewer must sometimes trudge. A party game is now being marketed that equates "BS" innocently with "Being Sneaky"—and presumably the object of the game is to fool or "snow" other players verbally without actually lying to them.

## Some Defining Characteristics

A mark of the newfound "respectability" of BS is that it's receiving academic attention. Harry Frankfurt, chairman of Yale's Department of Philosophy, recently speculated on the nature of BS.[16] His analysis suggests several practical insights for the journalistic interviewer:

❏ *BS is not lying, and must be treated differently.* Frankfurt claims that "the liar is essentially someone who deliberately promulgates a falsehood." Yet, he says, the "essence of bullshit is not that it is *false* but that it is *phony*."[17] In this view, the liar knows the statement is false, and inserts it strategically in order to accomplish a specific goal. To lie, a speaker must not only know the truth, but in effect, be guided by its power. The BS-er has "much more freedom."[18] The BS "artist" (lying is a craft, BS an art, to Frankfurt) simply doesn't care about the truth. Basically, liars are still playing a "truth game." BS-ers deny the viability of such a game. Neil Postman and Charles Weingartner identify some prominent varieties of BS as pomposity, fanaticism, inanity, superstition and sloganeering.[19] None is necessarily related to concerns of truth and falsehood, but all are related to personal posturing and fuzzy thinking.

❏ *BS, therefore, may be factual and accurate.* The BS-er's goal is not necessarily to withhold facts but to "misrepresent what he is up to."[20] The content of BS may be false, but the BS-er hides the fact "that the truth-values of his statements are of no interest to him; what we are not to understand is that his intention is neither to report the truth nor to conceal it." "His eye," Frankfurt claims, "is not on the facts at all, except insofar as they may be pertinent to his interest in getting away with what he says."[21]

❏ *BS usually exists as a "program."* Since lying is paradoxically so sharply focused on—and connected to—the truth, it tends to occur in episodes or packages of interaction that might be analyzed readily by a knowledgeable investigator. BS is more nebulous, more vague and more difficult to pin down. To BS, a person needn't concoct new strategies all the time; the line is already in place and therefore, with practice, comes almost naturally. The "artist" engages in ongoing self-presentation; though Frankfurt doesn't specifically discuss this, BS seems more like a lifestyle than what we usually label a behavior or an action. How do you "catch" a BS-er? You don't—at least not red-handed. There's neither a "lie" to uncover nor even at times a clearly deceptive motive. BS isn't just a single isolated tactic to be employed strategically; it becomes embedded in an individual's public persona.

❑ *BS undermines the truth more than lies do.* BS is insidious because its effects are cumulative. It changes our expectations about the quality of public discourse. It seduces us into settling for less. In fact, Frankfurt questions whether indeterminate attitudes about truth (this chapter presents some) haven't contributed to the prevalence of BS in contemporary society. If truth isn't ultimately knowable, he imagines the BS-er to reason, then why not abandon the ideal of *correctness* for the ideal of *sincerity* of personal image?

❑ *BS is necessitated by our attitudes about the opinions of public figures.* This should be especially interesting to journalistic interviewers, who are forever seeking opinions of public figures. A statement elicited by a question often becomes news; had there been no question, there would have been no news. Mass media appears fueled at least in part by such inquiry. But the issue is a nagging one: Whose news is it? Public figures respond to questions with their "sincerity" and "image" in mind and will always have opinions. Reporters know that any interview can thus metamorphose into a story. The danger is discussed by Frankfurt: "Why is there so much bullshit? Well, bullshit is unavoidable whenever circumstances require someone to talk without knowing what he is talking about. Thus the production of bullshit is stimulated whenever a person's obligations or opportunities to speak about some topic are more extensive than his knowledge of the facts that are relevant to that topic. This discrepancy is common in public life, where people are frequently impelled—whether by their own propensities or by the demands of others—to speak extensively about matters of which they are to some degree ignorant."[22]

Each time you ask a public figure for an interview, consider the ways you are also inviting BS. Perhaps the current popularity of the term could help to broaden our awareness of this style of talk and our sensitivities to how it might be avoided. BS is still a pejorative term, though. You should be quite careful in thinking of public figures in this way. The danger is cynicism, and listeners who too readily label others as BS-ers may find rationalizations to "write them off" or dismiss all they might say. Listening carefully and observing alertly are still your best approaches, as with outright liars.

## Functions of Ambiguity

Our modern cult of personality fuels the trend toward ambiguous image-based rhetoric. Journalist David Wise presents an interesting case study of a 1971 "Today" show interview with Richard Nixon, conducted by Barbara Walters. She mentions that there has been much discussion of the president's image, and that he is seen by many as "stuffy" and not "human." She hesitates to ask, but does so anyway: "Are you—Oh, dear. Are you worried about your image, Mr. President?"

Note that the question itself validates the emphasis on image, sincerity and personality. Who could be surprised that a president would utter the following reply?

> Not at all. When Presidents begin to worry about images . . . do you know what happens? They become like the athletes, the football team and the rest, who become so concerned about what is written about them and what is said about them that they don't play the game well . . . the President, with the enormous responsibilities that he has, must not be constantly preening in front of a mirror . . . I don't worry about polls. I don't worry about images . . . I never have.[23]

Wise notes to obvious irony. Nixon's statement made good emotional sense, may have reflected his self-evaluation accurately and sounded good to voters. It's what we hope presidents feel. In fact, millions of voters were hearing a politician being interviewed about his image, hearing his heartfelt denial that image was an important issue for him—but hearing it via the most potent image medium of our times. Actually, Nixon's aides had "persuaded him that he was not getting across to the public and that he needed more exposure."[24] During one 12-day period, Nixon therefore arranged, in addition to the "Today" show appearance, a lengthy ABC television interview and a long "folksy" interview for women reporters.

## How to Respond?

When confronted with either BS or ambiguous evasion, the interviewer has a number of effective responses available. Trying out these responses may make you a better "crap detector," to use Postman and Weingartner's phrase.[25]

❑ Press for details. Ask your respondents for examples, even hypothetical ones, of what they mean. If they're quoting or paraphrasing someone else's policy, ask them to put it in their own words. Don't let unusual or unfamiliar words intimidate you; seek immediate clarification even if it means admitting your ignorance. You'll be surprised by how many interviewees use technical or jargon language that they can't adequately define and might not themselves understand.

❑ Ask for criteria. When interviewees consistently evaluate other people or policies, encourage them to describe their standards. If an actor asserts that Hitchcock was the "best" director ever in Hollywood, and that Woody Allen is "worthless," will you have much of a story unless you specify what "best" means to this person? Best at what? Which tasks of directorship are being judged? Is there a decathlon for directors? Although "best" sounds absolute, probably the interviewee is basing his or her judgment on certain skills or characteristics. Incidentally, the actor is simultaneously—if indirectly—talking about *self* when making this judgment; you might want to inquire tactfully about the personal criteria by which the actor feels qualified to make the judgment in the first place. Has the actor worked with both directors? In what areas was Hitchcock especially effective compared with Allen?

❑ Expose inconsistencies. Do this judiciously, but do it. You're responsible for creating a sensible and credible story out of the interview. If you are confused, you owe it to your audience to resolve the confusion if possible. Describe why you might be confused by apparent inconsistencies, and invite your respondents to set you straight or give a plausible explanation. For example: "Coach, last week you told us that you'd bench Josephson if he missed practice again. I found out he missed Thursday, but started tonight against Lindenwood. I thought you should have a chance to explain this before I submit the story." Since full explanations may be difficult even for BS-ers, you risk becoming unpopular with some interviewees. You can live with it.

❏ Invite interviewees to evaluate their own statements, perhaps as their severest critics might hear them. This will not only give you a perspective on what this particular individual believes, but also on what he or she believes others believe. You might say to a political candidate: "You claim your opponent has been a liability to the district while he's been in Springfield. Yet he might be proud of the bill he introduced for state renovation of our local historical landmarks. What other evidence might he point to, and why isn't it significant from your standpoint?" Such a question takes a person momentarily away from his or her "ground" and may encourage less ego-involvement and/or more spontaneity. It's possible to learn much about people by listening carefully to how they characterize others' judgments. This is no foolproof antidote to BS or interview ambiguity, but it can be a powerful clarifier.

Who can possibly detect deceit each time it occurs or assess the motives of interviewees with certainty? Journalists must inquire, but they can neither read minds nor control the veracity and helpfulness of responses. The control you may exercise, however, is still powerful if you choose to apply it wisely. This control comes from an alertness to detail, a sensitivity to the possible signals of lying, and prior training in how to deal with evasion and BS by focusing questions on specifics, criteria, inconsistency and self-evaluation.

## Notes

[1]Bob Greene, *American Beat* (New York: Penguin Books, 1984), p. 202.

[2]William L. Rivers, *Finding Facts* (Englewood Cliffs, N.J.: Prentice-Hall, 1975), p. 62.

[3]Deborah Tannen, *That's Not What I Meant! How Conversational Style Makes or Breaks Relationships* (New York: Ballantine, 1986), p. 64.

[4]Tannen, *That's Not What I Meant!* p. 64.

[5]Sissela Bok, *Lying: Moral Choice in Public and Private Life* (New York: Vintage Books, 1979), p. 138; see also Roy J. Lewicki, "Lying and Deception: A Behavioral Model," in Max H. Bazerman and Roy J. Lewicki, eds., *Negotiating in Organizations* (Beverly Hills, Calif.: Sage Publications, 1983), pp. 68–90.

[6]Jody Powell, *The Other Side of the Story* (New York: William Morrow, 1984), p. 223.

[7]Paul Ekman, *Telling Lies* (New York: Berkeley Books, 1986), p. 91.

[8]Chris L. Kleinke, *Meeting and Understanding People* (New York: W.H. Freeman, 1986), p. 70.

[9]Ekman, *Telling Lies,* pp. 89 ff.

[10]Michael T. Motley, "What I Meant to Say," *Psychology Today,* February 1987, p. 25.

[11]Motley, "What I Meant To Say."

[12]John Weisman, "The Truth Will Out," *TV Guide,* Sept. 3, 1977, p. 13; cited in Ekman, p. 91.

[13]See Michael Cody, Peter Marston, and Myrna Foster, "Deception: Paralinguistic and Verbal Leakage," in Robert N. Bostrom, ed., *Communication Yearbook 8* (Beverly Hills, Calif.: Sage Publications, 1984), pp. 464–490; and the brief summary in Joseph A. DeVito, *The Interpersonal Communication Book,* 4th ed. (New York: Harper & Row, 1986), p. 196.

[14]DeVito, *The Interpersonal Communication Book,* p. 196; Kleinke, *Meeting and Understanding People,* p. 89.

[15]Ekman, *Telling Lies;* Paul Ekman and Wallace V. Friesen, *Unmasking the Face* (Palo Alto, Calif.: Consulting Psychologists, 1984).

[16]Harry Frankfurt, "Reflections on Bullshit," *Harper's Magazine,* February 1987, pp. 14–16.

[17]Frankfurt, "Reflections on Bullshit," p. 14.

[18]Frankfurt, "Reflections on Bullshit," p. 15.

[19]Neil Postman and Charles Weingartner, *The Soft Revolution* (New York: Delta Books, 1971), pp. 35–42.

[20]Frankfurt, "Reflections on Bullshit," p. 15.

[21]Frankfurt, "Reflections on Bullshit," pp. 15, 16.

[22]Frankfurt, "Reflections of Bullshit," p. 16.

[23]David Wise, *The Politics of Lying* (New York: Vintage Books, 1973), p. 275.

[24]Wise, *The Politics of Lying,* p. 275.

[25]Postman and Weingartner, *The Soft Revolution,* p. 41.

# CHAPTER SIX

# Handle with Care

## Interviews with Special Challenges

$A$ny job, when performed often enough and over an extended period of time, takes a particular shape. Routines are set, habits ingrained and workers begin to establish expectations. Journalists are no different. When will you likely work late? When will the editor demand a rewrite? Which assistants at city hall are most likely to talk with you? How will the prosecuting attorney react to a tough question? Part of your success will depend on fairly reliable expectations about such situations.

But a significant part of your success will also depend on situations in which these expectations could fly out the window. More than occasionally, it's not your normal *ability* that is tested—it's your *flexibility*. You may be able to perform well in a daily routine, but how about when unexpected challenges and unfamiliar settings place special demands on you? To use a baseball analogy, consider the distinction between a player's overall batting average and the new statistic showing how a player hits with baserunners in scoring position. It's nice when someone can hit .300, but managers also need to know how well players can hit in the clutch. A .300 hitter whose average is only .220 with runners on second and third, or in close games, could be of only marginal help to a team. Hitters who can produce in tense times, in unusually trying times, are known as the "money" players.

Can you be a "money" journalist? The answer is yes, but only if you have the flexibility necessary to adapt to a number of "handle with care" circumstances. In this chapter we'll examine these special tests of your communication skill as well as some of the knowledge needed to respond to them.

In one way, this chapter is inadequate. It won't tell you enough about what you need to survive as a competent "money" interviewer. Since we don't know specifically who *you* are, our specific readers, what we say must be somewhat general. You may be black or white, Hispanic or Asian, old or young, rich or poor, male or female, straight or gay. Our writing necessarily leaves out many crucial factors influencing how you personally might develop your interpersonal antennae. As you read, don't think of "receiving" information; think about supplying your own examples to supplement ours.

## RELUCTANT RESPONDENTS

Reporters occasionally encounter people who are hostile, uncooperative, evasive or rude. You shouldn't *anticipate* such treatment, but being prepared for it may help you open channels of communication where none previously existed. Here are some situations you might face—and advice on what to do.

### No Comment

A response of "no comment" to a reporter is like a red flag to a bull. Before flaring your nostrils, consider that a "no comment" may cover many hidden meanings. It might, for example, mean, "I'd really like to say something, but I'll lose my job if I do." Another "no comment" might translate to "I don't know the answer to your question, but I'm too proud to admit it." Or it could mean, "I can't tell you for good reason, but it's easier to say 'no comment' than to provide you with an explanation." In other words, "no comment" isn't necessarily an act of defiance. Explore the meaning of any "no comment" you receive. Knowing what the response represents will give you a fighting chance to persuade your interviewee to talk. You won't get very far saying, "Don't give me that 'no comment' stuff. You owe the public an answer." Instead you might say, "Are you under orders not to comment?" or "Are you afraid you'll get in trouble if you're quoted in the paper?"

## Evasiveness

Evasiveness comes in many forms, such as "stonewalling," "putting down a smokescreen" and "ducking the issue." At least that's how reporters often describe the behavior of people they believe aren't being forthright in answering questions. Again, you may profit from considering the other person's perspective. A public relations spokesman for an oil company explained, "What a reporter considers stonewalling may be what I consider a carefully phrased, responsible answer." At least try to deal diplomatically with apparent evasiveness. "Governor, could you be more specific in explaining why you vetoed the fair-housing bill?" A convoluted response may be deliberate; it may also be a case of muddled thinking. In any event, you're unlikely to win cooperation if you immediately resort to an admonition—"Don't dodge the question, please."

## Intimidation

Don't cower or back down if someone tries to deter you with intimidation tactics. Intimidation might come in the form of a sharp response: "That's a stupid question," or "I won't dignify that question with a response." When this happens, try to remain under control and calmly persist. You might rejoin: "I don't understand what's stupid about the question. Could you be more specific?" Another countertactic is to explore for causes of such behavior. "You are very upset with my questions. Do you think I'm trying to hurt you?" You might find out that you're dealing with someone with very real concerns, not a bully. Keeping your cool may not be easy; in fact, you may be pushed to the understandable breaking point. That happened to Oriana Fallaci when boxing legend Muhammad Ali belched in answer to one of her questions. She threw the microphone of her tape recorder at his face.[1]

## Hostility

Some people need to ventilate negative feelings. After the steam is released, they often regret their behavior, and a more open, helpful climate replaces the hostility, if you've been reasonably tolerant. Silent hostility poses a greater challenge—provided you are able to detect it accurately. There may be nonverbal clues, such as crossed arms or tight facial muscles. If you suspect silent hostility, it might have to be brought out into the open. You could say, "I sense I've said or done something to upset you. Am I right? Would you mind talking about it?"

## Hard Questions

Reporters can't shy away from hard questions. They can, though, take precautions. First of all, ask yourself if the question must be asked. Is it legitimate and fair? Would you take exception to the question if it were put to you? Don't be afraid to admit that some of your questions may be defective. Those you feel compelled to ask should be delivered sensitively. Minimize the sting if you can. You might try asking potentially embarrassing questions in a matter-of-fact manner. An indirect approach, described in Chapter 3, is another possibility. Some reporters prefer to blame the editor ("My boss insists that I ask this question") or distance themselves from the question ("As you know, Chief Murphy, there are those who think that your officers are racist"). Be prepared, however, for any of these methods to backfire. The interviewee might be annoyed and turn on the reporter ("Cut the crap. You're the one who thinks my officers are racists").

## Shock Treatment

In Chapter 3, we warned against overreliance on intentionally provocative questions simply to obtain an emotional response. But there will be times when all attempts to motivate an interviewee are futile. The animosity, indifference or rudeness is so severe that shock treatment may be the only recourse left to you. Don't throw notebooks or microphones, as Oriana Fallaci did in her interview with Ali. There are other methods. One is for the reporter to make an intentionally erroneous or outrageous statement. A reporter told us she had exhausted all means to get a response from dancer Rudolf Nureyev, who read a magazine throughout the "interview." Exasperated, she finally fabricated a deliberately provocative statement: "Is it true you are going to apply for American citizenship? To what country do you owe citizenship?" Nureyev came alive. "I am a citizen of the world," he replied haughtily. When feature writer Connie Fletcher ran out of tricks to get through to magician David Copperfield, she bluntly asked, "Have you always been such a wiseass?" Instead of ending the interview, Copperfield suddenly became expressive. "I used magic to hide behind because I was such a scared little kid," he confessed, going on to a series of self-revelations.[2]

The ultimate shock treatment is to close your notebook and leave.

Of course, you shouldn't be bluffing; you should be prepared to accept the consequences—no story. Sports reporter Wells Twombly walked out on baseball player Reggie Jackson after Jackson gave him a series of non-answers. But Twombly issued a parting shot: "I'm as good a writer as you are a home-run hitter. If you want me to write about you, you'll have to call me." Jackson did just that, and he was serious the second time around.[3]

## DIFFICULT INTERVIEWS, DIFFICULT PEOPLE

Each interview—because each is a unique event—poses its own special challenges. It is possible, however, to generalize about certain categories of people with whom communication frequently is difficult. We caution, though, against putting too much stock in generalizations. If you do, you may come to *expect* behavior from particular types of communicators and automatically develop defense mechanisms of your own. Try to approach all interviewees with an open mind.

### Celebrities

Some reporters would rather cover a Hell's Angels convention than interview an unfriendly celebrity. Horror stories are common. Oscar-winning actor Spencer Tracy, for example, often played warm-hearted roles in movies, but in life he could be cold and difficult, as one reporter painfully discovered. The reporter innocently asked Tracy what qualities make a woman attractive. Tracy found the question silly and said, "Young man, I'll give you 30 seconds to think of another question." The flustered reporter couldn't, and the interview ended.[4]

Celebrities, it seems, can be a pain, but before rushing to judgment, consider what their lives are like. If they venture into public, they usually are besieged by autograph seekers, hangers-on, opportunists, glad-handers—and the press. Although they owe a measure of success to fans, some people want too much—a pound of flesh, a piece of clothing or a 60-minute interview. If a celebrity is difficult to interview, try to analyze why. The reasons may range from boredom to shyness. And a lifeless interview may be more the product of exhaustion than rudeness.

Be sure to ask challenging questions based on thorough research. Celebrities are so frequently asked the same questions they either answer like a taped message ("I was 15 when I made my first movie . . .") or barely at all ("yeah" or "uh-huh"). Ask them something current, different and, if possible, thought-provoking. If the interviewee is a renowned journalist (preferably one with a sense of humor), you might borrow a line from author Gay Talese, who once asked if reporters are "restless voyeurs who see the warts of the world."[5] Asking biographical questions is a sure way to turn off a celebrity. Show you know something about him or her beyond what's been said in People magazine or even *Who's Who*. Is the celebrity an avid reader of mysteries? Is she an amateur poet? Is her daughter a budding scholar? Raise topics and questions that will build rapport and pique interest.

## Police

Police officers often erect a psychological screen between themselves and others, including the press. It's a case of "us vs. them." The interviewing experience of Mark Baker, author of *Cops,* help explain why reporters may find it hard to communicate with police. "Some cops could not overcome their xenophobia for anyone outside the police department. They remained suspicious of my motives."[6] Those who did talk were gregarious, Baker discovered, but despite signs of friendliness and openness, he knew he couldn't entirely enter their private preserve. In Baker's words: "A cop could stand drinking with me at a bar, regaling me with one funny story after another, but he still kept one eye on the door and everyone who came and went. He couldn't put his back to an aisle where strangers were passing back and forth. I realized this watchfulness carried over to the officer's relationship with me."[7]

The "watchfulness" extends to reporters, whom police often mistrust. The police expect support in battling criminals, and they can't understand it when reporters question their actions and methods. Police officers are not necessarily paranoid in seeing reporters as the enemy. As one police chief said: "Too many reporters suffer from a Woodward-Bernstein syndrome—they think public officials are crooks and police are brutes and on the take. On a percentage basis, there are more police loyal to the badge than there are [loyal] ministers, priests and rabbis." Reporters, the police chief said, frequently conclude that reticence by police is a sign of something amiss. "Their approach," he said, "is (a) I have something to hide, (b) it's intentional deception and (c) if I'm hiding something, it's a significant story."

Police do, indeed, hide things from reporters, which some reporters can't accept. A detective said reporters unrealistically may want every detail of a crime. "We have to hold back some information," he explained, "so we won't get bogus confessions. That's why we sometimes don't want to reveal the exact description of a murder weapon. But reporters aren't satisfied with a 'large-caliber pistol.' " It would help if reporters and police understood each other better. A give-and-take relationship may be needed at times.

## Military

Reporters and military represent two separate ways of thinking. The military accents conformity, control, discipline and loyalty. The press culture generally values competition, spontaneity, enterprise and advocacy. No wonder the two clash. In times of armed conflict or high-level alerts, reporters can anticipate disinformation from the military. During World War II, British Prime Minister Winston Churchill claimed, "In time of war, the truth is so precious, it must be attended by a bodyguard of lies."[8] To military officials, being true to duty, honor and country may necessitate being untrue to the press.

Even under normal conditions, you can expect delays and frustrations in dealing with the military. Requests for information may have to run up the chain of command. Usually, you will have to go through a public affairs officer, who, in turn, will have to check with superiors before providing answers to your questions.

## Politicians and Public Officials

Reporters and politicians often are in the throes of a love-hate relationship. What would reporters do without politicians, and vice versa? Generally, politicians are quite willing to talk. As a former city hall reporter said, "Politicians are very easy. You know, they're in the business. They are used to being interviewed and they're not quite so leery about talking [to reporters]." Politicians, however, don't always talk on reporters' terms, and that's what causes friction. When necessary, politicians can be masters of obfuscation. Although reporters ought to understand politicians' methods and motives, they occasionally display what The Nation described as "outraged innocence" when political figures lie or manipulate.[9] In some cases, reporters would be naive to expect full candor. Politicians will nearly always leave doors ajar, but don't count on doors to be flung wide open simply because the reporter says, "The public has a right to know." With politicians, skepticism and perseverance are necessary.

You may need to speak softly, but carry, if you must, the crowbar of the First Amendment. You *do* have a right and duty to raise tough questions and expect answers. Helen Thomas, UPI's veteran White House reporter, puts it well: "You can't have a democracy without an informed people, and sometimes people in government think information is their private preserve." She sees the press as making government accountable to the people. "We are the only institution that can question a president. The press keeps reminding the president there is a public trust."[10] Her words also apply to reporters who cover city hall, the school district or the library board.

## Athletes

Athletes are people. They can be shy and sensitive or spoiled and boorish. Bud Lea of the Milwaukee Sentinel related an especially unpleasant interview with running back Brent Fullwood, the No. 1 draft pick of the Green Bay Packers in 1987. Here's a sampling of how it went:

LEA: "Tell me about your first week here. Has it been easy? Hard? Long. . .?"

FULLWOOD: "Yeah, long."

LEA: "Is pro football as much fun as college?"

FULLWOOD: "Nope."

LEA: "Why not?"

FULLWOOD: "Don't ask me that question because I don't know why."

The interview didn't improve, and it finally ended when Lea asked, "Do interviews tick you off?" Fullwood replied, "I'm just tired. I don't want to be bothered. I've got to go."[11]

Lea's questions may not have been inspirational, but Fullwood did little to contribute to the interview. Was he truly tired? Is he just immature? Insensitive? Was he bored? Did Lea do something to upset him? We don't know what went wrong, but a general observation applies: Most athletes, like most people, respond well to someone who is considerate, reasonable, fair and interesting in approach. A public relations director for a National Hockey League team described a reporter respected by the players. "He's a person who is sensitive to people's time schedules, needs and moods." She explained why aggressive, insensitive reporters usually don't get far with players: "Aggressive tactics tend to alienate hockey players. [Hockey players] are, by far, the best interviews. They're accessible. They're reporters' dreams. But if you take an aggressive step toward them, it's like a confrontation on the ice and they deal in a very physical game, so their instincts are there."

An athlete who turns his back to a kid's plea for an autograph will probably ignore a reporter as well. Don't be too quick to write off athletes as jerks, though. Reporters can't expect them to endure patiently question after question and interview after interview. On the field of play, athletes usually perform well when challenged. They probably will respond better if reporters pose challenging questions, not trite, tired ones.

## Business Executives

Some executives believe business reporters exhibit an ugly combination of bias and ignorance in their coverage. To them, reporters are liberal reformers who prefer socialism to evil capitalism. What's more, they don't know the difference between stocks and bonds. That, of course, is a stereotype, just as business people are branded by media stereotypes as being "solely dedicated to the bottom line, justifying anything—be it to shut down communities and throw people out of work or to foul rivers and streams—in the mad pursuit of profit."[12]

Covering the economy and business in a time of hostile takeovers and insider trading is challenging enough without the complications of stereotypes. When stereotypes dictate, reporters begin to look for devious motives behind every corporate move. And executives see reporters as hostile muckrackers. Indeed, battles between business and the press are fought, and some rightly so. Reporters will dig deeper when executives stonewall or deceive, which they occasionally do. Business people will counterattack when reporters falsely accuse them, as reporters occasionally do.

Reporters who care about fairness—and who want to emerge with a good story—will take certain precautions in dealing with executives. Chief among these is to be prepared—not only to know the topic but to demonstrate your knowledge as a reassurance to the interviewee that you don't fit the stereotype. You may have to specify your topic and provide a list of some representative questions as a prerequisite to obtaining the interview. A veteran business reporter advises, "The CEO [chief executive officer] is not in the wish business; you'll have to be specific as to why you are requesting the interview *now*."[13]

During the interview, be alert for signs of anti-media tactics. Many of today's business executives are trained to parry and thrust in dealing with the press. Corporate America's leading proponent of an aggressive stance toward reporters is Herbert Schmertz, former vice president of public affairs for Mobil Oil. He warns business executives to be on guard for, among other ploys, the seductive, "you-can-trust-me" approach of reporters.[14] As a result, reporters, particularly broadcast journalists, should be prepared for defensiveness and argumentation in some business interviews. "When a TV journalist wants to interview me," Schmertz says, "I generally assume one of two things: either the story he's working on is hostile to me or my company, or else he wants to use me to attack somebody else. When a print reporter calls, I make no such assumptions."[15] If you face executives who share such an outlook, exercise self-control. You may not break down anti-media attitudes in the course of a single interview. But fairness and competent reporting eventually will encourage better relations.

## INTERVIEWS WITH DISABLED PEOPLE

An increasingly visible segment of our population is composed of the mentally or physically "disabled." More than 10 million children and 30 million adults in the United States are disabled in some way, and, increasingly, reporters are calling on members of this once neglected minority for news and feature stories. Unfortunately, reporters behave no differently from the rest of society in communicating with the disabled. They tend to be ill at ease in the presence of disabled individuals, especially those who are severely impaired, such as quadriplegics. The disabled are relatively tolerant of clumsy attempts by others to communicate with them. They would, however, respond more favorably to someone who is clearly attuned to their needs and feelings.

First of all, always try to think of the *person* first, not the *disability*. The Colorado Developmental Disablities Council advises reporters: "Emphasize the uniqueness and worth of the individual, rather than the [disability]; avoid making the disability larger than the person."[17] Overemphasis on the disability leads to what are called "pedestal images." Disabled persons, though, usually object to being portrayed as heroic or courageous. In the words of a paraplegic: "People put us on a pedestal for driving a car. After a while, you begin to start feeling like an idiot because you are doing something most adults are able to do." Obviously, disabled people don't want to be thought of as *extraordinary* for doing what they consider *ordinary* activities—raising a family, holding a job, participating in athletics. Their perspective suggests that reporters shouldn't do a feature, for example, on a blind teacher unless he or she is noted for innovation or talent in education. If the individual's accomplishments truly are noteworthy, even for a non-disabled person, reporters should *still* view the disability as merely *one* aspect of the story, not the whole story.

An important step toward fruitful communication with disabled persons is to avoid stereotyped, pejorative language—in interviews and in stories. Public consciousness has been raised to the point that most of us would never use words like "cripple," "idiot" or "deaf and dumb." But seemingly unobjectionable terms, such as the word "handicapped," remain part of the vocabulary of the non-disabled. By most accounts, "handicap" is no longer a proper synonym for a disability. One origin of the word is "cap in hand," as in begging.[18] The preferred usage is "disability" or "disabled," terms that are used to describe a variety of conditions which interfere with a person's ability to do something independently—walk, see, hear, talk. Disability may refer to a physical, mental or sensory condition. If reference to a disability is essential to your story, try to use the proper terminology for specific disabilities, like Down's syndrome or Huntington's disease, followed, if necessary, by a definition. Other commonly used phrases or words that may offend are those that are considered negative or suggest limitations, like "wheelchair-bound," "a victim of cerebral palsy" or "afflicted."

Reporters must also overcome attitudinal stereotypes. Some might fear interacting with disabled people because the disabilities are an unsettling reminder of human mortality and vulnerability. Fears lead to a range of reactions by the non-disabled. There are those, for example, who treat disabled people as if they carry a contagious disease that can be contracted through touch or close exposure. Others treat physically disabled people as though they are mentally disabled, too. According to James McDaniel, "It is assumed that the crippled in body are crippled in mind as well."[19] Attitudes like these may cause non-disabled people to relate to disabled people in obviously inappropriate, demeaning ways. (At least, the behavior will be obvious to the disabled person.) A pamphlet produced for reporters offers these suggestions for interviewing people with disabilities:

- Talk directly to the individual, even if he or she is using an interpreter.

- Use a normal tone of voice. If people cannot hear or understand you, they will let you know.

- If you do not understand what they are saying, say so. They will appreciate it.

- Sign or gesture to make yourself understood, if that is appropriate.

- When interviewing a person who is mentally retarded, speak in simple, clear sentences. Speak slowly, but not loudly. Remember, please, that simple language is not childish language.

- Be careful not to assume that a person with one disability has others. A person in a wheelchair is not necessarily hard of hearing, nor is a person who is blind particularly likely to be mentally impaired. People often speak to all disabled individuals as though they were talking to a person who is hearing impaired and mentally impaired.

- When interviewing a person who is in a wheelchair, try to sit across from them at eye level. If no chair is available, do not kneel—it may appear condescending.

- Ask if assistance is needed rather than assume it is.[20]

If you decide the disability is important to the story, don't be reluctant to bring up the subject. You probably won't upset or offend disabled people by asking thoughtful, well-intentioned questions. The mother of a disabled person explained, "It pains them more to see someone struggling through a conversation than to just have them come right out and ask about it." It would be appropriate, for example, to ask a disabled person about when and how she was injured—if it is relevant to the story. It also would be appropriate to ask a blind judge how he examines visual evidence in a case. If your questions reflect a sincere attempt to understand the disabled person, you probably won't damage the relationship.

## INTERVIEWS WITH PEOPLE IN NEED

Reporters can expect to communicate with people who have special needs, such as the victim of crime or the grief-stricken. We don't want to be misunderstood on this point. The people we're talking about seldom suffer from communication ailments of their own making, nor are they inherently "needy." If there are communication difficulties, they tend to be caused by the discomfort of other parties. Here are some suggestions for communication with "people in need."

### Communicating with the Grief-stricken

Asked to name their most dreaded assignment, many reporters would say, "Interviewing people in grief, especially someone whose spouse, son, daughter or parent has died in an accident." Most of us are uncomfortable, even awkward, when trying to talk to someone recently bereaved. Observe what happens at a wake when friends attempt to say something comforting to the family. Words of condolence seem inadequate or trite; people stammer, groping for something to say. Reporters share these feelings and more. They are conditioned to see themselves as guilty of privacy invasion or exploitation. No wonder. There is a great public perception of journalists as vultures who stick microphones in the faces of weeping parents and ask, "How do you feel?" That stereotype haunts journalists, who generally are considerate in dealing with the grief-stricken.

There is no need for reporters to feel like cads or ghouls. A newspaper ombudsman shared some reassuring experiences:

> Young reporters hate to do obituaries. They shouldn't. In a way it is a relief for the bereaved to talk to someone outside their sympathetic friends. It is almost a healing thing to do. I was once sent to the home of a sailor who drowned, and I also had to get a picture. His mother said, "I'm so glad to see you," and she brought out a scrapbook and told me all about her son. I thought I was invading her grief. I wasn't. I also talked to a father whose entire family was killed at a railway crossing. He was surrounded by a phalanx of friends who told me, "How dare you intrude." Later I saw him alone and I approached him. I said I was sorry, and his feelings spilled out. It was a beautiful story and not offensive to him or anyone else. [As ombudsman] I get complaints over "grief" stories, but the families usually don't object.

Grief, authorities say, is meant to be shared with others. Talking is a form of healing the hurt. Reporters, if they are sensitive and caring, can be part of the healing process and still fulfill their primary obligation to report the news. The key is to know what is appropriate behavior on your part and what to expect from bereaved persons. Here are some suggestions:

❏ Be prepared to encounter protective friends and relatives. Some people wrongly conclude that bereaved people don't want to talk about the loss of a loved one. If your path to the bereaved is blocked, suggest to the sentries that the sheltered person ought to be given the opportunity to decide whether to talk to a reporter. Emphasize that an obituary or sensitive news story is an epitaph and a tribute that will be appreciated by the family and friends alike. You face a stiffer challenge if seeking information about a tragic death or a suicide. Nevertheless, the bereaved generally still need to talk. Several informal surveys suggest that families of victims of tragedy are not nearly as adverse to news coverage as readers (or friends) assume. In one case, the executive editor of The Ledger in Lakeland, Fla., asked the mother of boy who was accidentally electrocuted by a high-voltage line if coverage by his newspaper upset her. "Nothing you did made me angry," she said. "Your reporter wanted to know what Dougie was like. That really touched me."[21] The story also helped the mother better understand what happened to her son. A veteran reporter said he finds this approach effective: "Your daughter (or husband or whatever) deserves more than just a little item in the newspaper, but I'm afraid that's how it's going to end up." In the event a family member does not want to talk, respect his or her feelings and withdraw. Usually someone close to the bereaved will act as a representative.

❏ Express condolences. A simple, sincere statement of sympathy—"I'm sorry about your loss"—is appropriate when you talk to the bereaved. There's no reason to be flowery or personal; you're a stranger who is there primarily to do a job, as cold as that might sound. Your approach and manner should be professional but compassionate. You might say, "I appreciate your willingness to talk about your husband." Don't be reluctant to refer to the deceased (a depersonalized term you should avoid) by name: "Did Bobby play on the football team?" or "I understand Mr. Willis was an avid fly fisherman."

❏ Ask questions with care. Your questions should be gentle probes, at least at first. You might begin with questions that will allow the bereaved to maintain composure. If a question appears to be painful, your options are to proceed gingerly, retreat or return to the question later. You'd be surprised, however, how often the grief-stricken draw upon reserves of emotional strength that enable them to speak lucidly and even eloquently about their loved one. Be guided by the knowledge that people want to share warm memories of happier times, not grim facts of a tragic death. If you must learn details about the death, be sure what you seek constitutes legitimate news rather than morbid curiosity.

❑ Expect tears. In an interview with Mamie Eisenhower, the widow of the former president, Barbara Walters saw Mrs. Eisenhower's eyes fill with tears as she talked about her husband's last years. Trying to spare her pain, Walters said, "Let's go back to talking about the happy years." To Walter's surprise, Mrs. Eisenhower said: "But Barbara, those were happy times. After all, Ike lived to see our son John's book become a success, he lived to see David and Julie married . . . and, most important, he lived to make a hole in one." She laughed through the tears, Walters said.[22] Crying is a common, essential part of expressing grief. But Richard Lewis Detrich and Nicola J. Steele, experts on the grieving process, say many people are afraid of tears, and frequently they try to prevent tears in others. Detrich and Steele advise: "You need to communicate, not necessarily verbally but at least by your attitude, 'It's OK to cry. It's part of your healing, and I understand.' "[23] As Barbara Walters discovered, even happy memories can elicit tears. Don't conclude that you're to blame for tears—or that you're inflicting pain. In themselves, tears aren't a reason to end or modify a conversation. Indeed, tears may result in a beneficial cleansing and releasing of feelings and a more memorable story. But always be attuned to the feelings of the bereaved, as Barbara Walters was with Mrs. Eisenhower.

❑ Listen compassionately but non-judgmentally. You ought to be prepared to allow grieving people time to express their feelings. Supportive words on your part, such as, "I understand," are appropriate. Listen sympathetically and patiently, even through long silences. You also should be prepared for a range of emotions—from laughter to sobs, from peacefulness to anger. Occasionally, people experiencing deep grief will say something like, "I wish I would have died in that crash instead of my daughter." Expressions of guilt by the bereaved often spring from self-blame for real or supposed wrongs done to the loved one. Keenly felt guilt may represent a danger signal—perhaps a sign that suicide is being contemplated. Resist the temptation to console or counsel the bereaved with pat, meaningless comments like, "Oh, you shouldn't feel that way." If you sense that the guilt or anger may warrant professional help, tell somebody close to the bereaved. Should you ever explore expressions of guilt? It might be best for you to simply acknowledge the bereaved's feelings in a neutral way, by saying something like, "I see." If you decide to probe, do so with an uncritical question such as, "Why do you say that?" or "I'm interested in why you feel that way." The answer might reveal a potentially important element of the story. "I blame myself for suggesting that Jane drive all the way on that Highway 19 death trap. She's only had her license for six months."

❏ Remember that you are a reporter, not a minister or psychologist. But you do have a reponsibility as a human being to help people in need, even if you might have to forget, for the moment, that you're a reporter. Remember, too, that the grief-stricken may be vulnerable. Don't exploit their grief. (Chapter 8 discusses ethical guidelines for interviewing people who are distraught.)

## Communicating with Victims of Crime

Reporters need to recognize that crime victims often feel ignored and misunderstood. Reporters sometimes contribute to these feelings by focusing their attention on the exploits of the police and criminals. The victim is left wondering, "Aren't I important?" Part of the problem is how people tend to define "victim." The definition is often based on whether there has been physical harm. Unless someone's been bashed or bloodied, a reporter may not realize that there are "victims" to be found in purse snatchings, burglaries or any "minor" crime. Morton Bard and Dawn Sangrey, authors of *The Crime Victim's Book,* note: "The exaggerated prominence given to physically violent crimes fosters a misconception about the injuries that crime victims can suffer."[24] Psychic and emotional injuries are just as real and painful as physical ones. Bard and Sangrey contend that a mugging victim, for example, may lose the capacity to trust people or become laden with guilt for not fighting back. Insensitive remarks like "At least you weren't hurt" compound the injury. Crime victims usually are hurt; their wounds may be invisible, but reporters should never assume they don't exist or compare them in significance to supposedly "worse" crimes.

People react differently to crimes. And different crimes cause different reactions. For instance, burglary victims frequently experience feelings of violation and fear. Someone—a frightening stranger—has been inside their home, and it may never be possible for them to feel safe or secure there again. With any crime, reporters should attempt to imagine what the victim feels. An assault victim, especially a male, may feel cowardly and ashamed for not resisting. A reporter, then, might take particular care in asking the victim if he defended himself.

Some crimes are so traumatic that reporters should take even greater precautions against causing further pain. Rape is an example. A psychiatrist who has worked with crime victims says some people benefit from telling their stories—the more they relive their experiences, the faster they recover. But others, he warns, may suffer a second victimization at the hands of the media. Reporters, he says, can't be expected to "diagnose and figure out who should and shouldn't receive attention."[25] If that's the case, reporters face a dilemma in interviewing some crime victims: will my questions help or hurt? An answer might be available, though, if the victim is being treated by a crime-victims center. If you're unsure about questioning a crime victim, it would be a good idea to seek advice from a professional counselor.

## INTERVIEWS ACROSS GENDER, AGE AND CULTURAL DIFFERENCES

Three principles are central to our understanding of any encounter involving people who have fundamentally different communication styles. First is the simple realization that *"I'm not you, and you're not me."* Actually, this insight seems almost painfully obvious—but don't dismiss it too readily. In practice, it means that you should expect differences, no matter how predictable or similar to you the other person appears. Even within quite cohesive cultural or ethnic groups, values vary and perceptions are persistently different. All communication depends on difference; otherwise, what would we have to communicate *about?* The inevitability of difference leads to what anthropologist Alfred G. Smith calls the "idiosyncrasy of objectives":

> When a teacher talks with a student about the grade on a term paper, the student is concerned with the grade he gets, while the teacher is concerned with the grade he gives. These are two different grades, even if

they are both represented by the same letter. There is a difference in the meaning of a *B*, and a difference in the objectives of the two people.[26]

The question an interviewer asks is not the question the other person hears. The vest a reporter wears is not the vest an assembly line worker sees. The headline a college graduate writes is not the headline a grade school dropout reads. The outward appearances can belie the vast differences in inward experiences. Of course, the greater the differences, the more potential misunderstandings are possible. Robert Kahn and Charles Cannell claim that, though there are obvious exceptions, "the fewer such characteristics as age, socioeconomic status, and education the interviewer and respondent have in common, the more serious will be the general problem of lack of shared experience."[27]

The second principle of intercultural communication is a complication of the first. That is, some of our differences are made up of prejudices, and *everyone is prejudiced.* Think about it. Not all of us are prejudiced in the everyday name-calling sense of unfair and negative overt behavior designed to put down another group of people; we aren't all "racists," or "sexists," for example. But clearly we are all prejudiced in the root sense of building our communication worlds around prejudgments. Humans have, in social psychologist Gordon Allport's words, "a propensity to prejudice. This propensity lies in the normal and natural tendency to form generalizations, concepts, categories, whose content represents an oversimplification . . . of experience."[28]

Third, *each person's cultural assumptions are essentially invisible to self.* We see our own culture only through comparing it with others. Until we encounter the "other ways," in effect becoming the "stranger," it's difficult to imagine how *our* ways are "other" and "strange" to *them.* An often-repeated aphorism in communication, attributed to the media theorist Marshall McLuhan, is that we're not sure who discovered water, but we're pretty sure it wasn't a fish. The idea is intriguing in its implications. Water forms a fish's only environment, and a living fish—if it imagines at all—couldn't imagine itself alive outside that environment, so the fish literally can't compare water to, say, air as an environment. If something is the only environment, the only assumption, then it becomes invisible for practical purposes. It is unexamined. And, without a different environment for comparison, it's unexaminable.

Because of the nature of the job, journalists especially need training in how to recognize possible interpersonal conflicts that are attributable to gender, age or cultural differences. This book obviously can't examine every possible conflict situation a journalist might encounter. With limited space, the best approach is to choose some common differences of style, and indicate potential hindrances to effective communication. Obviously, advice cannot always be tailored specifically to *your* gender, age or cultural situation; we will try to illuminate problem areas, and trust that readers will make their own applications. *All reporters should understand that there are essential differences in the communication styles of various social groups—and should be able to use this knowledge to adjust their personal styles of interviewing accordingly.*

## Gender Differences in Communication Style

In male-female conversation, as with all other crossing-difference situations, generalizations are dangerous in predicting or explaining specific cases, but they may be quite valuable overall. Let's consider some of the differences you might expect in the speech of the genders, and how those differences could affect interviewing. Although future research may well discredit or modify these findings, the shape of our current knowledge is fairly clear. These factors are all well-described in professional literature and reasonably well-established by research in communication, psychology and linguistics.[29]

The differences are presented primarily from the standpoint of women. We could easily have chosen the male point of view with only minor descriptive adjustments, but there are some good reasons to emphasize awareness of women's speech patterns. For one thing, women's variations in speech style are not often considered by the general population. The culture at large tends to elevate a male style of "controlling" talk as the "right" way to communicate—especially in a professional setting. In addition, a significant portion of this culture, both female and male, is disturbed and often offended by the "maleness" of many public assumptions about communication. If journalists become more sensitive to the differences of styles as perceived from a woman's perspective, they will be less likely to offend inadvertently, and more likely to accommodate language to the other's needs.

When compared, then, with men's speech style, women's conversation normally exhibits:

- More emotion words and statements.
- More attempts at empathy.

- More relationship- and people-oriented statements when compared with men's emphasis on content-orientation.
- More qualifiers ("It may be that . . ."), self-disparagement ("I'm probably silly to believe this, but . . ."), tag questions ("This is a good response to that lawsuit, *isn't it?*") and implicit requests for approval.
- More indirection ("Wouldn't it be nice if . . .") and euphemism.
- More self-disclosure of personal information.
- More sensitivity to "metamessages"—those mostly nonverbal and covert messages that tell people how to "take" another person's comments (examples would be a wink, smile or a raised eyebrow to signal another to take an insulting comment as "kidding" or "joke" rather than "put-down").
- More verbalized verifications of listening accuracy (described earlier as "perception checks" and "active listening").
- More reinforcement and encouragement of others' speech (for example, women tend to use affirmative nods and the verbalized "uh-huh" to indicate "I'm still following you," while men tend to nod and use "uh-huh" less frequently and primarily to signal agreement with the speaker.
- More reluctance to initiate conversational topics.
- More tendency to submit in confrontive arguments.
- More eye contact with a speech partner, coupled with an increased likelihood of averting gaze if stared at.
- More smiling.
- More body tension and rigid posture in social situations.
- More avoidance of power positions in meetings (women are less likely than men to sit at the head of a table, even if the seat is available).
- More defined and smaller personal space or "territory."

This information has important implications for interviewing. Consider the ways that assumptions can work to subvert communication. Whether you are a male or female reporter, are you tempted to assume that your respondent is "waffling" on an issue if there is averted gaze in response to your hard, intense question? Or if the respondent qualifies a position by saying, "You're kind of right, in a manner of speaking," or "Yes, but I'm not sure I'd say that, would

you?" don't assume these responses are directly tied to the toughness of your questioning or an interviewee's weakness of character;
they may simply be a natural part of the speech style of the woman
you're interviewing.

It's tempting for people to overestimate the similarities between
others' speech styles and their own. If you're a male reporter,
women interviewees may overestimate, for instance, your abilities
to receive subtle messages—thinking that their intended irony or
humor will be obvious to you. But you're more likely to miss it
than a woman reporter would be, perhaps being somewhat less
empathic and more inclined to overt, control-oriented messages. A
male reporter appears to be less likely to understand the emotional
tone and demands of tense interview situations, but more likely to
possess the assertiveness to press for answers. If you're a female
reporter, men interviewees may underestimate your seriousness if
you deliver a tough question with a smile. All these factors, and
others too numerous to detail here, make even more obvious the
need for interviewers to check out their interpretations with interviewees. (In fact, the demands of interviewing suggest that journalists could work to blend male and female styles—become androgy-
nous communicators in this sense—for maximum flexibility and
effectiveness.)

Knowledge is fine, but what does it mean in action for the working journalist? Several suggestions are important, *especially* for men
in the profession who have not yet understood the distinctions between male and female speech styles. Women, too, may need to
develop the same awareness.

First, recognize that many of the differences stem from simple
status inequalities in society. The characteristics of women's speech
in many ways correspond to the characteristics of any social group
with diminished power or prestige. The de-emphasis of speech for
control, the self-deprecation, the tentativeness, the vulnerability to
interruption, touching and persuasive power-plays—all these factors
point to a basic linguistic inequality that reporters, whether male or
female, need not perpetuate. Analyze the ways your speech and
nonverbal habits might contribute to it. Do you call *her* by her first
name before you'd do so to a man? If you're male, do you move
immediately to a "power seat" at the end of a table? Do you reach to
invade her space through inappropriate taps on the arm or pats on
the shoulder or head? Do you find yourself interrupting her in ways
you wouldn't interrupt a man?

If you have the opportunity, carefully and analytically compare a taped interview you've done with a man and one you did with a woman. Naturally, one such comparison won't "prove" anything, but it may indicate or suggest subtle behavioral changes in your personal style.

Second, monitor your speech, and, if necessary, change your labels for and references to women. This, of course, applies to female journalists as well as to males. Many women are rightly offended by such speech forms as the generic *he* used to refer to both genders ("the reporter finds *himself* surprised to learn that . . . "), or the blanket use of other male terms to refer to large groups. Do not use such words as *mankind* or *manpower,* and remember that adult women may well feel demeaned by being called "girls" when men of corresponding ages aren't called "boys." Make other references equal, too; it doesn't make much literal sense to refer differently to men and women in the very same context, but many covert commentaries about relative status are embedded in our references. An example: "Sam Purdy and Julia Brown were recently promoted. Purdy has been with the firm since 1965 and Julia since 1963."[30] You might ask yourself, too, why so many inanimate objects of desire (sports cars, for instance) are referred to as feminine ("She's really beautiful"), and if this is necessary. And we need not assume by our references that certain groups are wholly the province of men or of women ("a good nurse will always put her patients first," "a truck driver must spend long hours in his truck").[31]

Third, be wary of that differential treatment of men and women sometimes known as *politeness.* Many men, ironically, were taught this habit by their mothers. Politeness can frustrate communicators quickly if it is accompanied by a perceived attitude of one-up*man*-ship. Communication specialist Bobbye Sorrels Persing writes: "Even opening doors, holding chairs, lighting cigarettes, standing in the presence of a woman, and holding coats can be demeaning if done in a condescending manner or if accompanied by 'cracks' about 'women's lib.' If these acts are done naturally by one human for another equal human, the communication is positive, but all too often that is not the case when the act is done to or for a woman by a man."[32] Interviewers would be wise to consider whether their communication behaviors across gender differences consistently conform to Persing's criterion of "acts . . . done naturally by one human for another equal human." There *are* differences between male and female speech styles. But those differences are not ones that should ever signal inequality.

## Age Differences in Communication Style

Journalistic interviews often involve obtaining information from older adults who have communication habits and expectations very different from those of their younger questioners. This older population is increasing, both in numbers and in influence. Yet elderly citizens as a group have not been integrated successfully into the mainstream of American society, nor do we adequately understand the contributions they might make or their unique communication styles.[33] We are hindered by such myths as the expectation of memory loss, the "can't teach old dogs new tricks" assumption, the notion that intelligence declines with age and the expectation that older people will become increasingly lonely.[34]

In truth, recent research has shown it is not that memory or intelligence "decline" as much as it is that sensory information—the building blocks of memory and intelligence—may become increasingly unavailable to the elderly. Aging processes decrease the acuity of the senses, and some diseases and conditions, such as arteriosclerosis and strokes, impair the senses, too. But many of the problems of memory, intelligence, learning, loneliness and responsiveness we've believed to be related directly to aging are not inevitable at all.[35] They are communication problems partially induced by society's relatively negative attitude about aging.

Changing your attitudes about communicating with the elderly may change your results for the better. When you ask questions of and converse with older respondents, expect to spend more time in the interview, but also expect a unique perspective that you may not be able to get from a younger person. Anticipate wisdom and recollections in fascinating historical context. You may help facilitate what you expect. Given enough time for observation and recollection, elderly people can be quite reliable informants. But you'll notice some distinctive styles of interpersonal communication too, warns researcher Mark Knapp. He lists the following communication characteristics of older adults, paraphrased here to adapt to the interview setting:

❏ Some elders may have reduced their overall contact with people and will "talk your arm off" out of an enthusiasm for reestablished conversation. Allow enough latitude and time for such a person. Conversely, others may be out of the habit of talking opening and may need some gentle probing.

❏ Some will be afraid to say anything controversial because of the risk of further isolation, while others resent their life situation so much they're likely to take it out on you with their negativity. Be aware of the potential for each of these patterns. Don't take them personally.

❑ It will be harder for many elderly people to trust due to the insecurity of many of their living conditions. They may become highly uncooperative. Your assurances and sincere promises may need to be clearer to these respondents before they'll be willing to disclose. Again, Knapp notes the converse condition; insecure elders may also deal with their feelings by becoming highly docile, malleable and dependent. Be careful that this latter person isn't just telling you what you want to hear. Your empathic skills will be severely tested here.

❑ Many elders focus on themselves as the center of attention, due to a "constricted social world." This could happen to any of us (if it hasn't already). If you are a patient listener, gently guiding the respondent to imagine other viewpoints, you can counteract this potential "selfishness" factor.

❑ Many elders prefer to talk with only one person at a time. This may be because of declining sensory capabilities and the resulting insecurity. Effective interviewers of older adults work to focus and simplify the interview situation without condescending to the interviewee. They'll try to reduce competing stimuli (music, visual movements, passers-by) to a minimum.[36]

Noted salesman Ken Delmar adds some other suggestions that have worked for him when "selling older clients." He suggests a conservative style of dress, a slowed-down pace with fewer quick movements, a "deeper level of seriousness," calm eye gaze, close listening, extensive familiarity with your own point of view and an ability to compare alternative choices clearly for the respondent.[37]

## Black and White Differences in Communication Style

The Rev. Jesse Jackson has accused American journalism of being insensitive to black issues, in part because so many reporters are white. "Most reporters," he said, "have no sense of the [black] area so they can't report it." They don't live in the same neighborhoods, and are afraid of increased contact with blacks.[38] Even when events directly concerning minorities are covered, many reporters will seek out interpretive interviews not with minority respondents, but with whites.[39] Jackson is correct in identifying journalism as a fundamentally white occupation, and it's true that many white reporters have relatively little experience with blacks. But it's not ignorance of another group's neighborhoods and communities that is the major problem.

*Whether the reporter in search of a story is white or black—or, for that matter, of Hispanic or Asian heritage—there usually isn't a clear recognition of the effects of differing styles of communicating on interview outcomes.* Linguist Deborah Tannen observes that if communication "strains and kinks develop when there really are no basic differences of opinion, when everyone is sincerely trying to get along," the problem is likely caused by differences of conversation *style*. Few problems in life can be as frustrating, since conversational habits can be so subtle, and because we're not accustomed to identifying them as causes of misunderstanding. But the effects are profound: "Nothing is more deeply disquieting than a conversation gone awry. To say something and see it taken to mean something else; to try to be helpful and be thought pushy; to try to be considerate and be called cold; to try to establish a rhythm so that talk will glide effortlessly about the room, only to end up feeling like a conversational clod who can't pick up the beat—such failure at talk undermines one's sense of competence, and of being a right sort of person. If it happens continually, it can undermine one's feeling of psychological well-being."[40]

People often sincerely attempt to communicate but find their efforts quashed by differing assumptions of what "good" communication means. It is then we can observe the muted, undercover collisions of style. The communicators are doomed to continual misunderstandings until one or the other recognizes that the other's reluctance to answer (for example) may be related more to his or her cultural habits than to evasiveness.

Since black-white encounters are so common for journalists, it might be helpful to summarize in detail four basic conversational style areas especially relevant to the interview situation: information-seeking, negotiation of agreement, turn-taking, and nonverbal habit. Although the style that seems "right" or "wrong" to you in each area probably depends on which cultural group is your own, it's important to remember that styles themselves are neither better nor worse than any other; once you know that a style exists and how it functions, you can begin to take it into account more effectively. In highlighting these differences, we are not advocating black styles or white styles. We're simply advocating awareness and knowledge.

**Information-seeking Styles.** In the following discussion, we rely heavily on the influential work of Thomas Kochman, who was a participant-observer in the "ethnographic" research he conducted.[41] His findings are consistent with a wide variety of research studies and black experience.[42]

One of Kochman's major conclusions—especially interesting to journalists—was that, in America, black and white approaches to seeking information are fundamentally different. At initial meetings, whites typically begin with questions designed to obtain information about status, achievement and "social advancement." They want to "locate individuals . . . within some social, educational, and professional network or context,"[43] and they feel perfectly normal doing so by asking direct questions even of people they hadn't previously met. Blacks, on the other hand, tend to be surprised by such tactics. They "consider the inquisitiveness and probing that whites demonstrate in these contexts improper and intrusive."[44] The black style often is to avoid direct questioning, and, if faced with it, to show disdain through silence. White reporters whose questioning styles tend to be direct, focused and personalized are hereby forewarned. Asking "How old are you, Mrs. Jones, and when did you move to this neighborhood?" may provoke a response no fuller than "What?" Pressing the point might only generate more ill will. A black reporter, on the other hand, should understand that whites are generally more responsive to personal questioning from a stranger. When the reporter's cultural tendency might be to wait for the respondent to volunteer certain information, about family history, for example, a pointed question could save time.

**Agreement-Disagreement Styles.** In arguments, blacks tend to challenge others overtly—but not in a malicious manner. They challenge not as "antagonists," but with intense emotions as "contenders cooperatively engaged in a process that hopes to test . . . the validity of opposing ideas."[45] Blacks readily become advocates, investing their points of view with their personalities. The black style is to assume that a disagreement is between *people* at least as much as it is betweeen *ideas*. The white style is more oriented to divorcing the arguments from the arguers; the white arguer is much more likely to look to authorities, experts and published materials for support. Whites look much less to personal experience and verbal superiority as indicators of competence in argument.[46] Interestingly, this style is perceived by many blacks as insincere, since the arguer doesn't seem—from the black perspective—to *care* enough to be an emotionally involved advocate.[47] Black reporters are forewarned: An impersonal, analytical statement from a white may not indicate lack of commitment or lack of sincerity as much as a basic interpersonal style.

**Turn-taking.** Whites appear to regard maintaining the "floor" in conversations as a matter of "entitlement, to be granted only to one person at a time, and to be terminated only by that person or the person empowered to grant turns."[48] In other words, to whites a conversation is an orderly sequence of statements with minimal interruption; people can take their turns only when the other speaker clearly signals his or her willingness to yield the floor. Black cultural styles, however, emphasize that a "turn" of a speaker should be shorter, more interruptable, and with fewer points of contention. Blacks tend to "come in to argue a point before whites have 'finished.' " Whites consider this rude. However, blacks believe a turn is over when a point has been made on which others wish to comment. Consequently, they consider whites selfish for 'hogging the floor.' "[49] Black and white reporters both are forewarned: Some conclusions reached about your respondent might simply be misjudgments based on criteria that may not apply to a different group.

**Nonverbal Styles.** The dominant white culture in the United States expects certain nonverbal indicators of interest and involvement in conversations. Being "on time" is important. Direct eye contact is another such signal, as is the habit of facing each other while conversing. White reporters, for instance, typically assume that a tardy interviewee, or one who turns away, or who fails to maintain fairly consistent eye contact, is inconsiderate. Such a listener may even be thought disagreeable or hostile on the basis of the evidence. However, research shows that black assumptions are quite different. Precision in time of arrival is less keyed to respect for the people joined; thus, lateness is not necessarily a sign of disrespect. Averted gaze is often actually a sign of *respect* with blacks and certain other cultural groups, especially in an encounter with someone older or of higher status. Similarly, blacks may exhibit trust in social situations by briefly turning away from others; it is not meant as an affront.[50]

This matter is complicated by the fact that we are not consciously aware of many nonverbal behaviors. Attitudes and even prejudices leak out through this nonverbal system of messages, and we're hardly in control of them. For example, white reporters responsible for interviewing whites and blacks fairly should be sobered by a recent psychological study. In this experimental design, white job interviewers were the subjects, told to interview candidates (white and black confederates of the researchers). Through one-way mirrors, researchers recorded all aspects of the various interviews. As Nancy Henley summarizes the results, white interviewers "placed their chairs at a significantly greater distance from the blacks, and showed significantly less 'total immediacy,' a measure made up of combined scores for forward lean, eye contact, and shoulder orientation (directness). In addition, they ended the interview significantly sooner with blacks, and made more speech errors."[51]

If prejudice is this embedded in nonverbal behaviors and styles, then reporters representing dominant cultural groups—in this case, white—must be careful indeed to ensure that they don't make false assumptions about the source of others' behaviors and discomfort. It should be clear from even this cursory description that overassuming and overconcluding in interracial and intercultural interviews are extremely dangerous; there are too many legitimate variations in conversational style, and too many of us—black and white—are unaware of them.

## Other Intercultural Differences in Communication Style

Black-white communication style differences, of course, aren't the only interrcultural situations commonly encountered by working journalists. Native Americans are often prominent in the news, as are such other groups as Hispanic-Americans, Asian-Americans, Italian-Americans, Polish-Americans, Jewish-Americans and even non-ethnic groups that exhibit cultural distinctiveness, such as gays and some blue-collar groups. Hispanics and Asians are, in particular, such large and growing subgroups in the United States that non-Hispanic and non-Asian reporters should familiarize themselves with specific components of the interpersonal styles of these groups.

**Hispanic Communication Styles.** People of Latin descent form the second largest cultural minority (after blacks) in contemporary America, and are especially prominent in the urban centers of the Southwest, Southeast and Northeast. Some controversy surrounds the choice of identifying label for the group. *Hispanic,* though it is now commonly used in the national media and in governmental circles, does not enjoy universal support; *Latino* is growing in popularity as an overall term for all Spanish-surnamed Americans, and *Chicano,*

*Mexicano, Mexican-American* or other specific names might be preferred by particular populations.[52]

Obviously, generalizations are difficult. Even Mexican-Americans, Nobleza C. Asuncion-Lande says, "are not a homogeneous group. There are class differences and regional distinctions," despite a unitary and largely negative stereotype.[53] John Condon attempts to get beyond the stereotype, however, to describe differences between Mexican and general North American styles of talk.[54] Although most research has focused on Mexican-Americans, Condon's conclusions may be relevant for other Hispanic groups as well. Condon highlights the following tendencies that could be confusing or frustrating to a naive interviewer. Mexicans tend to:

- Value the "inner" uniqueness of a person so much that any slight to someone's dignity is understood as a matter of grave concern.

- Talk easily about inner spirit or individual soul and are suspicious of people who insist on avoiding such topics by substituting rational objectivity. "Americans are corpses," says a Mexican quoted by Condon.[55]

- Be very willing to disclose—and inquire about—family life. There is suspicion of people unwilling to do this.

- Place trust in individuals rather than large organizations or abstract principles.

- Be far more likely to flatter, praise effusively and compliment than is the general North American habit.

- Call attention to, and even exaggerate, differences between people of different sexes, ages or statuses. What many North Americans would label "sexist" talk, for example, is quite ingrained in the cultural assumptions of Mexicans and should not be taken automatically as insulting.

- Have a different definition for what "the truth" is for. That is, while the general habit of the United States is to criticize lying (if at times hypocritically), some Hispanic styles recognize broader social functions of lying. In contrast to using lies aggressively, defensively or misleadingly, Mexicans might tend to lie to entertain or satisfy a conversational partner. Condon cites Francisco Gonzales Pineda's point that lying has become a kind of "institution" in Mexican culture.[56] It's not reasonable to regard lying in this context, therefore, as a necessarily negative, improper or unethical behavior.

Obviously, then, interviewers ought to examine their assumptions carefully before feeling too confident about knowing what another person might "mean" by a comment or reaction. This advice also applies, of course, to Hispanic reporters who may, if not on guard, judge others through a cultural prism.

**Asian Communication Styles.** City journalists have long known about an extremely visible and energetic culture of Asian citizens. Many non-Asian reporters are aware of overt differences of culture (perhaps even becoming intimidated by them) without understanding how their view of conversation itself might differ from that of their Asian interviewees. Again, while recognizing the dangers of overgeneralization, we look to intercultural communication specialists to inform us about the overall assumptions and shape of Asian (and, by extension, much Asian-American) talk. K.S. Sitaram and Roy T. Cogdell have analyzed some of the major differences between non-Asian American and Asian speech styles[57]; their conclusions, paraphrased here, should guide reporters in developing more realistic expectations for interviews.

Asian speakers tend to:

❑ Use references to tradition as a form of support or evidence; the more Western approach is to elevate "newness" and not give an idea more weight just because it is entrenched or traditional.

❑ Make many more references to group welfare and the group's concerns than to a speaker's own opinions. Personal opinions are assumed to be relatively unimportant and subservient to the larger good of the group. Interviewers should be aware that pressing for such personal disclosures is likely to be counterproductive.

❑ Attempt to use a "higher" or grander level of language than native Westerners. Such language should not be taken automatically as pomposity or indifference.

❑ Seek to avoid direct criticism of others, even others who oppose them. Attempts to persuade are less valued than attempts to discover a truth that transcends both individuals. This does not signal an absence of a unique point of view, but is simply a different style of expression consistent with a concern for dignity.

❑ Assume that communication is a joint venture with shared responsibility between speakers and listeners, whereas a common Western belief is that communication should be primarily a *speaker's* responsibility. Imagine the implications for an interviewer who tries to "milk" specific information from such a respondent, but seems uninterested in the rest of what the speaker had to say—or, just as bad, an interviewer who continually interrupts.

❏ Respect and value silence much more than native Westerners. A period of silence in an interview, therefore, is much less likely to mean disinterest or conflict. Non-Asian interviewers must learn patience and the ability to tolerate what they experience as the ambiguity of silence.

❏ Assume a respect for older people that is relatively uncommon in Western culture. That is, younger speakers are supposed to be deferent and primarily interested in what elders say; a young person who is perceived as an "upstart" or seems interested in promoting himself or herself to an older one is not likely to gain much cooperation from an Asian interviewee.

Of course, such insights further indicate that what is appropriate for an interviewer in one situation is likely to contradict expectations in another situation. For example, an Asian-American reporter raised in a tradition of unquestioned respect for elders may be assigned to interview an elderly Caucasian politician who must be asked tough questions. Can the reporter transcend cultural difference to get the story? A reporter oblivious to the concerns of intercultural communication just invites trouble.

## STRATEGY FOR "HANDLE WITH CARE" INTERVIEWS

In this chapter we've asked you to consider circumstances that are most likely to challenge your interviewing abilities. Interviewers who are effective in most everyday situations can become extremely frustrated when confronted by the closed doors of governmental or military life, or when they must interview people who exhibit special needs, emotional involvements or disabilities. When gender, age or cultural differences divide interviewers from interviewees, communication quality can also deteriorate.

Interviewers need a clear and focused philosophy of communicating that will guide them through these mazes. We suggest a three-part approach. First, knowledge must be built about how meanings are created by different groups in such situations. "If we know nothing about the strangers' culture," write William Gudykunst and Young Yun Kim in their book on cross-cultural interaction, "it is highly probable we will make inaccurate predictions and interpretations of their behavior."[58] Second, there is no good substitute for alertness or sensitivity to the actual behaviors, statements and feelings as they emerge. The interviewer must account for and—to the extent possible—suspend personal stereotypes and avoid dismissing unfamiliar behaviors as meaningless or ridiculous. Finally, an interviewer must approach each respondent as a unique individual, not as a mere representative of a given social category. A reporter who isn't flexible in this way is one who isn't *competent* in a very crucial sense. Journalism is, among all its other characteristics, an enterprise of surprise.

## Notes

[1] Melvin Mencher, *News Reporting and Writing,* 2nd ed. (Dubuque, Iowa: Wm. C. Brown, 1981), p. 451.

[2] Connie Fletcher and Jon Ziomek, "How to Catch a Star," *The Quill,* December 1986, p. 35.

[3] Quoted in John Brady, *The Craft of Interviewing* (New York: Vintage Books, 1977), p. 107.

[4] Hugh C. Sherwood, *The Journalistic Interview* (New York: Harper & Row, 1969), pp. 36, 37.

[5] Denis Brian, *Murderers and Other Friendly People* (New York: McGraw-Hill, 1973), p. 183.

[6] Mark Baker, *Cops: Their Lives in Their Own Words* (New York: Pocket Books, 1985), p. 5.

[7] Baker, *Cops,* p. 5.

[8] "The Disinformers," *The Nation,* Oct. 18, 1986, p. 364.

[9] "The Disinformers," p. 363.

[10] Particia Corrigan, "Helen Thomas: Press' First Lady in White House," *St. Louis Post-Dispatch,* May 25, 1987, p. 1D.

[11] Bud Lea, "How's Fullwood Doing? No. 1 Keeps Silent," *Milwaukee Sentinel,* Aug. 15, 1987, Part 2, p. 1.

[12] Thornton E. Bradshaw, chief executive officer, RCA Corp., remarks before the 1984 Gerald Loeb Awards Banquet for Distinguished Business and Financial Journalism, New York, June 13, 1984.

[13] Warren Strugatch, "Prepping for the CEO: Ten tips for getting a better interview," *The Quill,* January 1988, p. 26.

[14] Herb Schmertz with William Novak, *Good-bye to the Low Profile: The Art of Creative Confrontation* (Boston: Little, Brown, 1986), p. 123.

[15]Schmertz, *Good-bye to the Low Profile,* p. 99.

[16]Cited in Charles J. Kokaska and Donn E. Brolin, *Career Education for Handicapped Individuals,* 2nd ed. (Columbus, Ohio: Charles E. Merrill, 1985), p. 4.

[17]"Fit to Print: A Terminology and Reference Guide for the Colorado News Media" (Colorado Developmental Disabilities Council, undated), p. 3.

[18]"Guidelines for Reporting and Writing about People with Disabilities" (Media Project of the University of Kansas, 1984).

[19]James W. McDaniel, *Physical Disability and Human Behavior* (New York: Pergamon Press, 1969), p. 19.

[20]"Fit to Print," p. 6.

[21]"Notes & Comment," *The Quill,* October 1986, p. 8.

[22]Barbara Walters, *How to Talk with Practically Anybody About Practically Anything* (Garden City, NY: Doubleday, 1970), p. 78.

[23]Richard Lewis Detrich and Nicola J. Steele, *How to Recover from Grief* (Valley Forge: Judson Press, 1983), p. 118.

[24]Morton Bard and Dawn Sangrey, *The Crime Victim's Book,* 2nd ed. (New York: Brunner/Mazel, 1986), p. 7.

[25]Dru Lipsitz, "Crime Victims and Press Coverage," unpublished paper, Southern Illinois University at Edwardsville, June 1983, pp. 14, 15.

[26]Alfred G. Smith, "Communication and Inter-Cultural Conflict," in Carl E. Larson and Frank E. X. Dance, eds., *Perspectives on Communication* (Milwaukee: University of Wisconsin–Milwaukee Speech Communication Center, 1968), p. 169.

[27]Robert L. Kahn and Charles F. Cannell, *The Dynamics of Interviewing* (New York: John Wiley and Sons, 1964), p. 11.

[28]Gordon W. Allport, *The Nature of Prejudice,* abridged ed. (Garden City, N.Y.: Doubleday Anchor Books, 1958), p. 26.

[29]See Cheris Kramerae, *Women and Men Speaking* (Rowley, Mass.: Newbury House, 1981); Nancy M. Henley, *Body Politics: Power, Sex, and Nonverbal Communication* (Englewood Cliffs, N.J.: Prentice-Hall, 1977); Robin Lakoff, *Language and Woman's Place* (New York: Harper Colophon Books, 1975); Barbara Westbrook Eakins and R. Gene Eakins, *Sex Differences in Human Communication* (Boston: Houghton Mifflin, 1978); Judy Cornelia Pearson, *Gender and Communication* (Dubuque, Iowa: Wm. C. Brown, 1985); Deborah Borisoff and Lisa Merrill, *The Power to Communicate: Gender Differences as Barriers* (Prospect Heights, Ill.: Waveland Press, 1985).

[30]Loisanne Foerster and Patricia Walsh Rao, "Created Equal: Toward Communication Free of Sexual Bias," in Judy E. Pickens, Patricia

Walsh Rao, and Linda Cook Roberts, eds., *Without Bias: A Guide-book for Nondiscriminatory Communication* (San Francisco: International Association of Business Communicators, 1977), p. 19.

[31]Examples taken from Mercilee M. Jenkins, *Removing Bias: Guidelines for Student-Faculty Communication* (Annandale, Va.: Speech Communication Association, 1983), pp. 24–25.

[32]Bobbye Sorrels Persing, *The Nonsexist Communicator: An Action Guide to Eradicating Sexism in Communication* (East Elmhurst, N.Y.: Communication Dynamics Press, 1978), p. 102.

[33]Carl W. Carmichael, "Cultural Patterns of the Elderly," in Larry A. Samovar and Richard E. Porter, eds., *Intercultural Communication: A Reader* (Belmont, Calif.: Wadsworth, 1985); Carl W. Carmichael, "Communication and Gerontology: Interfacing Disciplines," *Western Speech Communication,* 40 (Spring 1976), 121–129; Carl W. Carmichael, Carl H. Botan, and Robert Hawkins, eds., *Human Communication and the Aging Process* (Prospect Heights, Ill.: Waveland Press, 1988).

[34]Carmichael, "Communication and Gerontology," p. 137.

[35]Carmichael, "Communication and Gerontology," p. 139.

[36]Mark L. Knapp, *Interpersonal Communication and Human Relationships* (Boston: Allyn and Bacon, 1984), pp. 77–78.

[37]Quoted in *Inside Radio,* Nov. 17, 1986, p. 7.

[38]"Jackson Says White Reporters Can't Cover Black Issues," *Editor & Publisher,* June 6, 1987, p. 90.

[39]Clint C. Wilson II and Felix Gutierrez, *Minorities and Media: Diversity and the End of Mass Communications* (Beverly Hills, Calif.: Sage Publications, 1985), p. 138.

[40]Deborah Tannen, *That's Not What I Meant! How Conversational Style Makes or Breaks Relationships* (New York: Ballantine, 1986), p. 5.

[41]Thomas Kochman, *Black and White Styles in Conflict* (Chicago: University of Chicago Press, 1981), p. 97.

[42]Dorthy L. Pennington, "Black-White Communication: An Assessment of Research," in Molefi Kete Asante, Eileen Newmark, and Cecil A. Blake, eds., *Handbook of Intercultural Communication* (Beverly Hills, Calif.: Sage Publications, 1979), pp. 383–401; Donald K. Cheek, *Assertive Black . . . Puzzled White: A Black Perspective on Assertive Behavior* (San Luis Obispo, Calif.: Impact Publishers, 1976), pp. 51–72.

[43]Kochman, *Black and White Styles in Conflict,* p. 97.

[44]Kochman, *Black and White Styles in Conflict,* p. 98.

[45]Kochman, *Black and White Styles in Conflict,* p. 18.

46Kochman, *Black and White Styles in Conflict,* p. 24.

47Kochman, *Black and White Styles in Conflict,* pp. 21–22.

48Kochman, *Black and White Styles in Conflict,* p. 28.

49Kochman, *Black and White Styles in Conflict,* p. 28.

50Pennington, "Black-White Communication," p. 387.

51Henley, *Body Politics,* pp. 10–11. The original study was Carl O. Word, Mark P. Zanna, and Joel Cooper, "The Nonverbal Mediation of Self-fulfilling Prophecies in Interracial Interaction," *Journal of Experimental Social Psychology* 10 (1974), 10, 109–120.

52Frank Sotomayor, "A Box Full of Ethnic Labels," in George Ramos, Frank Sotomayor, and Noel Greenwood, eds., *Southern California's Latino Community: A Series of Articles Reprinted from the Los Angeles Times* (Los Angeles: *Los Angeles Times,* 1983), pp. 27–28.

53Nobleza C. Asuncion-Lande, "Chicano Communication: Rhetoric of Identity and Integration," *Association for Communication Administration Bulletin* (April 1976), p. 31.

54John Condon, " '. . . So Near the United States': Notes on Communication Between Mexicans and North Americans," in Larry A. Samovar and Richard E. Porter, eds., *Intercultural Communication: A Reader,* 4th ed. (Belmont, Calif.: Wadsworth, 1985), pp. 86–91.

55Condon, "So Near the United States," p. 88.

56Condon, "So Near the United States," p. 90.

57K.S. Sitaram and Roy T. Cogdell, *Foundations of Intercultural Communication* (Columbus: Ohio: Charles E. Merrill, 1976), pp. 118–124.

58William B. Gudykunst and Young Yun Kim, *Communicating with Strangers: An Approach to Intercultural Communication* (Reading, Mass.: Addison-Wesley, 1984), p. 193.

# CHAPTER SEVEN

# Technology and Interviewing

## The Implications of Telephone and Broadcast Talk

Police beat reporter Edna Buchanan knows the value of the telephone. While covering a murder at a Miami restaurant, Buchanan tried to follow a homicide detective inside, but she found her way blocked by a yellow crime-scene rope. As the detective entered the building, the phone rang. It was for him. The caller? Edna Buchanan, using a pay phone on the sidewalk. "I know this sounds foolish," says Buchanan, "but often people uncomfortable at being seen talking to a reporter will speak more freely over the telephone."[1] Her theory isn't foolish; it makes good sense.

Most reporters would attest to the importance of the telephone in news coverage. But the telephone, like other instruments of technology used by journalists, both aids *and* complicates human communication. Consider how television news choreographs satellite links to connect reporters and newsmakers electronically wherever they happen to be—a bar in Topeka or a government suite in Cape Town. Although face-to-face communication is usually preferred by reporters, technology has vastly expanded the range and extent of news coverage. The term "global village," popularized by Marshall McLuhan, certainly applies to modern journalism.[2]

If used improperly or naively, however, technology may depersonalize and diminish human communication. For example, print reporters, already isolated from certain segments of society, risk increased isolation if they rely excessively on the telephone. Instead of being an ally, the telephone becomes a crutch—an excuse to remain inside the protective cocoon of the newsroom. For television reporters, preoccupation with cameras, microphones and lights may lead them to function more like technicians than journalists, worried primarily about the audiovisual quality of an interview rather than its substance.

As you'll see, the hardware of mass communications forces journalists into a series of compromises with implications and consequences for interviews.

## TELEPHONE TALK

Our world is now webbed with lines of communication that potentially can link any two people, any two places. Certainly almost everyone a journalist would need to interview is immediately accessible by telephone, and this accessibility presents both vast opportunities and barely noticed challenges. The advantages of using the telephone to discover information are obvious enough, but reporters should be aware of the trade-offs.

Telephone talk falls between the personal involvement of face-to-face encounter and the relatively impersonal psychological distance of written documents. Exceptions come to mind, of course—intimate letters from loved ones aren't experienced as "distant," and complaining about your defective lawnmower in front of the department store manager isn't likely to feel informal, personal or "close." In general, though, communicators who seek a closer bond with others, who want to understand each other better, will attempt to arrange their direct presence. Except for specific strategic purposes, a phone call is a compromise of communication, while a letter (or questionnaire, document or memo) is an even greater one.

Reporters, however, often must conduct business by telephone. A study of British correspondents found that a reporter's day consisted of between 15 and 45 calls, with more calls being placed by the reporters than received. One reporter estimated daily telephone use as "15–20 [calls] made; 10 received. This is wild guessing. Sometimes there are so many calls that the left ear becomes positively painful. On other days the phone hardly rings."[3]

### Advantages of the Telephone

For better or for worse, the telephone is an indispensible tool for journalists. Four advantages are most obvious:

❏ Financial. Frequently, the telephone is the only realistic way to contact an interviewee from another city or country. Your employer will not fly you long distances for a single conversation, but many news organizations and corporations have WATS lines and sophisticated phone systems.

❏ Convenience. A journalist can explore many facets of the same story without ever leaving his or her desk. Facts may be discovered, reactions generated, contacts and relationships maintained and all in a matter of minutes. The phone is perfectly suited for the short informational interview, such as the verification by one official of another's account or the last-minute detail-checking so crucial to accurate news stories.

❏ Immediacy. The telephone facilitates the rapid dissemination of news. Fast-breaking stories—and the people who fuel them—won't necessarily linger for the reporter who wants to be on the scene. Think about making the necessary travel plans, then think about dialing. Many interviews depend so much on proper timing that to forego the phone means missing the story.

❏ Reliability. When your prime criterion is information, and your purpose is to survey and collect data on a specific issue, then the phone call can be as reliable as face-to-face interviewing. Communication authorities Charles Stewart and William Cash summarize the results of a number of studies that compare opinion polling by telephone with face-to-face interviewing:

  • The quality of data gained on complex attitudinal and knowledge items is the same with both interviewing methods.

  • The quality of data on personal items is about the same, with some respondents preferring the anonymity of the telephone.

  • Respondents are somewhat more likely to give socially acceptable answers in face-to-face interviews.

  • The interviewee rate of refusal to take part in or to complete interviews running 45 minutes or longer is about the same with either method.

  • Interviewees in certain neighborhoods prefer telephone interviews because they do not want to open their doors to strangers.

  • Telephone interviews remove dress, appearance and nonverbal communications as potential biasing factors.

- Interviewer preference for telephone and face-to-face interviews is nearly the same.[4]

Obviously, in many survey or basic information-seeking situations, the journalist is justified in pursuing stories by telephone; the results are comparable to what would be achieved by face-to-face talk.

## Disadvantages of the Telephone

Notice that Stewart and Cash specify the *survey* interview when discussing these points of comparability. Will most journalistic interviews fit this description? According to Stewart and Cash, "If 'precision' describes the survey interview, 'adaptability' describes the journalistic interview."[5] But the telephone is in some ways an ill-suited medium for communication that calls for adaptability. Telephone interviews are notable, too, for what they sacrifice.

These disadvantages need to be considered carefully by journalists before they begin to make telephone interviews habitual:

**A Diminished Sense of "Reality."** Perhaps the most subtle but pervasive disadvantage is that modern technological culture has further shifted our trust from what we hear to what we see—and the telephone's extension of our communication capabilities across distance sacrifices the believable visual connection between people. "In our society," writes Edmund Carpenter and Marshall McLuhan, " . . . to be real, a thing must be visible, and preferably constant. We trust the eye, not the ear. Not since Aristotle assured his *readers* that the sense of sight was 'above all others' the one to be trusted, have we accorded to sound a primary role."[6] This diminished credibility of aural communication may seem intangible and slight at first, but in the context of other disadvantages, it is extremely powerful.

The telephone diminishes reality in one other way. Reporters who can "work the phones" are admired in most newsrooms. But the telephone is a tempting excuse to stay in the office and avoid direct contact with people. Even exceptionally skillful telephone users need frequent excursions into the reality of different worlds.

**Fewer Nonverbal Cues.** As earlier chapters stress, it is important that the interviewer perceive bodily and context cues as indicators of a person's mood, intent, meaning and personality. Interpretation of such non-verbal messages becomes just as crucial as interpreting the words, since they are often truer indications of a person's disposition. Remember that between 65 percent and 93 percent of the meaning generated in social situations comes from non-verbal messages, and that many of those messages are visual ones. Facial expression, posture, dress, gesture, object manipulation and choices of decor are only a few obvious examples. Much of your ability to detect or suspect deception is based upon facial expression and body language. Your interviewee may be kidding you by "saying it with a wink," but you can't hear the wink. Your interviewee can attempt irony or sarcasm by manipulating tone of voice, but without the facial indicators to verify the intent, perhaps you're lost. When an interviewer is cut off from such cues, he or she is much more likely to miss the essence of a person, and more likely also to misinterpret crucial points. This could be an expensive price to pay for convenience.

**Less Interviewer Control.** The prospective telephone interviewer sacrifices a significant degree of control over interview access. If you arrive at the office of the police chief, it's often obvious if he or she is "in." Your request for time may not be granted, but in most cases, waiting will pay dividends. Phone calls are much more easily deflected. The person you're calling may have trained a secretary to "filter the calls for those which the person truly cares about, suggest times to call back that would be more convenient, extend promises (sometimes false) that the call will be returned, and simply lie about the presence of the person."[7] The resulting frustration unfortunately sometimes leads to a kind of journalistic ingenuity that could border on, or cross over to, unethical behavior. Reporters have been known to exaggerate the necessity of the conversation, lie about who they are and misrepresent their purpose just in order to be connected.

Phone interviews also give the journalist less control over the length, depth and quality of the interview. If you do get through, the person may be "called away" on a (spurious) "emergency that needs immediate attention." Since you have no way to check on this, phone interviewers must accede to such interruptions. (Be sure to arrange an alternate time for the talk, though, before you hang up.) Aside from this ploy, phone respondents can easily end a conversation with, "Well, I have to get going now. Hope you have enough for your story . . . thanks . . . goodbye." On the phone, tough questions or unpleasant topics are much more likely—compared to an in-person encounter—to result in an abruptly ended interview.

**Less Disclosure.** Interview topics are likely to be more superficial on the phone, too; people are less likely to engage in self-disclosure when their talk is mediated by a telephone. Researcher Edward Dickson refers to the "severely truncated self" presented in telephone talk, and the high degree of control most people have learned to exercise over their "aural images."[8] There is even some evidence, though dated, to indicate that telephone communicators use a very restricted vocabulary, with inordinate emphasis on words like "I" and "me."[9]

Another factor complicating the interviewee's willingness to disclose over the phone is the common occurrence of third-party bystanders in the presence of the called party. As an interviewer over the phone, you are unaware of who else is in the room with your interviewee, and what influence that person's presence has on your respondent's comments. Think of the typical topics of journalistic interviews—inquiries about opinions and criticisms, for example—and imagine yourself in the other person's situation. Imagine calling your friend, an executive for the power company, to ask about an unpopular rate-increase proposal, not knowing that your friend's boss is sitting across the desk. Under those circumstances, you are sure to receive only cautiously worded and safe answers to your questions.

Further, you are at the mercy of the person you've called even to disclose *whether* someone else is listening. Sociologist Erving Goffman's analysis of the interpersonal dynamics of this phenomenon should be sobering to the telephone interviewer.[10] When there is a bystander, your call likely interrupted an ongoing conversation; in this case, the called party "may feel a special need to deprecate the telephone encounter in favor of the immediate one."[11] A form of "collusion" between the called person and the bystander is what Goffman predicts—and it might manifest itself in "gestures of impatience, derogation, and exasperation" unknown to you.[12] Goffman goes on to explore the dilemmas faced by the called party, such as how to maintain a natural conversation on the phone without excluding or affronting the person who is sitting a few feet away. Managing these dilemmas can require "a tortuous kind of self-control" and a "close discipline. . . . Yet given the situation and the fact that the manner of conducting talk leaks information about relationships, this precarious line is structurally encouraged and often managed."[13] In practical language: You're likely to get a somewhat phony interview.

**Fewer Details.** When interviewing by phone, reporting essentially is one dimensional—communication without visual, sensual or symbolic contexts. Of course, color and backdrop scenes can be elicited by phone. Working from your downtown office you might call a neighboring community—one you've never visited—and ask, "Sheriff, what's the terrain like where you're searching for the missing child?" Still, there's no substitute for being at the scene and putting your senses to work. You may, for example, have a cordial and productive telephone conversation with the new principal of the high school, but you can't see that she's speaking to you from her desk in the main corridor of the school. In person, you'd recognize the symbolic and strategic implications of where she does business, and you'd explore those implications.

*Some guidelines.* When the need to use the telephone outweighs the disadvantages, you might want to follow these guidelines for telephone talk:

❑ Never schedule an important interview on the phone just because it is convenient to do so. The "necessity" criterion should be substituted for the "convenience" criterion.

❑ If possible, arrange ahead for the uninterrupted time of your respondent. This might involve a pre-interview call to the person or his or her secretary.

❑ Give the respondent a realistic assessment of the projected length of the interview, and be prepared to hold to that estimate. If the person chooses to be expansive or loquacious, follow that lead, but it's counterproductive to try to force a telephone respondent to prolong the interview.

❑ Identify yourself, discuss briefly why you're requesting the interview and inquire courteously about the other's willingness and ability to talk. If you can use the person's name periodically during the interview, you'll probably increase his or her willingness to listen and talk openly. Two caveats: (1) verify the pronunciation *before* you call, if possible; and (2) do not use overfamiliar names such as first names or nicknames unless you're invited to or you already know the person on that basis.

❑ Prepare your notes carefully beforehand, so the phone call isn't prolonged, and so that you'll be perceived as efficient. Rambling and failing to come to a point irritate phone interviewees perhaps more than in-person interviewees.

❏ Avoid other tasks (grocery lists, flirting, rearranging your desk, checking a ball score) while on the phone. Focus your full attention on the interviewee's words and implications.

❏ Speak distinctly, with a minimum of slang or overpersonal references. People usually expect (and offer) less "small talk" over the phone.

❏ Don't interrupt or talk over the respondent's comments. Though interruption is common in daily interpersonal communication, many of the cues to signal its appropriateness are visual ones— and they aren't available to you.

❏ If you must remind the interviewee that he or she has not answered the questions you asked, do so in an even, polite voice. There is rarely a need to scold, and even a little sarcasm risks becoming intensified by the medium. A simple repetition or close paraphrase of the question will suffice.

❏ Be prepared to paraphrase the other's statements to ensure you've understood them accurately. If you pause to write down quotes or take notes, you might explain any ensuing silences by referring to your concern for accuracy. ("Excuse me; just give me a moment to write down what you just said.")

❏ When appropriate, seek out descriptive details to bring life to your story. Covering a plane crash by phone, you might ask, "Could you describe the weather conditions?" Think of what you might be looking for if you could be at the scene.

❏ At the conclusion of the interview, you might want to offer to summarize your notes for your interviewee to demonstrate how carefully you've listened. Such assurances are especially important in this restricted-channel context. There's no visual evidence to assure the interviewee that you've been attentive. Finally, be sure to express your appreciation for the time and effort the respondent expended, and indicate what follow-up—if any—can be expected.

## Telephone Self-analysis

If you want to polish your telephone style, ask friends who frequently speak with you on the phone to help you with some self-analysis. Become politely persistent if they merely tell you how wonderful and effective you are. You need to request their honest feedback on some basic issues of telephone speech:

❑ Do you broadcast unintentional "mood" messages, such as tension, annoyance or impatience? In your own mind's ear, you sound normal, but those listening to you may interpret an emotional state from your tone. You may sound "peeved," "curt" or "preoccupied" to them. Testing how you sound with friends may reveal that your tone of voice is being misread.

❑ Is your volume appropriate? A soft voice makes others strain to hear; they'll rapidly tire of conversations with you. Or do you speak too loudly over the phone? According to communication consultant Abne Eisenberg, many people who exhibit this volume problem will overtly deny it. Yet "because the telephone normally amplifies the human voice, excessive volume becomes doubly objectionable," and others "are inclined to care less about what is being said."[14]

❑ Do you maintain an informal conversational tone, or does your telephone voice tend toward a more "stilted" or artificial sound? Eisenberg recommends that you shouldn't censor your normal gestures while talking on the phone—even though your interviewee can't see them, and you may feel slightly foolish using them. The result, surprisingly enough, simulates the normal free-flowing conversational style of face-to-face talk.[15]

❑ Are there times when you inadvertently cut people off, inserting your thoughts before they've finished, or ended conversations prematurely? In other words, do you help create enough comfortable "space" for the other person to contribute full thoughts? It's possible that, as with many of us, you are telephone-shy. Telephone shyness may cause you to avoid the phone if possible, or to foreshorten calls unnecessarily due to your own discomfort.

It should be obvious by now that the telephone interview is a difficult communication task. Reporters who accomplish it with style and efficiency will therefore earn the lasting respect of many interviewees. This respect translates into more than a mutually satisfying relationship; it increases the chances that additional information will be forthcoming. It increases the chances that the story you eventually write will be comprehensive and accurate. Simply bear in mind the advantages and necessities of telephone interviewing, account for the potential dangers, learn some basic rules of telephone talk and do a realistic self-assessment of your own telephone habits.

## BROADCAST TALK

Broadcast reporters labor under conditions that would unnerve the most hardened of print reporters. Broadcasters not only must *inform;* they also must *perform.* That's especially true of television reporters, who work in a hybrid field of news and show business. When the red light of the camera appears, they are on stage, and their "performance" may be watched by an audience that numbers in the millions—an audience, too, that undoubtedly includes the boss. Every blunder, stammer and blemish is noticeable. If the broadcast is live, there are no retakes and no opportunity to edit. Electronic journalists must be concerned even with the incidentals of broadcast interviewing—lighting, acoustics, backdrops and makeup, among others.

By its nature, broadcasting forces reporters to make compromises in communication. Television, in particular, is frustrating to reporters who care about interviewing. In television, visual images, especially those of dramatic action, are more valued than interviews, or "talking heads," as they say in the business. News crews are pressed into action at a moment's notice. They practice—not necessarily by choice—hit-and-run journalism: hit with a few questions to get usable sound bites and visuals, then scurry to the next assignment.

### Differences between Broadcast and Print Interviews

There is an array of differences between broadcast and print interviews. Here are a few examples:

❑ In broadcast interviewing, some norms of comunication are abandoned for the sake of expediency. Interruptions, for instance, are often necessary to maintain a lively pace. Loaded questions are more common and may be needed to add drama to a dry exchange. Elaboration and introspection are sacrified for slam-bang, punchy Q-and-A. Broadcast interviewing is far from ideal, and that bothers many electronic journalists. It pains them to employ strategies only to fit the limitations and demands of television or radio.

❑ Broadcast reporters sometimes feel like captives of their equipment. Television stations have invested so heavily in the latest electronic newsgathering hardware that the investments must be justified by live, remote broadcasts. Live reports put reporters and interviewees in a pressure cooker that strains communication. There's no opportunity to edit and little opportunity to probe, to confirm, to reconsider, to pause. Broadcast journalists who "go live" operate under the constant anxiety of making a mistake or not getting the whole story. What is said and done goes out over the air, whatever the quality.

☐ A print interviewer and interviewee can have the combined personality of a prune, and a decent story may still be salvaged if the journalist is a creative writer. A broadcast interviewer lives in fear of "dying" on the air. Television and radio interviewers work under the added strain of knowing that they must maintain a pace and excitement that will keep viewers or listeners involved. Once into a live interview, a broadcast reporter is, in a sense, at the interviewee's mercy. If stage fright or hostility turns an interviewee to stone, the problem is the reporter's, and, if it occurs on television, a problem for all to see.

☐ Broadcast reporters often face more difficulty obtaining interviews. There are, of course, people who are attracted to a camera like moths to fire; most people, though, have reason to be apprehensive. "Mike fright" and stage fright are common, especially if the broadcast is to be live. Fear of saying something stupid or embarrassing causes some people to shy away.

☐ Time is usually a greater enemy for broadcast reporters than for their print colleagues. Many broadcast interviews are done at fast-forward speed because the assignment desk says there's just 45 minutes to get to the next scheduled interview. Shortcuts are seductive. Then, too, broadcast reporters often must capture the essence of a story in two minutes or less. Experienced interviewees know this; unfortunately but unavoidably, they often come prepared with compact, prepackaged comments and quotations that bear little resemblance to natural communication.[16]

## Reminders for Broadcast Interviewers

Broadcast journalists need all the communication skills they can muster. Print reporters can stumble in an interview and still recover. But electronic reporters usually must get it right the first time. Planning and execution are more crucial for the broadcaster. Moreover, methods that will work well for print reporters won't always work for broadcasters.

**The Importance of Pre-broadcast Small Talk.** Broadcast reporters frequently deal with people who are petrified about being on the air. Small talk is especially important in establishing rapport and helping the interviewee feel comfortable. Small talk might focus on the studio or equpiment. ("Have you even been on camera before? There's really nothing to it. Let me show you around the set. . . .") Barbara Walters uses this approach: "Don't pay any attention to the lights and cameras and stage manager—just look at us and let the camera eavesdrop on our conversation."[17] Oprah Winfrey finds her "vulnerability" helps put people at ease. "I allow myself to be vulnerable," she explains. "It's not something I do consciously. But I am. . . . I'm vulnerable and people say, 'Poor thing. She has big hips, too.' "[18]

**Rehearsal.** Broadcast reporters should warm up interviewees if possible before going on the air. Topics for discussion may be previewed. The reporter might say, "I'd like to ask you about your role in passage of the anti-obscenity ordinance, and we might get into your objections to the sheriff's policies, too." Giving the interviewee an idea of what will be asked simply makes good sense. There's time to think about an intelligent answer so the interview's "flow" will improve. For broadcast interviewees, knowing what's to come helps reduce apprehension. But it's not fair to tell someone to anticipate one thing and then hit them with an entirely different question. The press secretary to a big-city mayor said that's like throwing a curve ball: "If they throw you a curve and you stammer to think of an answer, then that comes across on television like you're trying to hide something." Beyond the ethical questions such behavior raises, you may leave an inexperienced interviewee speechless. You're left with dead air.

Excessive rehearsal isn't advisable. If you go over questions too much and test answers, you remove spontaneity. Your rehearsal may end up being livelier than the actual on-air interview. Sounding rehearsed or "canned" is one of the cardinal sins of broadcasting. It's comparable to what happens when athletes over-prepare for a contest. When they fail to perform after the whistle sounds, commentators may say, "They left their game on the practice field."

**Pre-screening.** A broadcast reporter who fails to ensure that an interviewee is appropriate for the topic is asking for trouble. It doesn't matter if the interviewee is articulate and poised on camera; he or she still has to have something to say. On the night comic John

Belushi died in 1982, "Nightline" producers were having trouble lining up someone to comment. At the last minute, host Ted Koppel was told Milton Berle was standing by in Los Angeles. Koppel put Berle on the air and asked, "Tell me about your relationship with John Belushi." Berle replied, "Well, I didn't really know him."[19] That was a painful slip that rarely occurs on "Nightline." In most cases, a few elementary questions will determine whether you have a suitable interviewee or someone who will bomb.

**Questions.** Preparation, of course, is important in all interviews. Reporters ought to develop and refine questions carefully. But you don't want a script. Some broadcast reporters compromise by preparing questions that are deliberately simple: easy to ask, to understand and to answer. Their creativity comes in the follow-up questions. Veteran reporters like Sam Donaldson recommend asking questions to which you can anticipate answers. He suggests asking a question that suggests a response.[20] That way there are fewer surprises, and the reporter can more effectively control the results. Not all electronic journalists prefer that approach. Oprah Winfrey, for example, says: "How can I ask a question if I already know the answer? I'd look like I'm faking it."[21] Nevertheless, some electronic journalists don't feel secure enough to venture into unexplored territory in a live broadcast.

Working with a list of questions is recommended—but only to provide you with a backstop in case you draw a blank on what to ask next. Relying on advance questions is comforting, but it discourages the kind of free-flowing conversation that is often so rewarding.

In live broadcasts, reporters must be more careful in framing and delivering questions. A convoluted question delivered with a sprinkling of "uhmmms" and "errrs" will grate on the ears of interviewee and audience alike. But taped interviews lessen the pressure for broadcast reporters to pose flawless questions. You can always edit your question out of the tape or use the script as transition to the interviewee's answer.

Potent questions invite potent answers. That translates to dramatic television or radio, which is desirable. Be aware, though, that challenging questions, particularly early in an interview, may be received by some personalities like an unexpected punch to the jaw. Instead of stimulating the interviewee, you stun, leaving him or her dazed and staggering. An on-air interview can't be stopped to administer smelling salts. With potent questions, you run all sorts of risks that the public will see, including a walkout by the interviewee.

("Are you as promiscuous as they say you are?" or "You admitted you 'bent the rules.' Why isn't it fair to call you a cheat?")

Here are some other tips about broadcast questioning:

❑ Don't be so concerned about getting a "sound bite"—a talking head or a voice on tape—that you fail to gain a full understanding of the person or event you're covering. As broadcaster Don Oliver says, "I've seen reporters sit down with somebody and say, 'Tell me about it,' and give someone 15 seconds, and say, 'That's all I need.' You need the sound bite, but you also need to know as much as the person can give you that is germane to the story."[22]

❑ Don't become excessively concerned about either the brevity or expansiveness of answers. Inexperienced reporters are right to worry about monosyllabic responses. They should avoid questions that invite "yes" or "no" answers. But even a "no"—when accompanied by tight focus on the interviewee's expressive face—can be a potent answer. When interviewees ramble, serving up an answer that is too long or awkward to use, be prepared to rephrase the question to elicit a shorter, clearer answer. In a live interview, though, it may be best for you to move on to another question.

❑ Don't ask questions that supply answers. The result may be either a prompted answer, which is likely to be invalid, or an answer that merely results in a "Yes, that's right" or, worse, a "No, that's wrong." In neither case does an interviewer look good.

**On-air Sacrifices.** On-air interviewing may hobble your full range of interviewing techniques. For example, the typical passive probes that help encourage responsiveness ("I see," "Tell me more," "Uh-huh," "Really?") may be distracting to the audience. If you're off camera, you can still use nonverbal encouragement, like nodding, smiling or raising an eyebrow. But it's better to augment nonverbal messages with verbal ones. Broadcasting also discourages use of silence as a probe. Silence can induce fuller explanations and comments, and it is encouraged in most interviews. Silence on the air, particularly in radio, is so pronounced, though, that many broadcast reporters feel compelled to say something—anything—to break the silence.

When the interview is conducted via long-distance—the reporter and interviewee in separate locations—some of the same shortcomings of telephonic communication arise. Usually the journalist is the only party in the interview who can maintain visual observation. The interviewee is denied nonverbal signals—like the interviewer's puzzled expression—that might influence his or her remarks. Additionally, the interviewer can't send nonverbal probes to the interviewee, such as a nod that says, "Go on; I'm with you." In some ways, the long-distance interview gives the interviewer a potential advantage that he or she might be tempted to exploit.

**Instant Clarification.** Taped or live, broadcast interviews frequently consist of the unedited, spontaneous words of the interviewee. While print reporters can paraphrase, compress and clean up rambling, unclear quotations, broadcasters often can't. Print reporters can re-examine notes or replay tapes to better understand what was said; broadcasters usually can't. For on-camera interviews, immediate clarity is crucial. Otherwise you risk confusing—or losing—your audience. Broadcast reporters listen with great concentration for statements that are inconsistent, contradictory, illogical, inaccurate or muddled. Interruptions and short summaries are justified to ensure that both you and your audience understand what was said. ("I believe the Russian occupation of Afghanistan occurred in 1979, not 1976," or, "So your three objections to the proposal are . . .") Rephrasing answers may also be necessary. ("In other words . . ." or "Let me be sure I understand you . . .")

**Control.** Throughout this text you've heard that an interview is not *yours*—the reporter's. It belongs to both parties. Remember, however, a qualification: Broadcast interviewers generally must exercise more control that reporters who interview for newspapers or magazines. It's another one of the communication compromises broadcasters must accept. Control is more important to meet deadlines and stay within time constraints. Unless you're taping an in-depth interview that can be edited extensively, you may be forced to stop long-winded types. Ted Koppel and Phil Donahue break in frequently to keep an interview on track and on time. They risk hurting feelings when they say, "Senator, I'm going to have to stop you there. We need to hear from our other guest." It might help to prepare interviewees for possible interruptions before going on the air. "I hate to do it, but I may have to cut some of your answers short if we start running out of time."

Another facet of maintaining control is to guard against a takeover by the interviewee. In a live program, especially, an interviewee might try to monopolize or take charge. Executives, politicians and celebrities are being trained at countertactics in interviewing. A book that claims to be a "A Survival Guide for Media Interviews" encourages interviewees to take the initiative—challenge questions, put questions to the interviewer and build bridges to shift from unpleasant topics.[23] Broadcast reporters should be ready to respond to such challenges.

**The Unexpected.** Broadcast interviewers must expect the unexpected. A technical glitch might test the creativity of an interviewer's explanation. Or an interviewee's behavior might take a reporter by surprise. A St. Louis television reporter, Jennifer Blome, was interviewing comedian Bob Goldthwait, who starred in the "Police Academy" movies. She expected some zaniness from Goldthwait, but not what happened:

> I asked him, "How do you get warmed up for your (comedy) performances?" He said, "By looking at girls' legs. Your slip is showing." Calmly, I said, "Yes, it's blue." We talked another minute or two and then I said, "Well, let's go to the clips from your next movie." He screams, "OK, the interview's going downhill. Go to the clips! No more talk! Go to the clips!" I still didn't panic. He asked me if I was going to see him that night at the (theater) and I said, "Sure." But he screamed. "She's lying! She doesn't respect me! She wouldn't be seen in the same auditorium with me!" That's when I lost it. I started laughing and the director had to take over.[24]

Sometimes technology conspires with the human factor to produce the unexpected. That happened to Washington-based NBC correspondent Andrea Mitchell as she tried via satellite hookup to interview several immigrants who were in a Detroit studio. One interviewee was Hu Na, a Chinese tennis player who had defected a year before. Mitchell's first question was, "How do you like it here in America, Hu Na?" "Please," Hu Na said. Mitchell repeated the question. "Please," Hu Na said again. Mitchell tried again and again to get a response. Finally she told her audience there was a technical difficulty. It was more than that—Hu Na couldn't speak English. The second interviewee, a refugee from El Salvador, attempted to hide her identity by wearing a broad-brimmed straw hat that she pulled over most of her face. Linda Ellerbee said it looked as if Mitchell were interviewing a hubcap. But Mitchell kept her cool. According to Ellerbee, "Andrea went ahead with the interview. . . .

She probably was too grateful it could speak English to care whether it was a hubcap, illegal alien or a cauliflower quiche."[25]

Resourceful broadcast journalists prepare for an interview by listing the eventualities the situation or person being interviewed might present. Is the interviewee noted for being a cutup or for icy answers? Are bystanders going to encircle you and your interviewee? Anticipation may help you remain poised.

Despite the shortcomings of broadcast communication, memorable moments occur when words, voices and images combine to tell a story. Charles Kuralt skillfully and sensitively merges vivid writing, careful, respectful listening, and complementary visuals to create vignettes of people and places. Barbara Walters, even in the static setting of a living room, enables viewers to eavesdrop on intimate conversations. David Frost recorded 16 hours of interviews with former President Richard Nixon and then condensed the videotape to four 90-minute programs. It was essentially a "talking heads" approach, but the questions and answers created a tension of their own that was accented by Nixon's body language. Here's one exchange as recounted by Frost, opening with his question:

> Frost asked, ". . . [S]omeone has said—I wonder if you agree—that perhaps, you were the last American casualty of the Vietnam War?"
> Nixon's face suddenly became a mask of pain, as if somewhere deep inside himself an old wound had been reopened. He paused. He drew a deep breath. His lips tightened. And then he spoke. "A case could be made for that, yes," he began.[26]

Technology needn't debase communication. For each compromise there are corresponding benefits and invitations to foster communication. Kuralt, Walters and Frost understand that.

The electronic tools of reporting enable journalists to communicate far beyond the confines of newsroom or studio. Today's journalism is immediate and global, which, in itself, calls for journalists who are proficient communicators. Communication links, called "spacebridges," now permit a reporter in Moscow, Idaho, to interview people and public officials in Moscow, U.S.S.R. To cover news in what has become a global village, journalism needs reporters who can transcend barriers of nationality and culture to achieve understanding. Reporters who are technologically and communicatively sophisticated will capitalize on the advantages of their tools and know how to minimize the disadvantages.

Now that you have had the opportunity to examine, test and adopt various theories and techniques of communication, you are encouraged to apply what you've learned responsibly. Therefore, the final chapter focuses on ethics for interviews.

## Notes

[1] Edna Buchanan, *The Corpse Had a Familiar Face* (New York: Random House, 1987), p. 269.

[2] Marshall McLuhan, *Understanding Media* (New York: McGraw-Hill, 1964).

[3] Jeremy Turnstall, *Journalists at Work* (Beverly Hills, Calif.: Sage Publications, 1971), p. 152.

[4] Charles J. Stewart and William B. Cash Jr., *Interviewing: Principles and Practices,* 3rd ed. (Dubuque, Iowa: Wm. C. Brown, 1982), p. 120.

[5] Stewart and Cash, *Interviewing,* p. 137.

[6] Edmund Carpenter and Marshall McLuhan, "Acoustic Space," in Edmund Carpenter and Marshall McLuhan, eds., *Explorations in Communication* (Boston: Beacon Press, 1960), p. 65.

[7] Edward M. Dickson, "Human Response to Video Telephones," in Gary Gumpert and Robert Cathcart, eds., *Inter/Media: Interpersonal Communication in a Media World* (New York: Oxford University Press, 1979), p. 140.

[8] Dickson, "Human Response to Video Telephones," p. 141.

[9] Sidney H. Aronson, "The Sociology of the Telephone," in Gary Gumpert and Robert Cathcart, eds., *Inter/Media: Interpersonal Communication in a Media World,* 3rd ed. (New York: Oxford University Press, 1986), p. 307.

[10] Erving Goffman, *Relations in Public* (New York: Basic Books, 1971), pp. 220–222.

[11] Goffman, *Relations in Public,* p. 221.

[12] Goffman, *Relations in Public,* p. 221.

[13] Goffman, *Relations in Public,* p. 221.

[14] Abne M. Eisenberg, *Job Talk: Communicating Effectively on the Job* (New York: Macmillan, 1979), p. 56.

[15] Eisenberg, *Job Talk,* p. 57.

[16] See Mitchell Stephens and Eliot Frankel, "The counterpunch interview," *Columbia Journalism Review,* March-April 1983, pp. 38, 39.

[17] Barbara Walters, *How to Talk with Practically Anybody About Practically Anything* (Garden City, N.Y.: Doubleday, 1970), p. 132.

[18]Quoted in Robert Waldron, *Oprah* (New York: St. Martin's Press, 1987), p. 1.

[19]"America's Q&A Man," *Newsweek,* June 15, 1987, p. 53.

[20]Shirley Biagi, *Interviews That Work: A Practical Guide for Journalists* (Belmont, Calif.: Wadsworth, 1986), p. 110.

[21]Waldron, *Oprah,* p. 115.

[22]Shirley Biagi, *NewsTalk II: State-of-the-Art Conversations with Today's Broadcast Journalists* (Belmont, Calif.: Wadsworth, 1987), p. 205.

[23]See Jack Hilton and Mary Knoblauch, *On Television! A Survival Guide for Media Interviews* (New York: AMACOM, 1982).

[24]John J. Archibald, "No Ill Winds Blow for Jennifer Blome," *St. Louis Post-Dispatch,* Jan. 26, 1988, p. 7D.

[25]Linda Ellerbee, *"And So It Goes": Adventures in Televison* (New York: Berkley Books, 1987), pp. 225–227.

[26]David Frost, *"I Gave Them a Sword": Behind the Scenes of the Nixon Interviews* (New York: William Morrow, 1978), p. 142.

# CHAPTER EIGHT

# Interviewing Ethics

## Masquerades, Lies and Ambushes

**R**eporters are known to make jokes about ethics in journalism. "Journalism ethics?" a young editor said, followed by a wry smile. "That's like military intelligence, isn't it—a contradiction in terms?" Ethics is not a laughing matter, of course. When reporters joke about ethics, it's often done in a self-deprecating, self-conscious manner. Is there a low-grade guilt that many reporters carry from having their behavior and tactics questioned so frequently? If there is such guilt, it seems to require regular feeding. Colleagues will even turn on one another in a frenzy of soul-searching and public penance unheard of within other callings or professions.

Consider what happens when criticism of the press is especially intense, such as over the handling of the Gary Hart affair in 1987. A Miami newspaper had followed presidential candidate Hart and reported that model Donna Rice spent the night at Hart's townhouse. Columnist Steve Daley of the Chicago Tribune, for example, compared coverage of Hart's alleged womanizing to garbage collection. "The manner in which the Miami Herald pursued this story simply perpetuates the popular image of the press as a roving gang of thrillseekers."[1]

Why do journalists so eagerly condemn each other or voluntarily lock themselves in a pillory? Most reporters, including those at the Miami Herald who broke the Hart story, are very concerned about ethical behavior, provided they can determine what's ethical. There seldom are clear-cut answers to the serious questions reporters face. Journalism's codes of ethics offer minimal help; they usually speak in general terms of honesty, objectivity and fair play. For example, the code of the Society of Professional Journalists, Sigma Delta Chi, says: "Journalists at all times will show respect for the dignity, privacy, rights and well-being of people encountered in the course of gathering and presenting the news."[2] This is admirable, but such criteria are seldom easy to translate into practice. The codes tend not to provide specific ethical guidelines for *interviewing*. Consider the many moral issues an interview presents. Here is such a situation:

> A small-town merchant is found dead in the basement of his home, a revolver in his hand. A reporter for the local paper notices the merchant's obituary because a few months earlier, the man's convenience store burned down in a fire the insurance company called arson. At the time of his death, the man was suing the insurance company to collect on his policy. The day after the shooting, the reporter, without identifying herself, calls and asks to speak to the disoriented widow, who, mistaking the reporter for an acquaintance, at first speaks freely about her husband's problems and the circumstances of his death. As the questions move into the sensitive area of suicide, the widow becomes more alert, realizing the caller's voice is not familiar. "Who is this?" she asks. Only then does the caller say she's a reporter. "I didn't know that," the widow says. "I really don't want to talk to the press about this." The conversation ends, but the next day the reporter's story includes many of the widow's comments.

The widow feels victimized. The reporter believes she did her job well, and many of her peers concur. Ethical questions nonetheless cloud her work. First, was it right to press someone obviously left vulnerable by grief? Why not talk to relatives instead? Was the reporter wrong not to identify herself immediately? Were questions about suicide proper? And once the widow realized she was talking to a reporter and requested that her comments not be used, was it right to include them in the story? Does the impact or importance of a story ever work to justify ethical compromise? Although there are no easy or even "right" answers to these questions, reporters must weigh the moral implications and consequences of their behavior and methods. They can't, and shouldn't, shrug off ethical questions in the name of high-sounding principles like "truthseeking." Beneficial ends rarely justify dubious means. On the other hand, if journalists agonize over every step they take in pursuing a story, they risk becoming Caspar Milquetoasts—timid, apprehensive and indecisive.

Ralph L. Lowenstein and John C. Merrill identify two principal ethical orientations of journalists—people-oriented types and event-oriented types. The people-oriented journalist considers the impact of his (or her) actions on people, including the impact on himself: "He is either an egoist or an altruist—and sometimes a little of both." The event-oriented journalist, they say, "stands as aloof as possible, ever the 'neutralist,' telling the story and letting the proverbial chips 'fall where they may.' "[3] Although either type of reporter is capable of being ethical, the hard-boiled, fact-seeking neutralist may be less sensitive to the consequences of his or her choices.

In this chapter you'll explore a thicket of problems that typically complicate the work of reporters. We'll focus on the behavior of reporters as they *communicate* with others, an area that is relatively underemphasized in most mass media ethics books. After a discussion of how important ethical choices are for the sensitive journalist, we'll ask hard questions about such specific tactics as lying, misrepresentation of role and hiding intentions. We then will examine the ethical dimensions of questions themselves.

## ETHICS AND NEWSROOM DECISIONS

Some of the principles of "good" journalism are bound to put journalists into ethical dilemmas. Reporters are expected to seek the truth wherever it is to be found, even if that means asking a presidential candidate if he's always been faithful to his wife. But the public might also expect them to show compassion and honor the golden rule. Quite naturally, reporters often are confused about what road to follow. A Newsweek story analyzing coverage of the sexual conduct of public officials put the problem this way: "If [reporters] don't investigate, they are guilty of a kind of Potomac paternalism—we in the Capital are privy to information that the rest of puritanical America cannot be trusted with. If they do go out and dig, they risk feeling like they work for The National Enquirer."[4]

Damned-if-you-do-and-damned-if-you-don't schizophrenia is not limited to the Washington press corps. All reporters are subject to its grip. Still, confused or not, reporters must make choices daily, often quickly. Frequently, choices are based on "gut reactions" or what passes for "newsroom precedent." Even if a deadline is fast approaching, a commitment to ethics requires that newsroom decisions emanate from a deliberative process.

A five-step approach, adapted from the work of Philip E. Wheel-wright, won't necessarily make the journalist's life any easier, but it would help ensure that decision-making is thoughtful and reflective.[5]

STEP 1: Identify and examine all alternatives or options.

STEP 2: Identify and clarify the consequences of the proposed behavior.

STEP 3: Project yourself into the predicted situation and identify yourself with the points of view of those whom your proposed behavior will most seriously affect.

STEP 4: Determine and weigh the values involved.

STEP 5: Arrive at a decision.

You can see how this process works through a hypothetical example:

> Tom Brown, a youthful-looking reporter, is enlisted by his newspaper to pose as a student to investigate rumors of drug abuse and gang violence at the local high school. The plan is for him to cultivate friendships with students, so they will accept him as a peer and let him into their world. The paper intends to publish what he hears and sees.

STEP 1: Let's assume the proposed story is socially important; it should be told. The options, then, involve *how* to report it. In this case, the options are simple: Brown will either go undercover or not. By pretending to be a student, he probably will get a more unvarnished view of high school life. If Brown works out in the open, asking questions and observing in the conventional manner, will he get a comprehensive picture? Perhaps, but Brown and his editors believe that going undercover will be the more fruitful strategy.

STEP 2: What are the consequences, first, in terms of the young reporter? If he poses as a student and "infiltrates" the school will he have to break any laws? Probably not, unless he falsifies records to enroll in the school. Will he be at risk as he searches out drug users, dealers and gang members? Yes, he could get hurt, particularly if he pursues the story off campus. Will the reporter have to accept a "joint" or buy alcohol for underage students in order to be accepted? Given the focus of his investigation, these are obvious possibilities.

Larger ethical consequences can be seen in how the reporter treats those with whom he establishes relationships. For one thing, he may be forced to lie, and certainly deceive, to hide his identity.

The reporter may have to take advantage of those he meets, violating, along the way, trusts and new friendships. Moreover, many of those he "uses" to get the story will be susceptible victims of his deceit—malleable, impressionable and unsuspecting. Later, after the story is published, will the reporter be able to resist police and judicial pressure for him to "snitch" on students? Even more compelling, should he voluntarily identify those he believes are lawbreakers or those who may need drug-abuse counseling?

On the positive side of the ledger, what he learns and reports may, ultimately, dramatize ills at the school and result in significant reform. Drug dealers and gangs may be driven out of the school and lives saved.

Obviously, the situation becomes murkier as the various consequences are identified and weighed. And while our scenario certainly doesn't exhaust the possibilities, it should demonstrate the complexity of making newsroom decisions.

STEP 3: The saying suggests, "Walk a mile in my shoes." The point of Step 3 is to imagine yourself in the other person's place before you do something that might affect him or her. In our hypothetical case, the editors should project themselves into the reporter's "shoes," and the reporter should identify with the students he will encounter.

The editors, eager to get a story with bite, might be less enthusiastic if they see themselves as the reporter, trying to act "cool" and ask questions surrounded by tough-talking gang members in a smoke-filled restroom.

The reporter might ask himself how he would feel if he learned in the local paper that someone he trusted and confided in had lied about and manipulated their friendship. What if that "friend" got you or others in trouble? Suppose the stories about drugs and violence at the school kill a needed bond issue or cost several students a chance to get college scholarships? How would such people perceive the so-called "higher purposes" that motivated the story? Walking in the other person's shoes might dampen the reporter's initial excitement and lessen his sureness that masquerading is the "right" thing to do.

STEP 4: What values are at stake? An inventory of values is likely to begin with one of the rallying calls of journalism—the public's right to know. The public would seem to have a clear, overriding interest in knowing about what's happening in the community high school. The press, in telling the story, would be fulfilling a corollary value—that of ensuring a well-informed citizenry. But not all the values involved in this case are compatible. There is, for example, the value of journalistic honesty and fair play. In serving the value of informing the public, are you violating a value that says you shouldn't deceive and exploit people? Furthermore, if a news organization uses subterfuge to gain information, no matter how worthy the cause, will it, in the long run, undermine yet another value—trust between the press and its audiences?

STEP 5: Ultimately a decision must be made. Will it be "right"? That determination may have to wait until Judgment Day. But if each of the preceding steps is scrupulously followed, the decision should be one the journalist can defend in good conscience, which is about the best you can expect.

## ETHICAL CONDUCT IN TALKING TO PEOPLE

Let's not kid ourselves. Reporters sometimes resort to intimidation, lies or false pretenses to accomplish their goals. Unfortunately, the feelings and rights of others may be sacrificed in the pursuit of a story. When is, and isn't, this justified? Reporters cannot be truly ethical without considering the consequences of their actions. Here are some particulars:

### Lying

Reporters rarely *publish* or *broadcast* falsehoods; those who do are almost always exposed and punished. Yet journalists will lie on occasion to gain information. Carl Bernstein and Bob Woodward, for example, tell of using falsehoods to confirm details in their Watergate investigation.[6] Journalists—both before and since Watergate—have used similar tactics: "Alderman Burns, we have learned from another source that you were responsible for getting the police to drop the DWI charges against Senator Smith." Actually, there is no other source, but the reporter lies in the hope of getting Burns to either admit his involvement or implicate someone else.

In our society lying usually is considered wrong unless it is done to protect lives or spare people from harm. But what about a reporter who lies to uncover a story of great consequence? Were Woodward and Bernstein right to lie? Perhaps, but according to author Sissela Bok, no one at the Washington Post stopped to ask if there was a problem in using deceptive means. "There was no reported effort to search for honest alternatives, or to distinguish among different forms and degrees of deception, or to consider whether some circumstances warranted it more that others," she says. "The absence of such reflection may well result in countless young reporters unthinkingly adopting some of these methods. And those who used them successfully at a time of national crisis may do so again with lesser provocation."[7] The closest we can come to an answer about lying is a not really an answer. It is a statement: Reporters who lie should be thoroughly convinced that their behavior is morally defensible, not just convenient or pragmatic. Lying is very hard to justify, and it should be the rarest of journalistic practices. Otherwise the public will rightly wonder, "If they lied to get the story, how do we know the story itself isn't a lie?" and "How can journalists be so upset at governmental deceit when they lie all the time, too?" Will people speak freely to members of an institution noted for its lying?

## Hiding Identity

Masquerades, disguises and impersonations represent another form of falsehood. Such behavior is, however, a significant part of journalism, especially investigative reporting. A Los Angeles Herald-Examiner reporter, for example, pretended to be an illegal alien to report on sweatshops and won two national awards for her efforts.[8] Two National Enquirer reporters dressed as priests at singer Bing Crosby's funeral to comfort the widow and get a scoop, each unaware his colleague had the same plan.[9] The reporters who posed as clergy won no awards. Not surprisingly, journalists are split into two camps on use of false pretenses to get a story, provided they can decide to which camp they belong. Admittedly, it would be difficult to find reporters who condone the tactics of the National Enquirer's bogus priests—but not impossible. And even the most ethically strict journalists might be hard pressed to find fault in going undercover to expose a sweatshop. No matter where you stand on the issue, however, ethical implications are inescapable.

From the perspective of *communication* ethics, the most serious problem of deception is that it represents interpersonal exploitation. Relationships develop from trust and presumed mutual understanding. When a reporter pretends to be a friend, confidant or colleague, at least one person is being dishonest in the relationship. The relationship, in fact, is a lie, built on lies and maintained by lies. People seldom share feelings and intimacies with strangers, much less with potential adversaries. They open up to those they trust. Out of trust, people speak more candidly, sometimes sharing thoughts they'd never dare to reveal publicly. Reporters who violate that trust may rationalize that their objectives are honorable, but the victims of their deceit will correctly feel exploited. What do you think?

## Withholding Identity

Ethical problems also commonly arise when a reporter merely withholds his or her identity. A reporter is assigned to do a color piece on a charismatic revival. Before and after the services, she mingles, striking up conversations but never pretending to be a true believer. Although she's not masquerading or lying, she still is being less than honest as she *collects* quotes from people who aren't aware they're *giving* them. More seriously, she is limiting somewhat the communicative freedom of choice of others—the freedom of choosing whom to talk to and to what extent.

The problem is compounded in this situation: A reporter approaches a man waiting in the hotel lounge, knowing the man is in town, unannounced, to be interviewed for the city manager's job. Without identifying herself, the reporter initiates a conversation, casually asking questions ("What brings you to town?" "What do you think of this city?") that she hopes will reveal something about the man's prospects for being hired and his attitudes about the community. It's a case of "I know who you are, but you don't know who I am." Unaware the engaging woman who bought him a drink is a reporter, the news target, perhaps weary from a long day of meetings, probably will communicate with defenses down.

You could argue that anyone who speaks freely to strangers obviously isn't too concerned about confidentiality. But there's a big difference between talking to someone you *assume* is another hotel guest and someone you *know* is a reporter. When roles are identified and understood, communication often occurs on another intellectual and emotional plateau. To be completely fair, reporters on assignment ought to identify themselves as soon as possible. Then each party communicates on more equal footing. Do you agree?

## Hiding Intentions

A related problem arises when reporters are either dishonest or deliberately ambiguous about their reasons for asking questions. People talk more freely when they believe there's no risk involved in communicating. Two invasion of privacy suits illustrate this point. In one case, an unwed teenage father talked to a reporter who, he thought, was doing a "survey." When his name and comments appeared in print, he felt deceived, and subsequently, sued.[10] In the other case, a pair of American youths living in caves on the island of Crete said they thought they were talking to a reporter who was doing a travel piece. They were upset—and also sued—when the story turned out to be about "nomadic," "disenchanted" and "aimless" Americans living abroad.[11] The courts ruled in favor of both media defendants, finding no convincing evidence that the reporters misled anyone. Nevertheless, whenever a reporter feigns innocence to camouflage ulterior motives, ethical complications are inevitable. Reporters might ask themselves this question: Will the person I'm talking to respond quite differently if my true purposes are known? If the answer is "yes" or even "probably," then fairness calls for candor on the reporter's part. Can you think of exceptions?

## Unintentional Advantage

Ethical problems are apparent when reporters intentionally use trickery in communication relationships. But there are also ethical subtleties, even in apparently routine stories, that reporters may overlook simply because they underestimate their ability to engage people in candid conversation, especially people who are naive about how the press operates. Herbert Gans identifies the two categories of news subjects as the "Knowns" and "Unknowns."[12] The Knowns—public officials and public figures—are experienced at relationships with reporters. It's a different game with the Unknowns, and reporters often hold an unfair advantage, if they want to capitalize on it.

The world of law enforcement presents one way of looking at the relationship between reporters and news subjects. The best detectives and the best reporters share a common talent—they know how to get people to talk. A major difference, however, between their methods is the "Miranda warning" that police must administer when interrogating criminal suspects. Anyone who has watched televised police drama knows the essence of the warning: You have the right to remain silent; what you say might be used to prosecute you. Its intent is to safeguard a suspect's constitutional right against self-incrimination. Reporters aren't usually trying to put people in jail when they ask questions, but they frequently get people to say things they never thought would appear in the newspaper. In a Quill magazine article entitled "Think twice before talking to a reporter," a Virginia editor-ombudsman suggests the press might need a Miranda warning of its own. The story he relates is typical: A reporter obtained the name of a burglary victim from police reports and called her for additional information. The victim talked openly to the reporter; no misrepresentation was involved. But when her name, address and comments were published, she was upset. "I had no idea that all of that was going to be printed. . . . It leaves me and my neighbors wide open for another theft." The editor sided with the woman, noting: "Most people have no experience dealing with reporters. They have not thought about the consequences of sharing sensitive information with representatives of the news media. They make an assumption—which is not always justified—that the friendly, polite person asking the questions has their own best interest at heart."[13]

The editor suggested that reporters might preface interviews with this statement:

> I'm a newspaper reporter. You do not have to answer my questions. If you choose to answer my questions, any information you share with me may be revealed to hundreds of thousands of strangers to use in ways you may not approve of and over which you have no control.[14]

It's not likely that news organizations or individual reporters will adopt a similar statement—certainly not one that is so direct. Editors, understandably, would fear it might give otherwise willing interviewees a reason to be reticent. Still, a warning statement of some sort has merit. If distrust of reporters spreads from situations like the one we just described, then reporters increasingly can expect to receive guarded, cryptic comments that will do little to enhance communication between them and people they interview. Reporters must recognize that some people don't understand the rules. And they must realize there are times when there's an ethical responsibility to be clear about what's "for publication" and what's not. Interestingly, some veteran police detectives have found that a gently delivered Miranda warning has encouraged, not discouraged, communication with suspects. Associated Press reporter Mike Feinsilber said he will sometimes tell an inexperienced news subject, "Don't tell me anything you don't want in the newspaper."[15] Reporters who show such concern for interviewees might find their concern returned in the form of more open, trusting communication.

Even people experienced at talking to the press are vulnerable at times. Consider this episode: A reporter from the Ann Arbor News quoted the earthy language used by the commissioner of the Michigan bar association to describe his feelings about an attorney accused of fraud and embezzlement. The commissioner complained when his words appeared in print. "I just don't think that's the kind of thing that should be quoted in a paper of general circulation," he said. "I guess I wasn't thinking [the reporter] was going to quote me verbatim."[16] Perhaps the man should have known better. Indeed, public officials and others used to reporters seldom drop their guard. As a city manager explained, "I'm careful of the words I use with reporters, or at least some of them. [One reporter], I can clown around with him a bit. He knows if he quotes me saying something like 'Ah, the hell with it,' and that was part of our casual conversation, I'll cut him off at the knees." A key is a common definition of "casual conversation." When people communicate, there usually are understood divisions between "personal" and "business" talk. The divisions, though, aren't *always* clear. It should be your responsibility to ensure that there are no misunderstandings.

That responsibility is greatest on a beat when dealing with people who are likely to see you in two roles—reporter and acquaintance. If you regularly trade jokes with the mayor, would it be fair to decide that his racist "humor" is worth reporting but his other jokes aren't? Under the guise of friendly conversation, isn't a kind of journalistic entrapment possible? In this situation, *your* sexist or racist jokes and comments might "set up" and elicit reactions—later quoted—that would never have occurred if not for your presence. David Shaw of the Los Angeles Times takes this precaution: "I don't use information I pick up in casual conversation unless I first go back to the person and say, 'Look, I'd like to use what you said this morning. Is that okay?' "[17]

## Exploiting Weaknesses

Ironically, the better you become at interpersonal communication, the easier it will be to lead people to unintended, hurtful revelations. Barbara Walters has that ability, although her interviewees say she rarely abuses it. Walters once interviewed actress Betty White of the television show "The Golden Girls" and touched a sensitive spot when she brought up the death of White's husband to cancer. "Barbara kept probing a little farther and a little farther without my realizing it," White said. "And I started to choke up. She stopped immediately—pulled back and went in another direction. And, bless her heart, she didn't air that part."[18] While people in pain sometimes find catharsis in conversation, not everyone wants to share feelings with a mass audience.

How do you deal with people who are in less than full control of their emotions and thoughts? In this category are people who are angered, grief-stricken, defeated, vulnerable or incapacitated in some way. They may willingly pour out feelings, but is it right to take advantage of what may be a moment of weakness? Like most ethical questions, this one presents no simple answers. An example, however, might help you decide how to handle such circumstances. One reporter interviewed a National Football League coach moments after a particularly galling defeat. The coach lashed out, blaming the owner for the team's misfortune. If published, the angry words, the reporter knew, could cost the coach his job. So the reporter decided to hold off on the story until the coach had left the stadium and gone home to his family. Then he called and asked the coach if he still stood by what he said. (He did.) The reporter, concerned about exploiting a man under great stress, put compassion ahead of an obvious exclusive—at least until he was sure the coach had had a chance to collect himself.

Exploitation occasionally may come close to journalistic blackmail. Judge the behavior of the reporter in this situation:

> A reporter is trying to confirm that the 14-year-old son of a state legislator is in custody as a rape suspect. Thwarted in his use of official contacts, the reporter calls a clerk he knows in the juvenile detention center, asking general questions about "how things are going." Gradually, the reporter starts asking specific questions, and the clerk begins to reveal details about the youth—information that state law prohibits the clerk from releasing. Suddenly aware of what's happening, the clerk says, "Gee, I've said more than I should have. Please don't use what I've said." The reporter, however, plays tough guy. "I thought you knew we were talking for the record. I've got to go with this unless . . ." The unnerved clerk blurts out, "I can get in real trouble over this." The reporter presses in: "Look, I don't want to see you get hurt. Just let me see the kid's file and I'll keep your name out of it."

Was this resourceful journalism or exploitation?

Any number of situations may require you to balance the importance of the story against the needs and rights of vulnerable interviewees. When someone implores, "Please don't quote me," or "I didn't mean to say that," what do you do? Try asking yourself some questions: How important is the quote to your interviewee? How important is the quote to your story? Can you get the information you need elsewhere? Is the quote worth the injury or embarrassment it might cause? Asking such questions may help you determine what's ethical.

## Pseudo Stories

Reporters are supposed to report the news, not create it. But occasionally they will cross the line by becoming both the catalyst and the conveyer of a "dispute." Here's how it might happen:

> Reporter Swift calls Mayor Jones, and asks the mayor's opinion about a political rival, Alderman Davis. "Mayor Jones, do you think Alderman Davis has the best interests of the city at heart by opposing your plans for a bond issue to finance a new football stadium?" The mayor, touchy about his pet project, picks up on the reporter's "best-interests-of-city" theme and calls Davis, among other things, an "anti-progress obstructionist." Swift then calls Alderman Davis and relates what the major has said. Swift intentionally agitates Davis, eliciting juicy quotes like, "I think the mayor's been hitting too many tackling dummies. He should do the smart thing and punt." Back at his word processor, Swift drafts a lead: "Like opposing linemen, Mayor Jerry Jones and Alderman Don Davis are butting helmets over the downtown stadium proposal. . . ."

Is this the birth of pseudo story? If a reporter helps escalate a difference of opinion into a public battle, is he being unethical by exploiting the mayor, the alderman and the readers of his newspaper? On the other hand, if the conflict is festering beneath the surface, shouldn't the reporter ask probing questions that might bring an important issue to the public's attention? It's another instance in which the reporter must let conscience be a guide. Usually, though, reporters should know when they are igniting a feud or conflict; they should sense when they've crossed the line from reporting to creating the news.

A variation is the "reaction" story. Steve Daley of the Chicago Tribune uses the case of Jimmy "The Greek" Snyder to describe this practice. Snyder, then a CBS Sports analyst, made several remarks, later criticized as racist, about the athletic prowess of blacks. Snyder's comments came during an impromptu interview with a radio reporter, conducted while Snyder was having lunch. (Was Snyder drinking martinis, and would that fact complicate the ethics of this case?) Within hours, the interview became a major story and Snyder lost his job. It was the reaction story at its finest—or worst. As Daley noted: "The inflammatory statement is followed by a relentless quest for reaction: This is what the man said, what do you think, what are you going to do about it? The instantaneous reaction from those presumably offended is then carrried back to the principal character, and his or her employer, and another set of reactions is demanded."[19] Is this another form of the pseudo story—a creation of insensitive, overambitious reporters?

## Communication "Arrangements"

There are four standard agreements between reporters and interviewees on the use of information obtained in an interview: (1) on the record (everything said may be used); (2) not for attribution (the interviewee's statements may be used, but they will not be attributed to the person); (3) on background (the interviewee's statements may be used with attribution to a general source, such as a "city hall official"); (4) off the record (nothing said may be published; the information is a means of briefing a reporter on a topic or situation). Misunderstandings sometimes occur between reporters and newsmakers over what is for publication and what isn't. To avoid the possibility of being accused of unethical behavior, reporters ought to be sure to confirm and clarify any ground rules for the interview. This is especially important when the substance of the interview is quite sensitive. Otherwise a interviewee might stop in the middle of a statement and say, "By the way, this is all off the record."

Reporters who enter into agreements that involve confidential pledges invite ethical headaches. Confidentiality takes various forms. In one case it might be an agreement to keep a conversation "off the record." In another instance it might involve a reporter's pledge to protect an informant's identity at all costs, even if that means spending time in jail for disobeying a court order to reveal the name. Confidential relationships should not be entered into cavalierly. A pledge of confidentiality to a drug dealer would be put to a severe test if the police convince you that he's been exploiting elementary school children. Some newsmakers hide behind confidentiality to leak damaging information about an opponent. In such instances, reporters risk becoming accomplices to character assassination. Anonymity, however, is occasionally warranted. It may be needed to save the job of a government "whistle-blower" or the life of an informant inside a mob-ridden union. Ultimately, though, all pledges of confidentiality restrict a reporter's ability to report the news fully. Moreover, they tend to lead to shortcuts and dangerous assumptions in reporting. As Renata Adler observes in her account of the libel suits of Gen. William C. Westmoreland and Gen. Ariel Sharon, reporters who rely on anonymous sources tend to embrace "the notion that what is obtained in secret is most surely true."[20] To be ethically and legally proper, corroborate any information obtained in confidence with at least two other persons or through records or documents.

## Hidden Tape Recorders

Reporters who use concealed tape recorders usually do so to catch the candid, unrehearsed words of a news subject. The hidden tape recorder may be used in combination with other forms of deception—disguises or undercover operations. Surreptitious taping is ethically questionable and legally risky, at least in some states. But even when the reporter is honest in every other way of communication with another person, the hidden tape recorder still poses ethical problems. The acknowledged presence of a tape recorder quite often results in a more formal type of communication. Knowing their words are being permanently recorded for possible public dissemination, most people will attempt to construct their comments carefully, conscious of being grammatical, reasonable and tasteful. Reporters who secretly tape record apparently assume that the "off-the-cuff" person is somehow more real than the "considered" person. But what people feel and say in unguarded or less-guarded moments is still only a part of who they "are." Shouldn't most people be given the opportunity to decide which side of them—the "off-the-cuff" vs. the "considered" person—is going to be captured on tape? Reporters cannot easily dismiss objections to a concealed recorder with rationalizations like "If she's got nothing to hide, why should she object to a tape recorder?" or "I don't what to cause 'mike fright.' "

Secret taping may be justified in some instances. Frederick Talbott, a former reporter and now an attorney, argues persuasively for taping on the sly. "It's the evildoers, the shysters, the liars and their brethren that cause me to grimace each time I hear or read codes or caveats prohibiting all secret or 'surreptitious' tape recording."[21] You might have to use a concealed tape recorder, he says, to expose a policeman who reportedly sexually harasses female motorists he stops at a speedtrap. Women stopped by the officer are afraid to make a report, so putting a "wire" on a female reporter *might* be the only way of catching him. Remember, though, that law enforcement officials usually must meet the preconditions of a judicial warrant to conduct electronic eavesdropping. Reporters often have only their own conscience as a restraint.

Some final words on ethical conduct come from two award-winning reporters. "I'm worried about exploiting [people]," says Rheta Grimsley Johnson. "And I think your obligation goes beyond identifying yourself. I think you have to look back at what you've written. Compassion is involved. It's hard to decide where good reporting and compassion can meet."[22] Then there is the introspection of Thomas Plate. "Suppose a candidate makes a buffoon of himself. My emotional reaction is contempt. But how valid is that reaction? Was I predisposed to feel contempt for him? Was he in a trying situation and did the best he could?"[23] Neither Johnson nor Plate offers answers, but their thoughts reflect a common concern about the power of the press to take advantage of people. It's a power all reporters should treat with appropriate respect.

## ARE ALL QUESTIONS CREATED EQUAL?

Journalists are paid to ask questions—at times exceedingly tough ones. Questions, in fact, are so much a part of reporting that it's natural for journalists to lose sight of serious ethical problems that can crop up at the question-asking stage.

### Biased Questions

Let's return briefly to a theme developed in Chapter 3—questions are personal creations that often reflect the reporter's view of the world. Before you ask questions of news subjects, you should direct several questions to yourself: How do I feel about the person I'm about to question? Dislike? Contempt? Pity? Respect? How do I feel about the subject of my reporting? Positively? Negatively? Honest answers may reveal a bias that should be confronted and suppressed. If the feelings are especially strong, you might even consider disqualifying yourself from doing the story. An example will illustrate this point.

You're the police beat reporter. The school superintendent is arrested for shoplifting after being caught taking a cassette tape from a music store. You know the man, having once covered the education beat, and you view him as arrogant, self-righteous and vindictive. You aren't quite gloating, but you see some poetic justice in his arrest. Six months earlier he suspended three basketball players for the season after they were caught stealing a case of beer from a liquor store. Although you don't say it aloud, you feel he deserves to be held accountable. So you go after the story aggressively, and the scope and substance of your questions tend to reflect your feelings. You ask the superintendent's previous employer about any past problems—drinking, stealing, immorality. The questions you put to the school board president are framed in negative terms: "Won't the school district's image be hurt by this incident?" or "Since the basketball players were punished for stealing, shouldn't the superintendent be held to the same standards?" Many of your questions are equally loaded and subjective.

Now let's re-examine this case from another perspective. If the school superintendent is a friend instead of an enemy, you would, perhaps, approach the story carefully and sensitively. You might even find a reason to withhold the arrest report, waiting to see what school authorities are going to do. And if you do report the arrest, your questions will probably seek the barest details—the facts of the arrest and little more. Obviously there are many ways to report an incident like this one. But before you do any reporting, deliberation and introspection are needed to safeguard against a double standard on your part.

## Questions about Rumors

There's a story attributed to Lyndon Johnson that demonstrates the harmful potential of questions about rumors. When Johnson was running for statewide office in Texas, he suggested to an aide that "perhaps" his opponent could be accused of being intimate with a farm animal. "You can't prove that kind of thing," the shocked aide replied. "I don't want to prove it," Johnson drawled. "I just want to hear him deny it."[24] Johnson understood human nature; he knew many people will assume that where there's smoke there's fire. A denial or, worse, a "no comment" can sound like an admission of guilt. Reporters who ask rumor-based questions provide the "smoke." Rumors are tricky business, to be sure. Some rumors, because they are so persistent and pervasive, take on the force of fact. Reporters are duty-bound to confirm or refute significant rumors and communicate their findings. They are not, though, duty-bound to perpetuate unconfirmed rumors. Columnist Mike Royko, worried about the way half-stories and rumors are peddled by people, urges reporters to pull out a pencil and pad and say, "Fine, I'll quote you on that." If you follow Royko's advice you might see a rumor vanish before your eyes. As Royko puts it, "If they swallow their tongues or go into shock, that's their problem."[25]

Reporters who feel obliged to probe rumors may end up walking an ethical tightrope. When Washington Post reporter Paul Taylor asked presidential candidate Gary Hart, "Senator, have you ever committed adultery?" several notable journalists condemned his behavior as "nauseating" and "demeaning." Taylor defended his question, saying, "Sometimes this job demands that we raise questions we'd rather not ask."[26] Taylor is right. But the dilemma remains: By asking tough, distasteful or embarrassing questions, you risk damage to reputations, including your own. If questions about rumors are asked in a public forum, such as a press conference, the damage undoubtedly will be more severe. The hardest choices arise when the questions touch on private matters: health, sex habits or mental stability. "Are you being treated for prostate cancer?" "Are you gay?" "Have you ever had shock treatment?" Rumors about corruption or malfeasance appear to be fairer game for reporters; they're seldom considered verboten. But even private matters—dependency on a pain killer, for instance—often affect the public life of the newsmaker in some way. The most important consideration in asking questions about rumors is to never forget that rumors *may be untrue.* An ill-advised question can bring the rumor out of the shadows, magnify its importance and afford it a degree of respectability it doesn't deserve.

Before asking rumor questions, we suggest that you take two steps. First, try to determine whether the rumors are primarily private in nature. Unwarranted invasion of privacy is unethical and unlawful. If you conclude that the rumor is of bona fide public concern, then, as discreetly and confidentially as possible, investigate for evidence of what in law enforcement is called "probable cause"—reasonable grounds for suspecting guilt. Only then should you publicly raise questions about the rumor. Rumors and gossip are much too destructive to be addressed carelessly.

Sometimes even the most delicately handled inquiry can be injurious. What if, for instance, several operating-room nurses tell you they suspect that Dr. William Davis, a prominent surgeon, is a problem drinker? They fear people are at risk when Davis operates. You decide to poke around the edges to see if there's anything to the nurses' suspicions; you don't intend to talk to Davis unless you have something more solid. With honorable intentions, you proceed to discuss the allegations with several doctors you know on the hospital staff. What you fail to consider, however, is that your carefully worded questions may be planting seeds of doubt about Davis' competence. In the end, you find no evidence of alcohol abuse, and you move on to another story, unaware of the damage done to Davis' reputation. For his part, Davis, unaware of your inquiries, wonders why he's not getting as many referrals as he once did and why the hospital chief of staff seems to be watching him more closely. Was this a case of journalistic malpractice?

## Tough Questions

Is it ethical to provoke someone intentionally simply to obtain a livelier, more potent interview or to gain a fuller, more powerful answer? That problem is most crucial for broadcast journalists who must not only conduct an interview but also ensure that it holds an audience. Of course, questions that goad or provoke might be the only way for the reporter to initiate a frank conversation of substance.

In other words, goading may be OK. "Suggestions for the Television Interviewer," a handout once given to students at a major university, contains a section on "bear-baiting interviews." It says the interviewer's purpose "is to strip away the facade, the veneer, the pretense, the protective attitudes, to get at the real issues, the real character, the real problem." Provided the interviewee has indeed erected a facade, it is hard to argue with those purposes. But the list of suggestions also contains these words of dubious wisdom: "Objectives—to attack a person's actions, beliefs, or position in a problem or issue. Audience appeal—to shock, to appeal to the sadistic, to involve the audience in the conflict—in taking sides for or against the interviewee. Examples—A 'meet-the-press' type of situation in which the poor, harassed interviewee is the bear in the center of the amphitheater ring, with the interviewer, or interviewers, circling him like so many gladiators to harass, to cripple, or to eviscerate him."[27] Are reporters (or journalism instructors) who view an interview as a game of Christians vs. lions too bloodthirsty?

Perhaps the difference between questions that "probe" and questions that "bait" is to be found in the reporter's attitudes and objectives. Consider Mike Wallace's perspective in describing "Night Beat," a program he hosted early in his career. "We had no qualms whatsoever about putting our guests on the spot. After all, as we frequently reminded each other, no one was ever subpoenaed to appear on 'Night Beat.' "[28] True, but people under subpoena are supposed to be protected from harassment and badgering. Wallace, admitting it was a case of going too far, says he once mercilessly questioned cartoonist Al Capp, creator of Li'l Abner, about why Capp self-consciously giggled each time he made an acidic remark. Wallace describes what happened:

As I pressed on, Capp was palpably unnerved; sweat broke out on his face, and his hands and arms began to shake in jittery, jagged motions. The viewers were suddenly looking at a man in public torment. . . . That nervous laugh was apparently a signal from his psyche and I had called attention to it on television. In doing so, I had caused him pain and embarrassment.[29]

Reporters who ask painful questions primarily for the sake of seeing someone squirm and suffer engage in a low form of journalism. Painful questions may have to be raised, but ratings, glory or perverse pleasure shouldn't be the motivation.

## Ambush Questions

A variety of baiting questions can be found in what is called the "ambush interview." Reporters who engage in ambush tactics usually try to catch a news subject by surprise with questions flying and, in the case of television news, with cameras rolling. Ambush questions may be justified. Some news subjects are so evasive that an ambush may offer the only hope of a response. In other instances, the ambush might be needed to deny a news subject opportunity to prepare what may be an alibi. But ambush tactics invite abuse, particularly by broadcast reporters. A 1986 invasion of privacy suit provides an example. A television reporter confronted the owner of a small business about some leaking barrels of waste on the man's property. The owner politely said the barrels weren't his and that he had asked authorities to remove them. "I don't want to say anything more," the man said. But the reporter persisted until the man lost patience and said, "Get the hell off my property."[30] His angry response was broadcast; the earlier polite request was not. If you feel you must surprise someone with an issue, don't shoot him or her in the back by twisting the right to say "no comment" into an insinuation of guilt.

## FINAL THOUGHTS ON ETHICAL BEHAVIOR

Most reporters want to be ethical. Often, though, what's right or wrong, responsible or irresponsible, is difficult to determine. Professional codes are generally vague and imprecise about what should be done in everyday practice and which exceptions are justified. As a result, sensitive journalists find themselves in many ethical quagmires.

There are too many exceptions in the world of reporting to expect the profession to operate under universal, clear-cut rules. As a result, many ethical decisions must be made on an ad hoc, case-by-case basis. A commitment to ethical behavior, however, requires that newsroom decision-making be thoughtful and rational. The process should assess and evaluate alternatives, values and consequences. The decision you make may still trouble you, but at least you can feel it was arrived at in a fair, deliberative manner.

Reporters may believe that their job is to report the facts, report the truth and 'let the chips fall where they may." That credo dangerously simplifies a reporter's duties, and, in fact, may conveniently remove any responsibility for ethical choices. Ethical reporters must come to grips with serious problems of lying, misrepresentation and deceit. Rarely, a falsehood or a masquerade may be justified, but you shouldn't forget that when you hide your intentions or identity, you're exploiting a communication relationship. The exploitation may come back to haunt you. Lies and deceit are likely to entangle the profession in more lies and deceit.

Even forthright reporters can take undue advantage of news subjects. An important point to remember is that most people you deal with ought to be afforded a freedom of choice in communication relationships. They ought to know who you are and what are the potential consequences of their communication with you. Police use a warning statement to protect the rights of suspects; some critics believe reporters should use a form of warning, too.

Questions are not created equal. Some are intended to hurt and embarrass. Especially potent are questions that bring rumors into the public spotlight. Reporters should recognize the potential of questions to do damage. There are bad questions and improper questions.

Finally, we return to the theme of Chapter One. Today's journalists show signs of being an isolated, and at times, a self-righteous elite; it is possible that arrogance blinds them to the feelings of others. Undeniably, the public is not pleased with the behavior of journalists in general. If the profession has lost much of the public's respect, it probably is because journalists put "newsgathering" ahead of people. Few stories are so significant that they must be told no matter what the damage to people and institutions, including the institution of the press. In the long run, reporters who repeatedly disregard the communication rights of others will diminish not only their own effectiveness, but the reputation of their profession as well.

## Notes

1. Steve Daley, "Garbage collectors and the Hart press," *Chicago Tribune,* May 7, 1987, Sec. 2, p. 1.

2. The three principal codes of ethics in journalism are the Society of Professional Journalists, Sigma Delta Chi, Code of Ethics, adopted 1973; Associated Press Managing Editors Code of Ethics, adopted 1975; and the American Society of Newspaper Editors Statement of Principles, adopted 1975, supplanting the 1922 Canons of Journalism.

3. John C. Merrill and Ralph L. Lowenstein, *Media, Messages and Men,* (New York: David McKay, 1971), p. 244, 245.

4. "Sex and the Presidency," *Newsweek,* May 4, 1987, p. 26.

5. Philip E. Wheelwright, *A Critical Introduction to Ethics,* 3rd ed. (New York: The Odyssey Press, 1959), pp. 4–9.

6. Carl Bernstein and Bob Woodward, *All the President's Men,* (New York: Warner Books, 1975), p. 180.

7. Sissela Bok, *Lying: Moral Choice in Public and Private Life,* (New York: Vintage Books, 1979), p. 128.

8. H. Eugene Goodwin, *Groping for Ethics in Journalism,* (Ames, Iowa: Iowa State University Press, 1983), p. 146.

9. Sid Kirchheimer, "Enquiring Minds Want to Know," *Chicago Tribune,* Feb. 15, 1987, Sec. 2, p. 3.

10. *Hawkins v. Multimedia,* 12 Med. L. Rptr. 1878, March 11, 1986.

11. *Goldman v. Time, Inc.,* 336 F.Supp 133 (N.D. Calif., 1971) at 136.

12. Herbert J. Gans, *Deciding What's News: A Study of CBS Evening News, NBC Nightly News, Newsweek, and Time* (New York: Pantheon Books, 1979), p. 8.

13. Richard P. Cunningham, "Think twice before talking to a reporter," *The Quill,* May 1987, p. 10.

14. Cunningham, "Think twice before talking to a reporter," p. 10.

15. Goodwin, *Groping for Ethics in Journalism,* p. 245.

16. Richard P. Cunningham, "A taste of South Africa in Minneapolis," *The Quill,* February 1987, p. 12.

17. David Shaw, *Press Watch* (New York: Macmillan, 1984), p. 54.

18. Roderick Townley, "Does She Push Too Hard? A Report Card on Barbara Walters," *TV Guide,* July 4, 1987, p. 5.

19. Steve Daley, "Rush to judgment on 'the Greek'?" *Chicago Tribune,* Jan. 21, 1988, Sec. 2, p. 1.

20. John Gregory Dunne, "Trials and Errors," *Esquire,* November 1986, p. 245.

21Frederick Talbott, "Taping on the Sly: Nasty business—or sound journalistic technique?" *The Quill,* June 1986, p. 43.

22Roy Peter Clark, ed. *The Best Newspaper Writing of 1983* (St. Petersburg, Fla.: The Poynter Institute, 1983), p. 79.

23Roy Peter Clark, ed. *The Best Newspaper Writing of 1981* (St. Petersburg, Fla.: The Modern Media Institute, 1981), p. 101.

24Steve Daley, "The Hart caper: Return with us now to the '50s," *Chicago Tribune,* May 12, 1987, Sec. 2, p. 5.

25Mike Royko, "Mario Cuomo has a right to be mad," *Chicago Tribune,* Dec. 14, 1987, Section 1, p. 3.

26"Adultery Query Was Proper, Reporter Says," *St. Louis Post-Dispatch,* May 24, 1987, p. D17.

27Anonymous, "Suggestions for the Television Interviewer," Southern Illinois University at Edwardsville.

28Mike Wallace and Gary Paul Gates, *Close Encounters: Mike Wallace's Own Story,* (New York: William Morrow, 1984), p. 32.

29Wallace and Gates, *Close Encounters,* p. 34.

30*Machleder v. Diaz,* 801 F.2d 46 (2d. Cir. 1986).

# Index

224 • Index

White, Betty, 203
Whyte, William Foote, 83
Wible, Arthur, 4
Winfrey, Oprah, 184, 185
Withholding identity, 200
Woodward, Bob, 11, 198

Young, Brigham, 112

Zich, Arthur, 31
Zinsser, William, 2, 80
Ziomek, Jon, 114
Zunin, Leonard, 27

**DATE DUE**

| | |
|---|---|
| OCT 27 1992 | |
| DEC 12 1992 | |
| ILL: 6/10/94 | |
| OCT 10 1998 | |
| IU - due 6-27-99 | |
| | |
| APR 30 2004 | |

DEMCO, INC. 38-2931